SignalR Blueprints

Build real-time ASP.NET web applications with SignalR and create various interesting projects to improve your user experience

Einar Ingebrigtsen

BIRMINGHAM - MUMBAI

SignalR Blueprints

First published: February 2015

Production reference: 1200215

Published by Packt Publishing Ltd.
Livery Place
35 Livery Street
Birmingham B3 2PB, UK.

ISBN 978-1-78398-312-4

www.packtpub.com

Credits

Author
Einar Ingebrigtsen

Reviewers
Dejan Caric
Anup Hariharan Nair
Michael Smith

Commissioning Editor
Usha Iyer

Acquisition Editors
Richard Harvey
James Jones

Content Development Editor
Sumeet Sawant

Technical Editor
Shashank Desai

Copy Editors
Janbal Dharmaraj
Relin Hedly

Project Coordinator
Purav Motiwalla

Proofreaders
Stephen Copestake
Faye Coulman
Maria Gould

Indexer
Tejal Soni

Production Coordinator
Aparna Bhagat

Cover Work
Aparna Bhagat

About the Author

Einar Ingebrigtsen has been working professionally with software since 1994, ranging from games development on platforms such as the PlayStation, Xbox, and PC to the enterprise line of business application development since 2002. He has always kept his focus on creating great products with great user experiences, putting the user first. Einar received the Microsoft MVP award in October 2008, awarded for his work in the community and in Silverlight space with open source projects such as Balder—a 3D engine for Silverlight. Today, Einar runs a company called Dolittle together with his partners, doing consultancy and building his own products with their own open source projects at the heart of what they do. The clients that Dolittle has had in the last couple of years include NRK (the largest TV broadcaster in Norway), Statoil (a Norwegian oil company), Komplett (the largest e-commerce company in Norway), and Holte (a leading Norwegian developer for construction software).

A strong believer in open source, Einar runs a few projects in addition to Balder, the largest being Bifrost (`http://bifrost.dolittle.com/`), a line of business platform for .NET developers, and Forseti (`https://github.com/dolittle/forseti`), a headless auto-running JavaScript test runner.

Additionally, Einar loves talking at user groups and conferences and has been a frequent speaker at Microsoft venues, talking about different topics—the last couple of years mostly about architecture, code quality, and cloud computing. His personal blog is at `http://www.ingebrigtsen.info/` and the company blog is at `http://blog.dolittle.com/`.

Einar is also the author of the book *SignalR: Real-time Application Development, Packt Publishing*.

Acknowledgments

It might sound like a cliché, but seriously, without my wife, Anne Grethe, this book could not have happened. Her patience with me and her support is truly what pretty much makes just about anything I do a reality. My kids, Mia and Herman, you rock! Thanks to them for keeping me mentally younger and making me playful. I'd also like to thank my colleagues, who have been kind enough not to point out the fact that I've had too much going on in the period of writing this book. I'll be sure to buy a round the next time we're having a company get together.

Last but not least, thanks to my clients for their patience and flexibility during the busiest periods of this process.

About the Reviewers

Dejan Caric is a software developer at Laboremus Oslo AS. He has extensive experience in a wide range of industries. Some of his work includes software to manage HDTV routers over network using SNMP, telnet, and SSH protocols, information systems for insurance companies, online banking solutions, public websites, intranets, and enterprise search solutions.

His main interests are enterprise search, software architecture, clean code, and agile software developer. He blogs frequently at `http://www.dcaric.com/`.

He currently resides in Oslo, Norway, with his wife, Marija, and son, Aleksa.

Anup Hariharan Nair is an experienced developer based in the New York metropolitan area with a passion for automation and software craftsmanship. Currently, he works as an IT consultant at KPMG. He has spent most of his time in Microsoft and Java camps, writing everything from console apps to large distributed systems and has extensive experience in web and mobile development, deployment automation, and continuous delivery. He is mild mannered developer by day and hopeless technology junkie by night. He blogs frequently at `http://hificoding.com/` and drinks tea while trying to look busy. You can reach him at `anup@hificoding.com`.

Michael Smith is a developer and consultant with 15 years of experience who has worked in a broad range of industries, including banking, finance, e-commerce, and oil. He is passionate about delivering high-quality software that meets and exceeds clients' needs. To this end, he is an advocate of putting the business in front when developing software.

He is involved in various open source projects, including the line of business application framework Bifrost.

www.PacktPub.com

Support files, eBooks, discount offers, and more

For support files and downloads related to your book, please visit www.PacktPub.com.

Did you know that Packt offers eBook versions of every book published, with PDF and ePub files available? You can upgrade to the eBook version at www.PacktPub.com and as a print book customer, you are entitled to a discount on the eBook copy. Get in touch with us at service@packtpub.com for more details.

At www.PacktPub.com, you can also read a collection of free technical articles, sign up for a range of free newsletters and receive exclusive discounts and offers on Packt books and eBooks.

https://www2.packtpub.com/books/subscription/packtlib

Do you need instant solutions to your IT questions? PacktLib is Packt's online digital book library. Here, you can search, access, and read Packt's entire library of books.

Why subscribe?

- Fully searchable across every book published by Packt
- Copy and paste, print, and bookmark content
- On demand and accessible via a web browser

Free access for Packt account holders

If you have an account with Packt at www.PacktPub.com, you can use this to access PacktLib today and view 9 entirely free books. Simply use your login credentials for immediate access.

Table of Contents

Preface

The purpose of software is to be a tool for us humans to help us perform tasks. A lot of software is also a replacement for something physical for which we had an opportunity to increase productivity by making it digital and also more accessible. When replacing a paper form with a digital solution, we as developers pretty much just copied the form field by field and never really thought through what we were trying to solve. This made the improvement all about the data rather than what the users were really trying to do. One of the benefits of having the forms digitally is that multiple users can see the same data at the same time and even edit it at the same time. However, since it has all been modeled as data, with often a single, large model representing it, we introduce new problems we never had in the real world on paper. Things such as transactions and data staleness make our software more complex and they never make sense at all for the user. These are technical requirements that we, as developers, have introduced to make sure the data is correct at all times.

Users are becoming better; they have new requirements based on their experience with software. Even in the enterprise, users are now demanding more of their IT systems. With the advent of the real-time Web, driven by services such as Facebook, Twitter, and other social media, our users are now used to different experiences that are more responsive and user friendly.

What is the state of the Web?

The Web has changed a lot over the years, but the core protocol, HTTP, has been pretty consistent since its first documented version was released in 1991. The protocol was optimized for the document delivery system that makes up the World Wide Web. Later, the protocol included information that helped us keep a session state on the server and be able to link subsequent requests coming into the same session state. Later with DHTML and AJAX, we didn't have to do full post backs to get the full document but get parts of the document, or maybe even just get the data and perform the necessary rendering or manipulation of the document in the client.

With the introduction of standards such as WebSockets, server sent events, and the like, we can go even further. We can now make our web solutions come even more alive by having persistent connections with a server and get notified from the server when something happens. This solves some of the problems discussed earlier, such as transactions and data staleness. By basically getting the changes continuously from any other users as they are doing them, we don't need to run into any conditions that put the system in a mode that it can't get out of. This will increase the user experience and make our job as developers a lot easier.

SignalR Blueprints will allow you to utilize SignalR to its fullest, showing you how to create different application types on the Web and mobile devices, along with a few tips and tricks along the way. In addition, this project book aims to show you the patterns that are not only good for SignalR but generally with cloud scale in mind. Most significantly, you will learn to think differently about software for users, keeping them in focus all the time.

Personal style

Throughout the book, you'll run into things you might disagree with. It could be things in naming the classes or methods in C#, for instance, at times, I like to drop camel casing, both upper and lower and just separate the words with an underscore yielding "some_type_with_spaces". In addition, I don't use modifiers, without them adding any value. You'll see that I completely avoid private as that is the default modifier for fields or properties on types. I'll also avoid things such as read-only, especially, if it's a private member. Most annoyingly, you might see that I drop scoping for single line statements following an IF or FOR. Don't worry, this is my personal style; you can do as you please. All I'm asking is that you don't judge me by how my code looks. I'm not a huge fan of measuring code quality with tools such as R# and its default setting for squiggles. In fact, a colleague and I have been toying with the idea of using the underscore trick for all our code, as it really makes it a lot easier to read.

You'll notice throughout that I'm using built-in functions in the browser in JavaScript, where you might expect jQuery. The reason for this is basically that I try to limit the usage of jQuery, in fact, it's a dependency I'd prefer not to have in my solutions as it is not adding anything to the way I do things. There is a bit of an educational, quite intentional reason for me not using jQuery as well; we now have most of the things we need in the browser already.

What this book covers

Chapter 1, The Primer, shows us that in order to hit the ground running with SignalR, it is important to understand why we need SignalR, but even more importantly, the architectural decisions that lead to the thinking behind SignalR. For the remainder of this book, there will be patterns and practices applied; this chapter covers that. In addition, it also covers the libraries being used.

Chapter 2, Overheating the Discussion, starts gradually by getting to know the basics, without introducing too much technology and patterns and practices. This chapter goes through the building of a forum that benefits from SignalR.

Chapter 3, Extra! Extra! Read All About It!, introduces e-newspapers—a great scenario for SignalR and a quite common feature found on the Web. Having SignalR at the core could be the tiny thing that differentiates you from the crowd. You'll learn how to scale to meet demand when things go viral.

Chapter 4, Can You Measure It?, introduces increasingly popular dashboards that will give you numbers at a glance. Often, the aim is to have the dashboards as up to date as possible but without having to do a timer that refreshes. SignalR can help here and light it all up, and with the right technique, make it visually appealing.

Chapter 5, What Line of Business Are You In?, shows that enterprise line of business apps are often referred to as where user experiences go to die, leaving users out of the equation when the software is designed and implemented. There are no reasons whatsoever for this. This chapter investigates how can we start to think differently about things and make them twinkle, like the stars discovered by the many voyages of the Starship Enterprise.

Chapter 6, An Architectural Taste, shows that software architecture is very important for many reasons, and this chapter looks more closely at a particular flavor that lends itself to the idea of real-time applications.

Chapter 7, The Three Screens - Mobile First, teaches how to connect the phone as a frontend for what we built in the previous chapter. SignalR is not only for the Web; it supports a wide variety of platforms, one of them being the Windows Phone.

Chapter 8, Putting the X in .NET - Xamarin, builds a frontend for the forum in *Chapter 2, Overheating the Discussion,* for the iPhone.

Chapter 9, Debugging or Troubleshooting, shows a few techniques that you can apply to find out why the code gets broken or systems in general don't do what they are told to. Then, you need to figure out what went wrong.

Chapter 10, Hosting and Deployment, walks through the varieties and particularly focuses on cloud and Microsoft Azure. An important fact here will be how one scales.

Who this book is for

This book is written for developers with experience in C# and JavaScript. At this stage, the developer should also have a basic knowledge of how SignalR works as well as what the developer needs to rethink when designing applications that have a persistent connection to the server.

Some of the things that we will discuss in the book are architectural in nature. Software architecture, patterns, and practices surround us; this book will present some less "mainstream" ideas that are ideal for the world of small changes. You don't need to be an architect to get this; the book will keep it at an intermediate level.

What you need for this book

The book uses C# and JavaScript in the samples and we will be using Visual Studio 2013 as the IDE of choice. You will be able to use Visual Studio 2013 Express, the free edition as well. You will need to have NuGet installed, which can be accessed at `http://www.nuget.org/`. For the Xamarin part of this book, you will need to have access to a Mac with Xcode installed plus Xamarin Studio, which you can download at `http://xamarin.com/`. Xamarin does provide a plugin for Visual Studio, but it needs to work in conjunction with a tool running on Mac OS X that compiles the code for use on iOS and also runs it either on the iOS Simulator or a real device.

Conventions

In this book, you will find a number of styles of text that distinguish between different kinds of information. Here are some examples of these styles, and an explanation of their meaning.

Code words in text are shown as follows: "At the core level of SignalR sits something called a `PersistentConnection` class; hubs build on top of this."

A block of code is set as follows:

```
@Scripts.Render("~/bundles/jquery")
@Scripts.Render("~/bundles/bootstrap")
```

New terms and **important words** are shown in bold. Words that you see on the screen, in menus or dialog boxes, for example, appear in the text like this: "To add a reference to a project, we start by right-clicking on the **References** of your project and selecting **Manage NuGet Packages**."

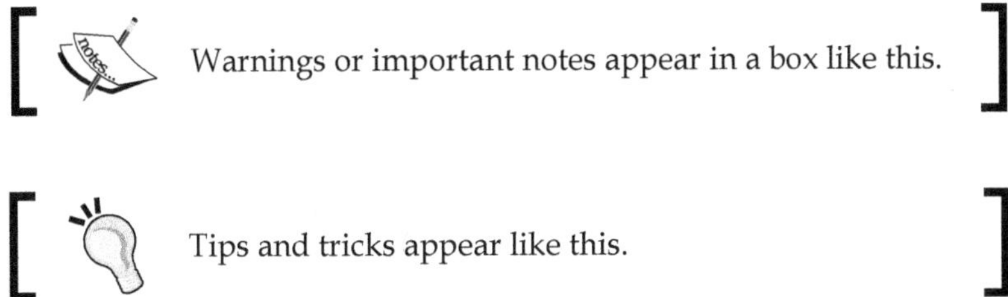

[Warnings or important notes appear in a box like this.]

[Tips and tricks appear like this.]

Reader feedback

Feedback from our readers is always welcome. Let us know what you think about this book—what you liked or may have disliked. Reader feedback is important for us to develop titles that you really get the most out of.

To send us general feedback, simply send an e-mail to `feedback@packtpub.com`, and mention the book title via the subject of your message.

If there is a topic that you have expertise in and you are interested in either writing or contributing to a book, see our author guide on `www.packtpub.com/authors`.

Customer support

Now that you are the proud owner of a Packt book, we have a number of things to help you to get the most from your purchase.

Downloading the example code

You can download the example code files for all Packt books you have purchased from your account at `http://www.packtpub.com`. If you purchased this book elsewhere, you can visit `http://www.packtpub.com/support` and register to have the files e-mailed directly to you.

Errata

Although we have taken every care to ensure the accuracy of our content, mistakes do happen. If you find a mistake in one of our books—maybe a mistake in the text or the code—we would be grateful if you could report this to us. By doing so, you can save other readers from frustration and help us improve subsequent versions of this book. If you find any errata, please report them by visiting `http://www.packtpub.com/submit-errata`, selecting your book, clicking on the **Errata Submission Form** link, and entering the details of your errata. Once your errata are verified, your submission will be accepted and the errata will be uploaded to our website or added to any list of existing errata under the **Errata** section of that title.

To view the previously submitted errata, go to `https://www.packtpub.com/books/content/support` and enter the name of the book in the search field. The required information will appear under the **Errata** section.

Piracy

Piracy of copyright material on the Internet is an ongoing problem across all media. At Packt, we take the protection of our copyright and licenses very seriously. If you come across any illegal copies of our works, in any form, on the Internet, please provide us with the location address or website name immediately so that we can pursue a remedy.

Please contact us at `copyright@packtpub.com` with a link to the suspected pirated material.

We appreciate your help in protecting our authors, and our ability to bring you valuable content.

Questions

You can contact us at `questions@packtpub.com` if you are having a problem with any aspect of the book, and we will do our best to address it.

1
The Primer

This chapter serves as a primer covering of all the terms, patterns, and practices applied in the book. Also, you will learn about the tools, libraries, and frameworks being used and what their use cases are. More importantly, you will find out why you should be performing these different things and, in particular, why you should use SignalR, and how the methods you employ will naturally find their way into your software.

Where are we coming from?

By asking where we are coming from, I'm not trying to ask an existential question that dates back to the first signs of life on this planet. Rather, we are looking at the scope of our industry, and what has directed us to where we are now and how we create software today. The software industry is very young and is in constant movement. We haven't quite settled in yet like other professions have. The rapid advances in computer hardware present opportunities for software all the time. We find better ways of doing things as we improve our skills as a community. With the Internet and the means of communication we have today, these changes are happening fast and frequently. This is to say that we are changing a lot more than any other industry. With all this being said, a lot of these changes go back to the roots of our industry. Computers and software are the tools meant to solve problems for humans, and often in the line of business applications that we write, these tools and software are there to remove manual labor or remove paper clutter. The way these applications are modeled is therefore often closely related to the manual or paper version, not really modeling the process or applying the full capability of what the computer could do to actually improve the experience of the particular process.

The terminal

Back in the early days of computing, computers lacked CPU power and memory. They were expensive, and if you wanted something powerful, it would fill the room with refrigerator-sized computers. The idea of a computer, at least a powerful one, on each desk was not feasible. Instead of delivering rich computers onto desks, the notion of terminals became a reality. These were connected to the mainframe and were completely stateless. The entirety of each terminal was kept in the mainframe, and the only thing transferred from the client was user input and the only thing coming back from the mainframe was any screen updates.

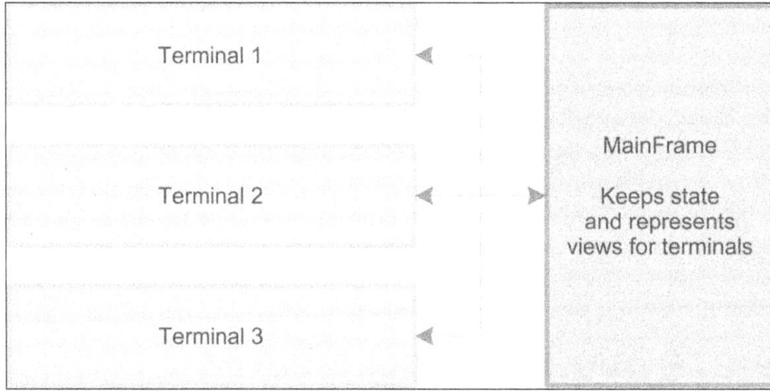

The relationship between multiple terminals connected to a mainframe and all terminals exist without state, with the mainframe maintaining the state and views

Fast forwarding

The previous methods of thinking established the pattern for software moving through the decades. Looking at web applications with a server component in the early days of the Web, you'll see the exact same pattern: a server that keeps the state of the user and the clients being pretty limited; this being the web browser. In fact, the only thing going back and forth between them was the user input from the client and the result in the form of HTML going back.

Bringing this image really up to speed with the advancement of AJAX, the image would be represented as shown in the following diagram:

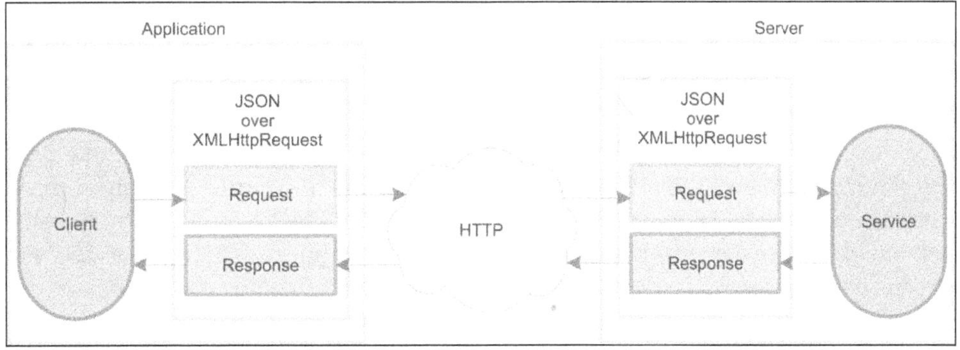

A representation of the flow in a modern web application with the HTTP protocol and requests going to the server that yields responses

Completing the circle

Of course, by skipping three decades of evolution in computing, we are bound to miss a few things. However, the gist of most techniques has been that we keep the state on the server and we have to go from the client in the sense of request, be it a keystroke or a HTTP request, before receiving a response. At the core of this sits a network stack with capabilities beyond what the overlying techniques have been doing. In games, for instance, the underlying sockets have been used much more in order for us to be able to actually play multiplayer games, starting off with games on your local network to massive multiplayer online games with thousands of users connected at once. In games, the request/response pattern will not work as they yield different techniques and patterns. We can't apply all the things that have been achieved in games because a lot of it is based on approximation due to network latency. However, we don't have the requirements of games either to reflect the truth in an interval of every 16-20 milliseconds. Accuracy is far more important in the world of line of business application development where it needs to be accurate constantly. The user has to trust the outcome of their operations in the system. Having said this, it does not mean that the output has to be in synchrony. Things can eventually be consistent and accurate, just as long as the user is well informed. By allowing eventual consistency, you open up a lot of benefits about how we build our software and you have a great opportunity to improve the user experience of the software you are building, which should be at the very forefront of your thinking when making software.

Eventual consistency basically means that the user performs an action and, asynchronously, it will be dealt with by the system and also eventually be performed. When it's actually performed, you could notify the user. If it fails, let the client know so that it can perform any compensating action or present something to the user. This is becoming a very common approach. It does impose a few new things to think about. We seldom build software that targets us as developers but rather has other users in mind when building it. This is the reason we go to work and build software for users. The user experience should therefore be the most important aspect and should always be the driving force and the main motive to apply a new technique. Of course, there are other aspects to decision making (such as budget) as this gives us business value, and so on. These are also vital parts of decision-making, but make sure that you never lose focus on the user.

How can we complete the circle and improve the model and take what we've learned and mix in a bit of real-time thinking? Instead of thinking that we need a response right away and pretty much locking up the user interface, we can send off the request for what we want and not wait for it at all. So, let the user carry on and then let the server tell us the result when it is ready. But hang on, I mentioned accuracy; doesn't this mean that we would be sitting with that client in an incorrect state? There are ways to deal with this in a user-friendly fashion. They are as follows:

- For simple things, you could assume that the server will perform the action and just perform the same thing on the client side. This will give instant feedback to the user and the user can then carry on. If, for some reason, the action didn't succeed on the server, the server can, at a later stage, send the error related to the action that was performed and the client can perform a compensating action. Undoing this and notifying the user that it couldn't be performed is an example. An error should only be considered an edge case, so instead of modeling everything around the error, model the happy path and deal with the error on its own.
- Another approach would be to lock the particular element that was changed in the client but not the entire user interface, just the part that was modified or created. When the action succeeds and the server tells you, you can easily mark the element(s) as succeeded and apply the result from the server. Both of these techniques are valid and I would argue that you should apply both, depending on the circumstances.

SignalR

What does this all mean and how does SignalR fit into all this?

A regular vanilla web application without even being AJAX-enabled will do a full round-trip from the client to server for the entire page and all its parts when something is performed. This puts a strain on the server to serve the content and maybe even having to perform rendering on the server before returning the request. However, it also puts a strain on the bandwidth, having to return all the content all the time. AJAX-enabled web apps made this a lot better by typically not posting a full page back all the time. Today, with **Single Page Applications** (**SPA**), we never do a full-page rendering or reloading and often not even rely on the server rendering anything. Instead, it just sits there serving static content in the form of HTML, CSS, and JavaScript files and then provides an API that can be consumed by the client.

SignalR goes a step further by representing an abstraction that gives you a persistent connection between the server and the client. You can send anything to the server and the server can at any time send anything back to the client, breaking the request/response pattern completely. We lose the overhead of the regular request or response pattern of the Web for every little thing that we need to do. From a resource perspective, you will end up needing less from both your server and your client. For instance, web requests are returned back to the request pool of ASP.NET as soon as possible and reduce the memory and CPU usage on the server.

By default, SignalR will choose the best way to accomplish this based on the capabilities of the client and the server combined. Ranging from WebSockets to Server Sent Events to Long Polling Requests, it promises to be able to connect a client and a server. If a connection is broken, SignalR will try to re-establish it from the client immediately.

Although SignalR uses long polling, the response going back from the server to a client is vastly improved rather than having to do a pull on an interval, which was the approach for AJAX-enabled applications before.

You can force SignalR to choose a specific technique as long as you have requirements that limit what is allowed. However, when left as default, it will negotiate what is the best fit.

Terminology

As in any industry, we have a language that we use and it is not always ubiquitous. We might be saying the same thing but the meaning might vary. Throughout the book, you'll find terms being used in order for you to understand what is being referred to; I'll summarize what these terms mean.

Messaging

A message in computer software refers to a unit of communication that contains information that the source wants to communicate to the outside world, either to specific recipients or as a broadcast to all recipients connected now or in the future. The message itself is nothing but a container holding information to identify the type of the message and the data associated with it. Messaging is used in a variety of ways. One way is either through the Win16/32 APIs with WM_* messages being sent for any user input or changes occurring in the UI. Another is things affecting the application to XML messages used to integrate systems. It could also be typed messages inside the software, modeled directly as a type. It comes in various forms, but the general purpose is to be able to do it in a decoupled manner that tells other parts that something has happened. The message and its identifier with its payload becomes the contract in which the decoupled systems know about. The two systems would not know about each other.

Publish/Subscribe

With your message in place, you want to typically send it. Publish/Subscribe, or in shorthand "PubSub", is often what you're looking for. The message can be broadcasted and any part of your system can subscribe to the message by type and react to it. This decouples the components in your system by leaving a message. This is achieved by having a message box sitting in the middle that all systems know about, which could be a local or global message box, depending on how your model thinks. The message box will then be given message calls, or will activate subscriptions, which are often specific to a message type or identifier.

The message box can be made smarter, which for instance could be by persisting all messages going through so that any future subscribers can be told what happened in the past. This is presented by the following diagram:

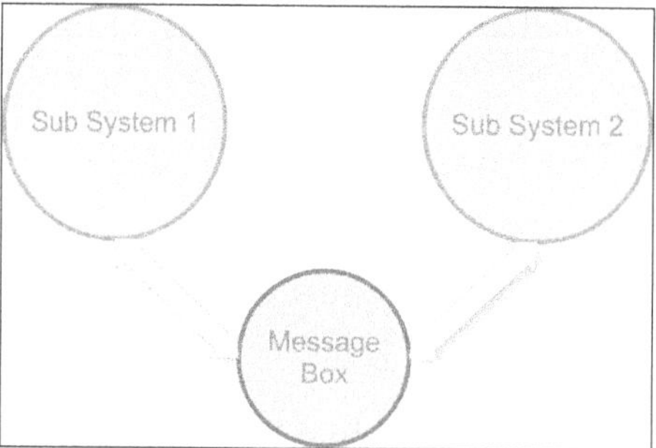

A representation of how the subsystems have a direct relationship with a message box, enabling the two systems to be decoupled from each other

Decoupling

There are quite a few paradigms in the art of programming and it all boils down to what is right for you. It's hard to argue what is right or wrong because the success of any paradigm is really hard to measure. Some people like a procedural approach to things where you can read end-to-end how a system is put together, which often leads to a much coupled solution. Solutions are things put together in a sequence and the elements can know about each other. The complete opposite approach would be to completely decouple things and break each problem into its own isolated unit with each unit not knowing about the other. This approach breaks everything down into more manageable units and helps keep the complexity down. It really helps in the long term velocity of development and explains also how you can grow the functionality. In fact, it also helps with taking things out if one discovers one has features that aren't being used. By decoupling software and putting things in isolation and even sprinkle some **SOLID** on top of this (which is known as a collection of principles; this being the Single responsibility principle - Open/closed principle - Liskov substitution principle - Interface segregation principle - Dependency inversion principle). You can find more information about this at `http://www.objectmentor.com/resources/articles/Principles_and_Patterns.pdf`.

By applying these practices with decoupling in mind, we can:

- Make it easier to scale up your team with more developers; things are separated out and responsibilities within the team can be done as well.
- Make more maintainable solutions.
- Take resource hungry parts of your system and put them on separate servers, something that is harder to accomplish if it all is coupled together.
- Gain more flexibility by focusing more on each individual parts and then compose it back together any way you like.
- Make it easier to identify bottlenecks in isolation.
- Have less chance of breaking other parts of the system when fixing or expanding your code.
- Gain higher development pace.
- Finally, this might be a bold claim, but you could encounter fewer bugs! Or at least, they would be more maintainable bugs that sit inside isolated and focused code, making it easier to identity and safer to fix.

The ability to publish messages rather than calling concrete implementations becomes vital. These become the contracts within your system.

This book will constantly remind you of one thing: users are a big part in making this decision. Making your system flexible and more maintainable is of interest to your users. The turnaround time to fix bugs along with delivering new features is very much in their interest. One of the things I see a lot in projects is that we tend to try to define everything way too early and often upfront of development, taking an end-to-end design approach. This often leads to overthinking and often coupling, making it harder to change later on when we know more. By making exactly what is asked for and not trying to be too creative and add things that could be nice to have, and then really thinking of small problems and rather compose it back together, the chance of success is bigger and also easier to maintain and change. Having said this, decoupling is, ironically enough, tightly coupled with the SOLID principles along with other principles to really accomplish this. For instance, take the S in SOLID. This represents the **Single Responsibility Principle**; it governs that a single unit should not do more than one thing. A unit can go all the way down to a method. Breaking up things into more tangible units rather than huge unreadable units makes your code more flexible and more readable.

Decoupling will play a vital role in the remainder of the book.

Patterns

Techniques that repeat can be classified as patterns; you probably already have a bunch of patterns in your own code that you might classify even as your own patterns. Some of these become popular outside the realms of one developer's head and are promoted beyond just this one guy. A pattern is a well-understood solution to a particular problem. They are identified rather than "created". That is, they emerge and are abstracted from solutions to real-world problems rather than being imposed on a problem from the outside. It's also a common vocabulary that allows developers to communicate more efficiently. A popular book that aims to gather some of these patterns is *Design Patterns: Elements of Reusable Object-Oriented Software, Erich Gamma, Richard Helm, Ralph Johnson, John Vlissides, Addison-Wesley Professional.* You can find a copy at `http://www.amazon.com/Design-Patterns-Elements-Reusable-Object-Oriented/dp/0201633612`.

We will be using different patterns throughout this book, so it's important to understand what they are, the motivation behind them, and how they are applied successfully. The following sections will give you a short summary of the patterns being referred to and used.

Model-View-Controller

Interestingly enough, most of the patterns we have started applying have been around for quite a while. The **Model-View-Controller** (**MVC**) pattern is a great example of this.

MVC was first introduced by a fellow Norwegian national called Dr. Trygve Reenskaug in 1973 in a paper called Administrative Control in the Shipyard (`http://martinfowler.com/eaaDev/uiArchs.html`). Since then, it has been applied successfully in a variety of frameworks and platforms. With the introduction of Ruby on Rails in 2005, I would argue the focus on MVC really started to get traction in the modern web development sphere. When Microsoft published ASP.NET MVC at the end of 2007, they helped gain focus in the .NET community as well.

The purpose of MVC is to decouple the elements in the frontend and create a better isolated focus on these different concerns. Basically, what one has is a controller that governs the actions that are allowed to be performed for a particular feature of your application. The actions can return a result in the form of either data or concrete new views to navigate to. The controller is responsible for holding and providing any state to the views through the actions it exposes. By state, we often think of the model and often the data comes from a database, either directly exposed or adapted into a view-specific model that suits the view better than the raw data from the database. The relationship between model, controller, view, and the user is summarized in the following diagram:

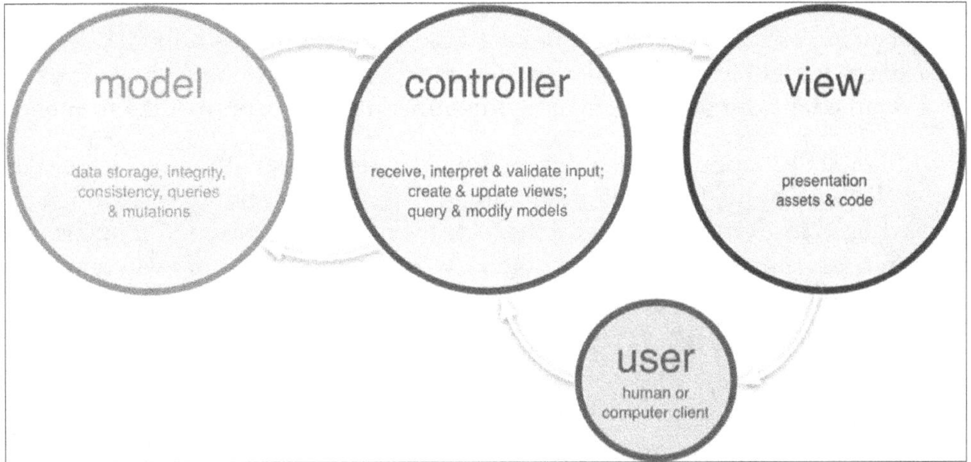

A representation of how the artifacts make up MVC (don't forget there is a user that will interact with all of these artifacts)

With this approach, you separate out the presentation aspect of the business logic into the controller. The controller then has a relationship with other subsystems that knows the other aspects of the business logic in a better manner, letting the controller only focus on the logic that is specific to the presentation and not on any concrete business logic but more on the presentation aspect of any business logic. This decouples it from the underlying subsystem and thus more specialized. The view now has to concern itself with only view-related things, which are typically HTML and CSS for web applications. The model, either a concrete model from the database or adapted for the view, is fetched from whatever data source you have.

Model-View-ViewModel

Extending on the promise of decoupling in the frontend, we get something called **Model-View-ViewModel** (**MVVM**); for more information, visit `http://www.codeproject.com/Articles/100175/Model-View-ViewModel-MVVM-Explained`. This is a design pattern for the frontend based largely on MVC but it takes it a bit further in terms of decoupling. From this, Microsoft created a specialization called MVVM, as it is called today.

MVVM was presented by Martin Fowler in 2004 to what he referred to as the Presentation Model (which you can access at `http://martinfowler.com/eaaDev/PresentationModel.html`).

The ViewModel is a key player in this that holds the state and behavior needed for your feature to be able to do its job without it knowing about the view. The view will then be observing the ViewModel for any changes it might get and utilize any behaviors it exposes. In the ViewModel, we keep the state, and as with MVC, the state is in the form of a model that could be a direct model coming from your data source or an adapted model that is more fine-tuned to the purpose of the frontend.

The additional decoupling, which this model represents, lies within the fact that the ViewModel has no clue to any view, and in fact should be blissfully unaware that it is being used in a view. This makes the code even more focused and it opens an opportunity of being able to swap out the view at any given time or even reuse the same ViewModel with its logic and state for the second view.

The relationship between the Model, View, ViewModel, and the user is summarized in the following diagram:

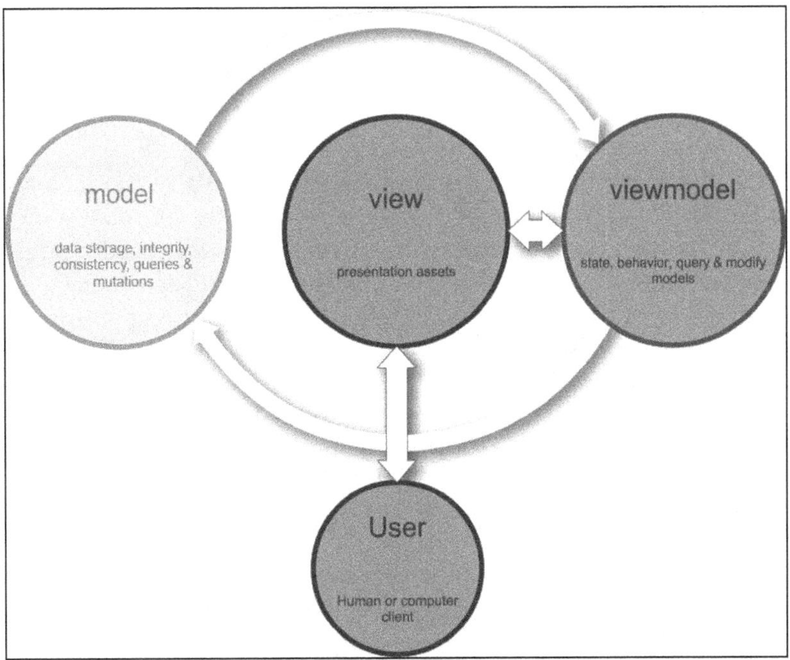

The artifacts that make up MVVM (don't forget the user interacts with these artifacts through the view)

Command Query Responsibility Segregation

Back in 1988, Betrand Meyer published a book, *Object-oriented Software Construction* (`https://archive.eiffel.com/doc/oosc/page.html`). In this book, one of the things being addressed was the separation of actions being performed in the system and data being returned. The data displayed and the actions performed are, in fact, two completely different concerns and it's described as commands for the tasks being performed and queries for the data one gets. At its core, there are no methods or functions that can perform an action and return data. These are separated out as two different operations, leading to the concept of **Command Query Separation** (**CQS**); more information can be found at `http://codebetter.com/gregyoung/2009/08/13/command-query-separation/`. Greg Young and Udi Dahan reached the conclusion of refining CQS into something called **Command Query Responsibility Segregation** (**CQRS**). At the heart of this sits the SOLID principles, especially with SRP, whereas the ideas of separation of concerns is on top (more information is available at `http://deviq.com/separation-of-concerns`). The evolution in CQRS over CQS was to take what was identified by Bertrand Meyer on the functional level and apply it to the object and architectural levels.

The basics of this is to really treat read and the write as two different pathways and to never mix them. This means that you never reuse any code between the two sides. Getting data through queries should never have side effects on the data as it can't write anything. Commands do not return any data as they only get to perform the action it is set out to do. A command is a data holder that holds the data that is only specific to this command. It should never be looked on as a vessel for large object graphs that gets sent from the client.

Going beyond the separation of read and write, CQRS is really about creating the models needed for the different aspects of your solution (never reuse a model between them). This would mean that you will end up having read models, write models, reporting models, search models, view models, and so on. Each of these is highly specialized for their purpose, leading again to decoupling your system even further. CQRS can be deployed with or without events that connect the segregated parts at its core; this all depends on whether or not your organization can be event driven or not. We will discuss CQRS in more depth later in this book.

CQRS is often seen as complementary to **Domain Driven Design** (**DDD**)—a practice that focuses on establishing the model that represents the domain you're making the software for (for more information, visit `http://dddcommunity.org/learning-ddd/what_is_ddd/`). It holds terminology for how you do this modeling and defines well-defined patterns for the different artifacts that make up your domain model. At the core of this sits the idea of a ubiquitous language that represents your domain; a language that is not only understood by a developer, but also by the domain experts and ultimately the users of the system. Some key facts that you need to bear in mind are as follows:

- Avoid unwanted confusion and also avoid having the need for translations between the different stakeholders of a software project.
- Capture the real use cases and how you should focus on capturing them while not focusing on technical things. Often, we find ourselves not really modeling the business processes accurately, leading to monster domain models that potentially could bring the entire database into memory. Instead of this, focus on the commands or tasks, if you will, which the user is performing. From this, you will reach different conclusions for things (such as transactional boundaries).
- Bounded contexts, another huge aspect of DDD, is the idea that you necessarily don't have one big application but rather many small ones that don't know about each other and live in isolation only to be composed together in the bounded context of the composition itself. Again, this leads to yet another level of decoupling.

The following diagram shows the division found in a full CQRS system with event sourcing and the event store and how they are connected together through events being published from the execution side.

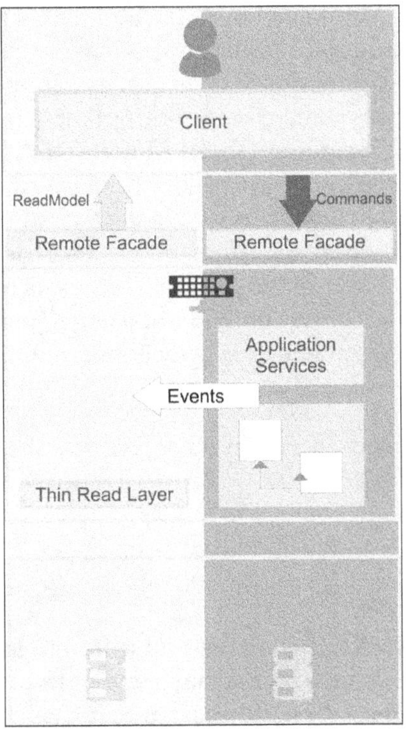

Libraries and frameworks

We will not be doing much from scratch in this book as it does not serve our purpose. Instead, we will be relying on third-party libraries and frameworks to do things for us that don't have anything to do with the particular thing we will perform. The range of libraries will be big and some of these represent architectural patterns and decisions sitting behind them. Some of these are in direct conflict with each other and for consistency in your code base, you should be picking one over the other and stick to it. The chapters in this book will make it clear what I consider as conflict and why and what libraries are right for you, whereas your architecture is something you will have to decide for yourself. This book will just show a few of the possibilities.

jQuery

Browsing the Web for JavaScript-related topics often yields results with jQuery mentioned in the subject or in the article itself. At one point, I was almost convinced that JavaScript started with `$`, followed by a dot, and then a function to perform. It turns out that this is not true. jQuery just happens to be one of the most popular libraries out there when performing web development. It puts in place abstractions for parts that are different between the browsers, but most importantly, it gives you a powerful way to query the **Document Object Model** (**DOM**) as well as modify it as your application runs. A lot of the things jQuery has historically solved are now being solved by the browser vendors themselves by being true to the specifications of the standards, along with the standards. Its demand has been decreasing over the years, but you will find it useful if you need to target all browsers and not just the modern ones. Personally, I would highly recommend not using jQuery as it will most likely lead you down the path of breaking the SOLID principles and mixing up your concerns.

SignalR has a dependency on jQuery directly, meaning that all the web projects in this book will have jQuery in them as a result.

ASP.NET MVC 5

Microsoft's web story consists of two major and different stories at the root level. One of these is the story related to web forms that came with the first version of the .NET Framework back in 2002. Since then, it has been iteratively developed and improved with each new version of the framework. The other is the MVC story, which was started in 2007 with the version 1 release in 2009 that represents something very different and built from the ground up from different concepts than found in the web forms story. In 2014, we saw the release of version 5 with quite a few new ideas, making it even simpler to do the type of decoupling one aims for and also making it easier to bring in things (such as SignalR). We will use ASP.NET MVC for the first samples, not taking full advantage of its potential, but enough to be able to show the integration with SignalR and how you can benefit from it.

KnockoutJS

It seems that over the last couple of years, you can pretty much take any noun or verb and throw a JS behind it, Google it, and you will find a framework at the other end of it. KnockoutJS (`http://www.knockoutjs.com`) represents a solution to MVVM for JavaScript in the web browser. It's a focused library with the aim of solving the case of having views that are able to observe your ViewModel. It also takes advantage of any behavior being exposed.

Bifrost

In some of the chapters, a platform called Bifrost (which you can access at `http://bifrost.dolittle.com/`) will be used. It's an end-to-end opinionated platform that focuses on CQRS and MVVM. It also shows a few other things, such as convention over configuration (`http://www.techopedia.com/definition/27478/convention-over-configuration`), along with a few ways of decoupling your software. The platform is open sourced and it's worth mentioning that I am the lead developer, visionary, and initiator of the project. The project got started in 2008 as a means to solve business cases while working on different projects.

Within Bifrost, you will only find things that are based on real business value, rather than imagined solutions to problems that have never been experienced.

When Bifrost is applied, there are other dependencies it pulls in as well, which will be discussed when they are being used. A few of these dependencies introduce a couple of other aspects of software development and will be explained once they are used.

Making it look good – using Twitter bootstrap

In the interest of saving time and focus more on code, we will "outsource" the design in this book and layout to Twitter bootstrap (which you can access at `http://getbootstrap.com`). Bootstrap defines a grid system that governs all layouts and it also has well-defined CSS to make things look good. It comes with a predefined theme that looks great, and there are other themes out there if you want to change the themes.

Tools

As with any craft, we need tools to build anything. Here is a summary of some of the tools we will be using to create our applications.

Visual Studio 2013

In this book, you will find that Visual Studio 2013 professional is being used for all cases for development except for *Chapter 8, Putting the X in .NET – Xamarin*, which makes use of Xamarin Studio. You can use the community edition of Visual Studio 2013 if you don't have a license Visual Studio 2013 professional or higher. It can be downloaded from `http://www.visualstudio.com/`.

NuGet

All third-party dependencies and all the libraries mentioned in this chapter, for instance, will be pulled in using NuGet.

In the interest of saving space in the book, the description of how to use NuGet sits here and only here. The other chapters will refer back to this recipe.

If you need to install NuGet first, visit `http://www.nuget.org` to download and install it. Once this is done, you can use NuGet by following these steps:

1. To add a reference to a project, we start by right-clicking on **References** of your project and selecting **Manage NuGet Packages**, as shown here:

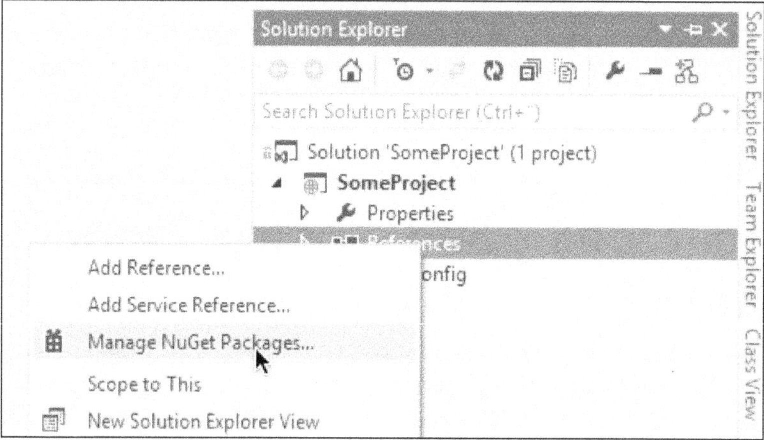

2. Next, select **Online** and enter the name of the package that you want to add a reference to in the search box. When you have found the proper package, click on the **Install** button, as shown in the following screenshot:

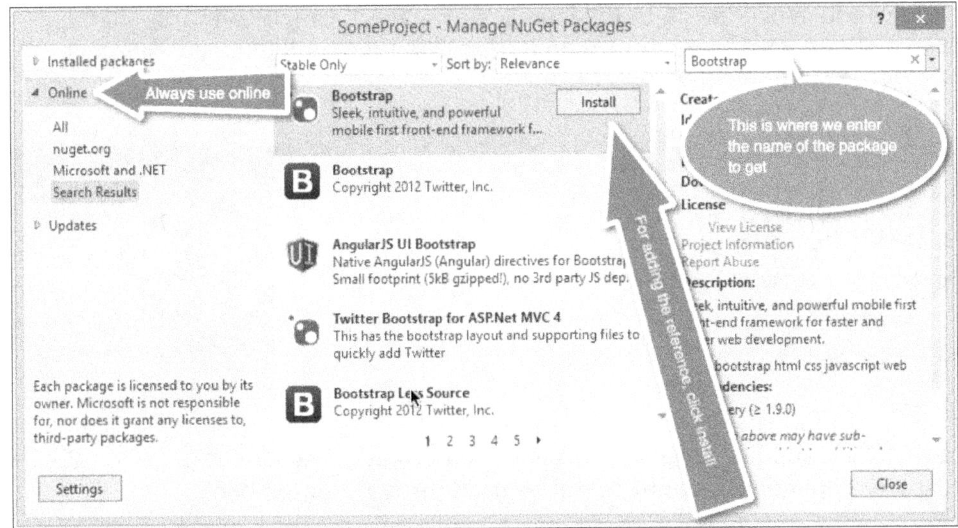

In some cases, we will need a specific version of a file. This is not something we can do through the UI, and we will need the package manager console.

3. Following this, go to **TOOLS** and then **NuGet Package Manager**. Click on **Package Manager Console**, as shown here:

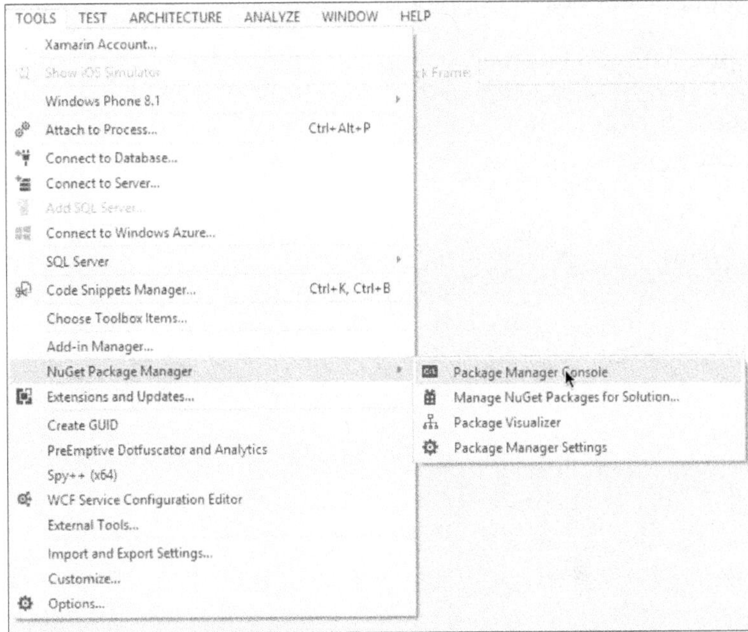

4. You then need to go to the **Package Manager Console** window that appears and you need to make sure that the project that will have the reference is selected:

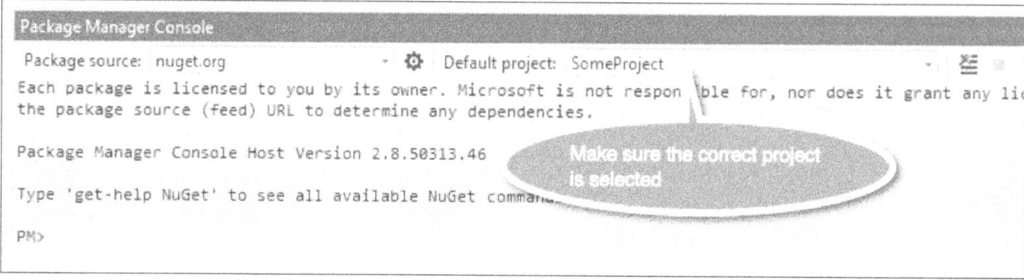

By now, you should be familiar with how you can add NuGet packages to reference third-party dependencies, which will be used throughout the book.

Summary

You now have a backdrop of knowledge, if you didn't already know it all. We explained the terminology in this chapter so that the terms will be clear to you throughout. It's now time to get concrete and actually start applying what we've discussed. Although this chapter mentions quite a few concepts and they might be new to you, don't worry as we'll revisit them throughout the book and gain more knowledge about them as we go along.

The next chapter will start out with a simple sample, showing the very basics of SignalR so that you get the feeling of what it is and how its APIs are. It will also show you how to do this with ASP.NET MVC and throw in the mix of the usage of bootstrap and jQuery.

2
Overheating the Discussion

This chapter will cover the basics of getting started with SignalR and at the same time will show the potential to improve the user experience in a simple way. We will begin with something simple, which is making your own forum discussion site. As a consequence of creating this, you will learn more about the following topics:

- Using simple ASP.NET MVC 5
- Enabling security
- Using simple jQuery
- Using Entity Framework 6
- Utilizing a hub
- Using SignalR groups

The goal – how to create a basic forum discussion site

Forums have been around since the dawn of computing, taking on many forms: bulletin board systems, user groups, and also web-based forums on different sites. In this chapter, we'll build our own forum and light it up with SignalR, improving the overall user experience and also scalability of the solution. We'll use the top-level abstraction within SignalR called a **hub**. The hub enables us to expose methods from the server directly to the client and also makes it possible to call functions on the client side from the server directly.

By the end of the chapter, you'll understand the basics of SignalR and how to use the top-level abstraction: hub. Also, you will briefly look at what MVC gives you in combination with Entity Framework.

So, let's just jump straight into it!

Hub

At the core level of SignalR sits something called a `PersistentConnection` class; hubs build on top of this. We won't be covering `PersistentConnection` as it is far more convenient to be working with the hub. In my opinion, a hub is the preferred abstraction to use; most applications really don't need to go any lower than this. It provides functionality to define functionality on the server in a C# class, much like an MVC or a Web API controller with the exception of it being persistently connected, leaving it possible to also call functionality on the client as well. The clients consume the hub and can directly call the methods on them. However, these clients can also register the client functions it responds to and create a subscription from the client that makes it respond to what it registered when the server calls it.

Getting started – creating an MVC template

Firstly, you'll need to open up your Visual Studio installation and create a new project by clicking on **New Project** from the **File** menu. The following dialog box will show up. Click on **Web** from the left-hand side menu and then select **ASP.NET Web Application**. Enter `Chapter2` in the **Name** textbox and select your location, as shown in the following screenshot:

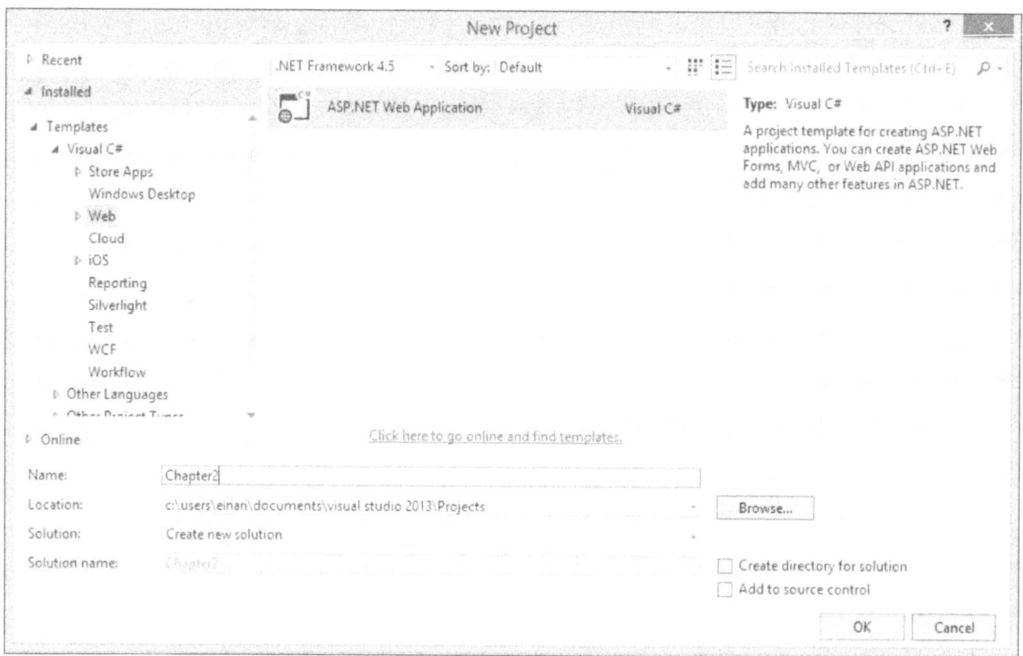

As we want to create an MVC app, select the **MVC** template from the template selector and make sure you deselect the **Host in the cloud** option. Before clicking on **OK**, click on the **Change Authentication** button, as shown in the following screenshot:

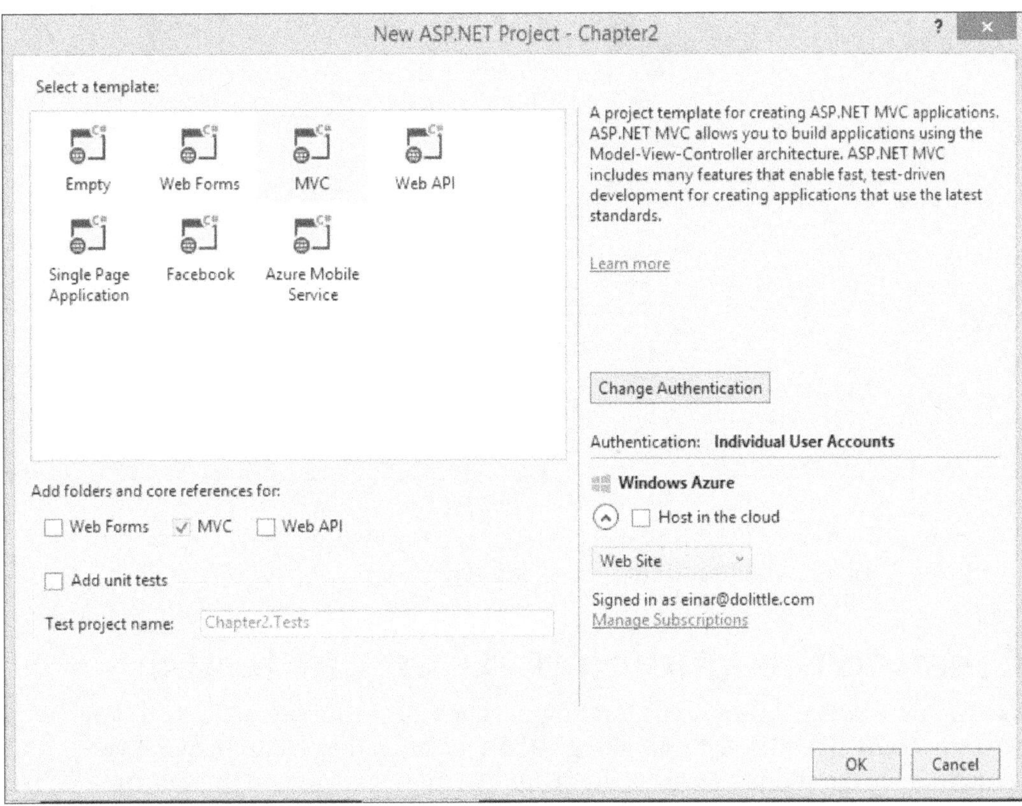

As you can see from the following screenshot, a dialog box will pop up. Make sure the **Individual User Accounts** option is selected and click on **OK**, followed by **OK** in the template selector dialog box you came from:

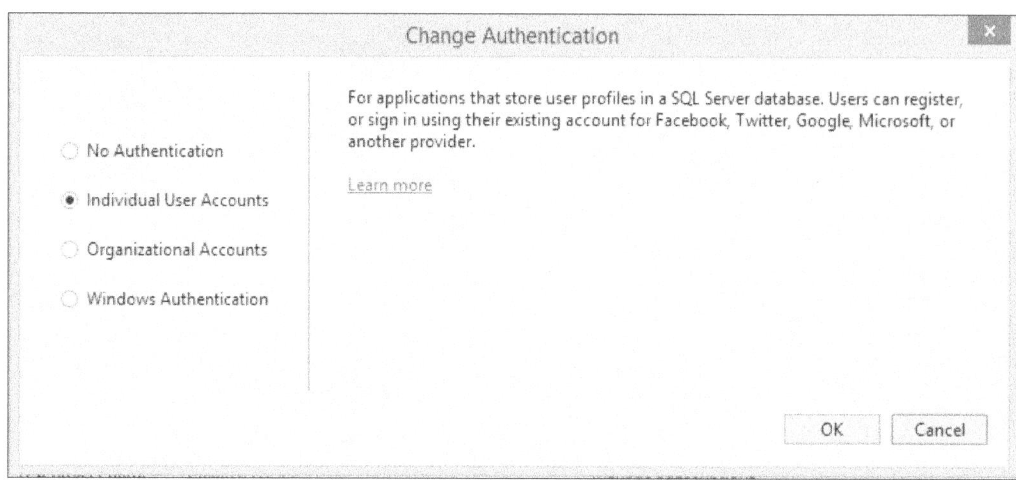

You now have your MVC template created, which enables authentication with its own user database. The foundation has been set!

Creating the landing page for our forum

We want to start off by getting a landing page for our forum. In order to do this, we need an MVC controller that will give us the action that will return the view, which we will be working from. This is done by right-clicking on the **Controllers** in the project inside **Solution Explorer** and selecting **Controller** from the **Add** menu, as shown here:

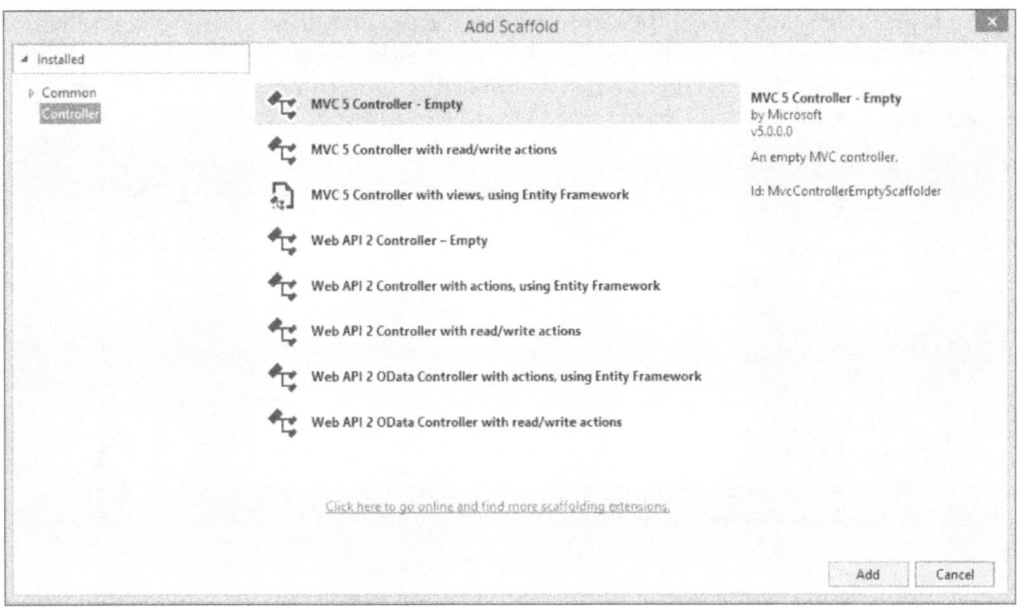

You can then name the controller as `ForumController` in the **Add Controller** dialog box. Next, click on **Add**, as shown in the following screenshot. Notice that the controller holds a method called `Index()` that returns a `View()`, which is the default view we will have for our forum.

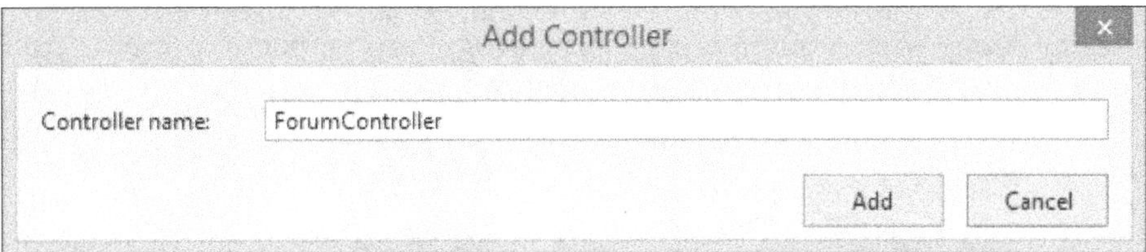

Leave the controller as it is; we won't require anything in it just yet.

Now, we want to establish a folder for any views related to the forum. Right-click on the `Views` folder in **Solution Explorer**, select **New Folder** from the **Add** menu, and name the folder `Forum`.

In the folder, we want to add the default view for the forum, so right-click on the newly created forum folder and select **View** from **Add**. Name the view as `Index` in the **View name** textbox. Leave the rest as default, as you can see in the following screenshot:

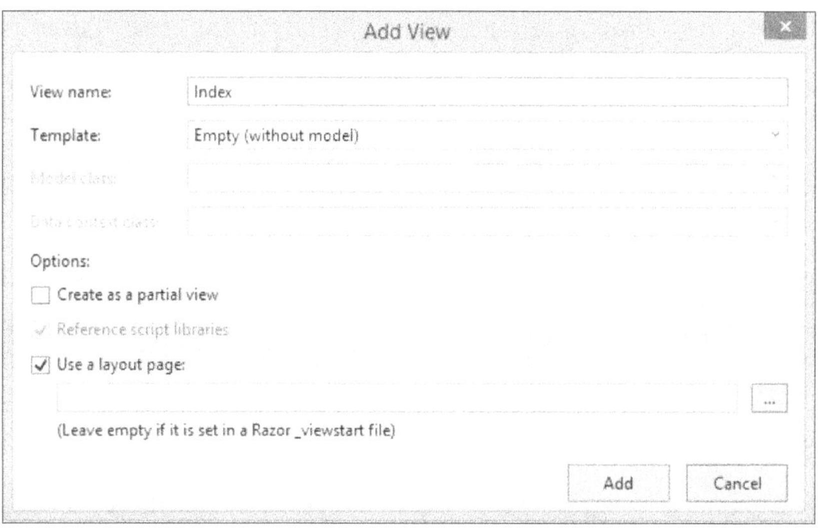

It's now time to build and run it by selecting the **Run Without Debugging** option from **Debug** (*Ctrl* + *F5*). When the site is running, navigate to `http://localhost:<port>/Forum/Index`. The port is generated by Visual Studio so just leave this as it was when you first started the project and append `/Forum/Index` at the end. You will see the following screenshot:

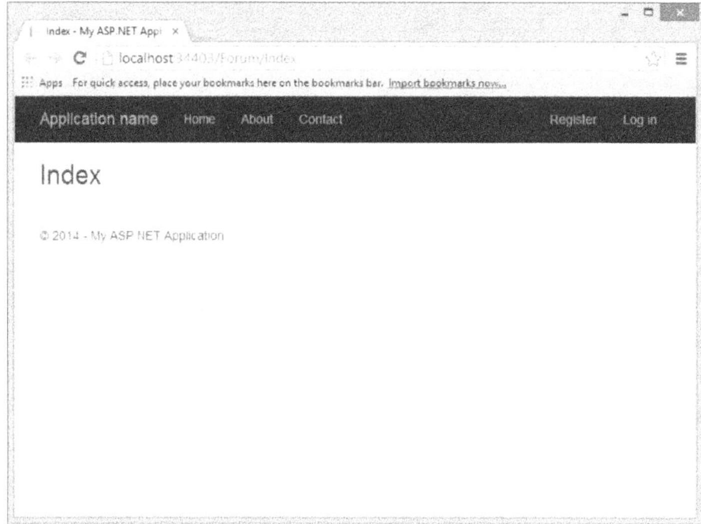

Setting up the packages

Now, we're going to need some packages to light things up. Let's start off by adding Entity Framework so that we can easily store the forum threads and posts in a database. We will be pulling this using NuGet, as described in *Chapter 1, The Primer*. Right-click on the **References** in **Solution Explorer**, select **Manage NuGet Packages**, and then type `EntityFramework` in the search box. Select it and click on install. We'll need a second package, which is the most important one: SignalR. Add a NuGet package reference as shown in the previous step, but this time, type `SignalR` in the search box. You should now find a package called **Microsoft ASP.NET SignalR**, select it, and click on **Install**. This will pull down a few other packages that SignalR depends on.

At this point, we have the project prepared with dependencies needed and a view and controller to start putting in a user interface our logic.

Preparing our web application for SignalR

We now have the dependencies set up as required so all we need now is to prepare our web application for SignalR.

Making your SignalR hubs available for the client

Any hubs that we create need to be exposed to any connecting client so that they can be used. Let's start by exposing any SignalR hubs that we add from this point to automatically be available for our client. Open up the `Startup.cs` file. At the bottom of the `Configuration` method, we need to add a call to map any SignalR hubs, as shown in the following code:

```
public void Configuration(IAppBuilder app)
{
ConfigureAuth(app);
App.MapSignalR();
}
```

It's possible to specify a base URL in the `MapSignalR()` method call that enables you to expose SignalR at whichever route you see fit.

By default, SignalR uses something called **Open Web Interface for .NET** (**OWIN**) and it needs to be told what the starting point is. Notice this is at the top of the `Startup.cs` file, above the namespace declaration but right below the using statements:

```
[assembly: OwinStartupAttribute(typeof(Chapter2.Startup))]
```

This will then, by convention, find the method called `Configuration` and call it when the signature matches.

> OWIN defines a standard interface between .NET web servers and web applications.

How to add JavaScript references to views

Now, we need to have the JavaScript references added to all our views. In ASP.NET MVC, you'll get a `Shared` folder within the `Views` folder in your project. This folder holds a `Layout.cshtml` file that represents the view template and layout for your site. In addition, this file defines the structure of your views and includes the JavaScript files you want for all views as well. Open this file and navigate to the bottom where you will find the following code snippet:

```
@Scripts.Render("~/bundles/jquery")
@Scripts.Render("~/bundles/bootstrap")
```

Add the following script references to the preceding code snippet:

```
<script src="~/Scripts/jquery.signalR-2.1.0.min.js"
type="text/javascript"></script>
<script src="~/signalr/hubs" type="text/javascript"></script>
```

The last script tag pulls in code that is generated by SignalR for all the hubs. This is really convenient because we get all the methods on the server automatically exposed to us without having to define anything ourselves. During the configuration we did in C# with exposing the hub to the client, this is also part of that exposure.

> The version that you get while adding the SignalR NuGet package might be different than the one described here. As we're not specifying a version when adding the package, you will get the latest released version, which is likely to be newer than what is in this book as they churn out new versions quite often. So, look in your `Scripts` folder to reflect the version you have for the script tag.

Creating a simple template mechanism

In addition to adding in SignalR and the hubs, we will create a very simple template mechanism, which we will use later to take data and expand it onto visual elements. Add a JavaScript file to the `Scripts` folder by right-clicking on the `Scripts` folder and selecting **New Item** from the **Add** menu. Then, select **Web templates** and then **JavaScript file**. Call it `templating.js` and click on **Add**. Finally, insert the following code in the file:

```
function expandTemplateWithData(templateName, data) {
    var template = document.getElementById(templateName);
    if (template == null) return; document.createElement("span");
    var templateString = template.innerHTML;

    for (var property in data) {
        templateString = templateString.split("%"+property+"%").
join(data[property]);
    }

    return $(templateString)[0];
}
```

The purpose of this code is to have something that can take a template, typically defined in a script tag and given a name, and expand the data we're giving it onto the template. In this template, you can basically have properties that you want to get filled with the data from the given data, and the format is that you specify the name of the property surrounded with `%`. So, if you have a property called `Title` in the data, you can have `%Title%` in the template, and it will be replaced by the actual value in the data given to the function.

We then want this to be included on all pages; go back to the `_Layout.cshtml` file and add another script reference block below the `"~/signalr/hubs"` reference, as shown here:

```
<script src="~/Scripts/templating.js"
type="text/javascript"></script>
```

Securing the forum

Now that we have things set up and are ready to go, we want to secure our forum. Only registered members should be able to see and use it. Open `ForumController`. At the top of the class, right above the class declaration, we will add an attribute that tells the ASP.NET pipeline to require an authorized user in order to execute any of the actions, as shown here:

```
[Authorize]
```

Everything inside the forum will now be locked down and you need a user to go there. Run the solution (*Ctrl + F5*), go to the **Register** link at the top-right corner of the window and register yourself as a user.

At this point, we have prepared the solution for SignalR, got all the JavaScript references needed, and also added a simple template solution.

How to create your UI for threads on your forum

Let's go back to the `Index.cshtml` view that was added to the `Views/Forum` folder and start building the user interface for the thread view and creation of new threads. Start by changing the headline from `Index` to `All threads` by finding the `<h2>` tag close to the top of the file, as shown here:

```
<h2>All threads</h2>
```

Creating the thread list – adding a table

Now, we want to add a table that will serve as the thread list, and yes it actually is a good use of the table. In HTML, table was abused for years to deal with layout instead of being used for listings like this. We use bootstrap CSS classes to make it look good. Add the following code right after the `<h2>` headline:

```
<table class="table table-bordered table-striped table-condensed
table-hover">
<thread>
<tr>
   <th>Title</th>
   <th>Started</th>
      <th>Started by</th>
      <th>Last post</th>
      <th>Last post by</th>
      <th>Post count</th>
</tr>
</thread>
<tbody id="threadTableBody">
</tbody>
</table>
```

Notice the `"threadTableBody"` ID for the `<tbody>` element (this will be the place where we add rows for the listing). Above the `<table>`, add the following `text/html` script template:

```
<script id="threadRowTemplate" type="text/html">
    <tr data-thread="%ID%">
        <td>%Title%</td>
        <td>%Started%</td>
        <td>%StartedBy%</td>
        <td>%LastPost%</td>
        <td>%LastPostBy%</td>
        <td>%PostCount%</td>
    </tr>
</script>
```

This template represents the template for each item in the table; each thread basically. The `expandTemplateWithData` function is the one that will be used to expand the properties based on the syntax explained earlier.

Adding a modal for creation of new threads

A vital part of the system will be the ability to start a new thread. We want to make this a modal dialog. After the table, at the end of the file, add the following markup:

```
<div id="createThreadModal" class="modal fade" role="dialog"
tabindex="-1">
    <div class="modal-dialog">
        <div class="modal-content">
            <div class="modal-header">
                <button type="button" class="close" data-
dismiss="modal"><span aria-hidden="true">&times;</span><span
class="sr-only">Close</span></button>
                <h4 class="modal-title">New thread</h4>
            </div>
            <div class="modal-body">
                <form role="form">
                    <div class="form-group">
                        <label for="title">Title</label>
                        <input id="title" type="text" class="form-
control" placeholder="Enter title">
                    </div>
                    <div class="form-group">
                        <label for="content">Content</label>
                        <textarea id="content" class="form-
control" rows="3"></textarea>
```

```
                    </div>
                </form>
            </div>

            <div class="modal-footer">
                <button type="button" class="btn btn-default" 
data-dismiss="modal">Cancel</button>
                <button id="saveThreadButton" type="button" data-
dismiss="modal" class="btn btn-primary">Save</button>
            </div>
        </div>
    </div>
</div>
```

The bootstrap-based modal dialog box recognizes `role="dialog"` and all you need is a button that opens it up. Through a `data-toggle=""` attribute, we will be able to make it thread our dialog box as a modal one and by specifying `data-target="";` we can point it to the correct target through CSS selectors. Add the following button and horizontal line above the table:

```
<button id="newThreadButton" class="btn btn-primary" data-
toggle="modal" data-target="#createThreadModal">New 
thread</button>
<hr />
```

Enabling the interaction for the view

We want to have a JavaScript file associated with the view; it will represent the "code-behind" the view and will deal with the interaction of the view and later the connection back and forth with the server. Expand the `Scripts` folder in the project and add a folder in it by right-clicking on the `Scripts` folder, selecting **New Folder** from **Add**, and naming it `Forum`.

Right-click on the new `Forum` folder, click on **New Item** from **Add**, select the **Web templates** on the left-hand side, and then **JavaScript file**. Finally, name it **Index.js** and then click on **Add**.

Now, we need to include our JavaScript file for the view. The layout template renders a section called scripts, something we can use on our concrete view and put in any script references for the page, placing them in the correct location in the finished HTML output. For this view, we want to have:

```
@section scripts {
    <script type="text/javascript" src="~/Scripts/Forum/Index.js"></
script>
}
```

Creating threads

Before we can populate the list with thread entries, we must be able to actually create one. We will need two models: `Thread` and `Post`. The `Thread` model will be the top-level container, establishing the subject for one or more post. Inside the `Models` folder of the project, we want a folder called `Forum`. Inside this, we want a C# file called `Thread.cs` (right-click on the `Forum` folder and select **Class** from **Add**). Open the `Thread.cs` file and make the file look like the following:

```
using System;
using System.ComponentModel.DataAnnotations.Schema;

namespace Chapter2.Models.Forum
{
    public class Thread
    {
        [DatabaseGenerated(DatabaseGeneratedOption.Identity)]
        public int ID { get; set; }
        public string Title { get; set; }
        public DateTime Started { get; set; }
        public string StartedBy { get; set; }
        public DateTime LastPost { get; set; }
        public string LastPostBy { get; set; }

        public int PostCount { get; set; }
    }
}
```

The thread type represents the information needed to be able to display the thread in the listing; it does not hold any posts as it gives no value to keep these together. We will model these on our own. Again, add a class to the `Models\Forum` folder, call this file `Post.cs`. Add the following code in it:

```
using System;
using System.ComponentModel.DataAnnotations.Schema;

namespace Chapter2.Models.Forum
{
    public class Post
    {
        [DatabaseGenerated(DatabaseGeneratedOption.Identity)]
        public int ID { get; set; }
        public int ThreadID { get; set; }
        public string Content { get; set; }
```

```
            public DateTime Created { get; set; }
            public string CreatedBy { get; set; }
        }
    }
```

Now that we have the two models, we will need, throughout this sample, a way of working with them so that they can be inserted into a database and also be able to retrieve them when needed. Go and add a folder at the project root called `DAL` (Data Access Layer). In this folder, add a C# file called `ForumContext.cs`. Add the following code in the file:

```
using System;
using System.Data.Entity;
using Chapter2.Models.Forum;
namespace Chapter2.DAL
{
public class ForumContext : DbContext
{
public ForumContext() : base("DefaultConnection") { }
public DbSet<Thread> Threads { get; set; }
public DbSet<Post> Posts { get; set; }
}
}
```

We now have something that enables us to retrieve `Threads` or `Posts` from the database. The `DbSet<>` type does contain the ability to add and delete new things to it. It also holds a method to save any changes to any objects related to the `DbSet` type. We will use this functionality to create a couple of convenience methods to create a thread and a post to a thread. Put the following methods right after the last `Posts` property in the `ForumContext` class:

```
        public Thread InsertThread(string title, string content)
        {
            var currentUser =
System.Threading.Thread.CurrentPrincipal.Identity.Name;

            var thread = new Thread
            {
                Title = title,
                Started = DateTime.UtcNow,
                StartedBy = currentUser,
                LastPost = DateTime.UtcNow,
                LastPostBy = currentUser
            };
```

```
            Threads.Add(thread);
            SaveChanges();

            return thread;
        }

        public Post InsertPost(int threadID, string content, out
Thread thread)
        {
            var currentUser =
System.Threading.Thread.CurrentPrincipal.Identity.Name;

            var post = new Post
            {
                ThreadID = threadID,
                Content = content,
                Created = DateTime.UtcNow,
                CreatedBy = currentUser
            };
            Posts.Add(post);

            thread = Threads.Find(threadID);
            thread.LastPost = DateTime.UtcNow;
            thread.LastPostBy = currentUser;
            thread.PostCount++;

            SaveChanges();

            return post;
        }
```

At this point, we have the functionality in our server code that enables us to create threads and posts for these threads. This will come handy in the hubs that we will create.

Our first hub – threads

Now that we have our data access layer and the models in place, we want to expose our first SignalR hub, enabling us to actually work with this from the client. At the root of the project, add a folder called `Hubs`, and inside this folder, create another folder called `Forum`. In this folder, we want to add a C# class called `ThreadHub.cs`. Start by adding the following code in it:

```
using System;
using System.Collections.Generic;
using System.Linq;
```

```
using Chapter2.DAL;
using Chapter2.Models.Forum;
using Microsoft.AspNet.SignalR;

namespace Chapter2.Hubs.Forum
{
    public class ThreadHub : Hub
    {
        ForumContext _forumContext;

        public ThreadHub()
        {
            _forumContext = new ForumContext();
        }

        protected override void Dispose(bool disposing)
        {
            if (disposing)
            {
                _forumContext.Dispose();
            }
            base.Dispose(disposing)
        }
    }
}
```

Being a good citizen means you need to clean up. Implementing `IDisposable` is good practice when you instantiate objects that need to be cleaned up. This way, the garbage collector will make sure to call your `dispose` method enabling you to clean up. Hub already implements this interface but leaves a `protected` method virtual that can be overridden to deal with this.

By just putting in the hub and running the application, it's now automatically exposed to the client through JavaScript proxy generation. The `"/~signalr/hubs"` script reference we put in earlier will pull down the generated proxy for any hubs in the system. However, the hub is not exposing anything interesting yet.

Enabling the data access for threads

Let's add a method to insert a thread. Add the following method right underneath the constructor of the `ThreadHub`:

```
        public void Create(string title, string content)
        {
            var thread = _forumContext.InsertThread(title,
content);
            var post = _forumContext.InsertPost(thread.ID,
content, out thread);

            Clients.All.threadCreated(thread);
        }
```

We now have a method that will make use of the `ForumContext` and insert `Thread` and `Post` into the database and also broadcast it to all connected clients that there was a thread created. When the application starts, this won't be of any use if there is already data in the database, so we want to expose a way of getting to existing threads as well. Add the following method right under the `Create` method:

```
        public IEnumerable<Thread>   GetAll()
        {
            var all = _forumContext.Threads.ToArray();
            return all;
        }
```

Let's move back to the frontend. Open up the `Index.js` file created in the `Scripts\Forum` folder. We want to hook into the document-ready event of the browser, create an instance `threadHub`, and then get data from it. Add the following code in the file:

```
$(function () {
    var threadHub = $.connection.threadHub;

    $.connection.hub.start().done(function () {
        threadHub.server.getAll().done(function (threads) {
        });
    });
});
```

At this point, we should be able to use the debuggers to see some result. You can now run this in a browser of your choice and put a breakpoint using the JavaScript debugger in the browser on the `threadHub.server.getAll()` line and see whether you are connected to the hub. Likewise, running with the debugger in Visual Studio, you will be able to set a breakpoint in the `threadHub` inside the `getAll()` method and see whether it gets called.

Making the threads become visible

Now, we need something that can take data coming from the server and then create a row in the table of the view. We will now make use of the template mechanism that we put in earlier. At the top of the `index.js` file, add the following code:

```
function addOrReplaceRow(thread) {
    var tableBody = document.getElementById("threadTableBody");
    var row = expandTemplateWithData("threadRowTemplate", thread);

    row.addEventListener("click", function (e) {
        document.location = "/Forum/Thread/" + thread.ID;
    });

    var $existingRow = $("[data-thread='" + thread.ID + "']");
    if ($existingRow.length == 1) {
        tableBody.replaceChild(row, $existingRow[0]);
    } else {
        tableBody.appendChild(row);
    }
}
```

The function adds a click event listener to the row it creates from the template that will navigate us directly into the thread. We will add the appropriate controller action and view for this later.

The data we get from the server contains fully expanded dates, but we want them formatted slightly different on the client. To do this, we need a mapping method that takes the data and modifies it slightly. Below the `addOrReplaceRow` function, add the following function:

```
function mapThread(thread) {
    thread.Started = new Date(thread.Started).toLocaleString();
    thread.LastPost = new Date(thread.LastPost).toLocaleString();
}
```

Hooking up the user interaction

Now, we really want to get to the magic: take the data, create rows to put it into the table, and also react to events coming in when threads are being created. Modify the document; the `$(function() { ... })` block at the bottom will look like the following code:

```
$(function () {
    var threadHub = $.connection.threadHub;
```

```
    var button = document.getElementById("saveThreadButton");
    var title = document.getElementById("title");
    var content = document.getElementById("content");

    button.addEventListener("click", function () {
        threadHub.server.create(title.value,
content.value).done(function () {
            title.value = "";
            content.value = "";
        });
    });

    threadHub.client.threadUpdated =
    threadHub.client.threadCreated = function (thread) {
        mapThread(thread);
        addOrReplaceRow(thread);
    };

    $.connection.hub.start().done(function () {
        threadHub.server.getAll().done(function (threads) {
            threads.forEach(threadHub.client.threadUpdated);
        });
    });
});
```

What we just added here was a hookup for `saveThreadButton` that connects back to the hub on the server and starts a new thread. In addition to this, we hook up two client functions that the server will be capable of calling: `threadUpdated` and `threadCreated`. The way we make a function available on the client is by going to the client property on the hub instance on the client and adding the function you want to expose. Calling this from the server will then automatically call it on the client. The function used by the update and created event is the same that we give to the `forEach` function. This way, we don't have to repeat the same code of mapping the thread object and adding or replacing the row.

At this point, running this (*Ctrl* + *F5*) will actually be a functional application. Creating a thread should result in the thread coming back. Refreshing the browser should also give you data coming back.

The detail view – posts on specific threads

Now that we have a list of threads, it's time to enable us to view a single thread and its posts. We want to click an item in the thread list and then be taken to a view that shows the content in the form of posts for this thread.

Navigating to a thread to see the posts

With a functional thread list, we now want to create the view to click a thread in the list. Let's start by adding another controller action that will take us to the view. Open the `ForumController.cs` file in the `Controllers` folder. Add the following method at the bottom of the class:

```
public ActionResult Thread(int id)
{
return View();
}
```

The `Thread` action needs a `Thread` view. Add, as before, a view by right-clicking on the `Forum` folder sitting in the `Views` folder of the project and select **View** from **Add**. Name it `Thread`, leave the defaults, and then click on **Add**.

Adding the view content for a thread

The new `Thread` view will be similar to what we had for the `Index` view, only this will be focused around posts for the thread, rather than the thread itself. Open the `Thread.cshtml` view and replace the entire content of the file with the following code:

```
@{
    ViewBag.Title = "Thread";
}
@section scripts {
<script type="text/javascript" src="~/Scripts/Forum/Thread.js"></
script>
}
<h2>Thread</h2>

<script id="postRowTemplate" type="text/html">
    <tr data-post="%ID%">
        <td>%CreatedBy%</td>
        <td>%Content%</td>
```

```
            <td>%Created%</td>
        </tr>
    </script>

    <table class="table table-bordered table-striped table-condensed
    table-hover">
        <thead>
            <tr>
                <td width="100">Author</td>
                <td>Content</td>
                <td width="150">Posted</td>
            </tr>
        </thead>
        <tbody id="postTableBody">
        </tbody>
    </table>

    <div class="modal-body">
        <div role="form">
            <div class="form-group">
                <label for="content">Content</label>
                <textarea id="content" class="form-control"
    rows="3"></textarea>
            </div>

            <button id="postReplyButton" class="btn btn-
    primary">Reply</button>
        </form>
    </div>
```

The `Thread` hub we created was focused on threads, now we need one that is focused on posts. Add a C# class in the `Hubs\Forum` folder called `PostHub.cs` and add the following code in the file:

```
using System;
using System.Collections.Generic;
using System.Linq;
using Chapter2.DAL;
using Chapter2.Models.Forum;
using Microsoft.AspNet.SignalR;

namespace Chapter2.Hubs.Forum
{
    public class PostHub : Hub
    {
```

```
        ForumContext _forumContext;
        public PostHub()
        {
            _forumContext = new ForumContext();
        }

        protected override void Dispose(bool disposing)
        {
            if (disposing)
            {
               _forumContext.Dispose();
            }
            base.Dispose(disposing)
        }


        public IEnumerable<Post> GetForThread(int threadID)
        {
            var group = ThreadHub.GetGroupNameForThread(threadID);
            Groups.Add(Context.ConnectionId, group);

            return _forumContext.Posts.Where(p => p.ThreadID ==
threadID);
        }

        public void AddPostToThread(int threadID, string content)
        {
            Thread thread;
            var post = _forumContext.InsertPost(threadID, content,
out thread);
            PostAdded(post);
            ThreadHub.ThreadUpdated(thread);
        }

        public static void PostAdded(Post post)
        {
            var hubContext =
GlobalHost.ConnectionManager.GetHubContext<PostHub>();
            hubContext.Clients.Group(ThreadHub.
GetGroupNameForThread(post.
ThreadID)).postAdded(post);
        }
    }
}
```

A major difference with this code compared to the code in the `ThreadHub` is the fact that we are not broadcasting to all clients but rather to the clients that are looking at the thread. The way we join the group as it's called is by adding the connection to the group, which is named based on the thread identifier. The thread identifier is pulled from the URL of the browser.

You might have noticed that the code in the `PostHub` is calling into `ThreadHub`, but the methods it is calling do not exist. Open the `ThreadHub` and add the following methods at the bottom of the class:

```
        public static string GetGroupNameForThread(int threadID)
        {
            return string.Format("Thread-{0}", threadID);
        }

        public static void ThreadUpdated(Thread thread)
        {
            var hubContext =
GlobalHost.ConnectionManager.GetHubContext<ThreadHub>();
            hubContext.Clients.All.threadUpdated(thread);
        }
```

Adding the thread view logic

At the top of the `Thread.cshtml` file, you will notice that there is a script section that refers to another JavaScript file, which we will have to create. Add a JavaScript file called `Thread.js` to the `Scripts\Forum` folder. Add the following code in the file:

```
function getCurrentThreadID() {
    var elements = document.location.toString().split("/");
    var threadID = parseInt(elements[elements.length - 1]);
    return threadID;
}

function addOrReplaceRow(post) {
    var tableBody = document.getElementById("postTableBody");
    var row = expandTemplateWithData("postRowTemplate", post);

    row.addEventListener("click", function (e) {
        document.location = "/Forum/Thread/" + post.ID;
    });

    var $existingRow = $("[data-post='" + post.ID + "']");
    if ($existingRow.length == 1) {
```

```
            tableBody.replaceChild(row, $existingRow[0]);
        } else {
            tableBody.appendChild(row);
        }
    }

    function mapPost(post) {
        post.Created = new Date(post.Created).toLocaleString();
    }


    $(function () {
        var postHub = $.connection.postHub;

        var postReplyButton = document.getElementById("postReplyButton");
        postReplyButton.addEventListener("click", function () {
            var threadID = getCurrentThreadID();
            var contentTextArea = document.getElementById("content");
            postHub.server.addPostToThread(threadID, contentTextArea.
    value);
            contentTextArea.value = "";
        });

        postHub.client.postAdded = function (post) {
            mapPost(post);
            addOrReplaceRow(post);
        };

        $.connection.hub.start().done(function () {
            var threadID = getCurrentThreadID();
            postHub.server.getForThread(threadID).done(function
    (posts) {
                posts.forEach(postHub.client.postAdded);
            });
        });
    });
```

As you'll notice, the code is very much similar to what we did in the `Index.js` file. The goal is the same: get data at startup and add it to a table in the view. When data gets added in the server, we want to respond to the client and add it to the table.

Running the solution now should give you two different views: a thread view that will respond to new threads being started by other users and also respond to users adding new posts. Clicking on a thread in the thread list should take you to the thread view that lists all posts and will respond to new posts being published by other users.

Summary

In this chapter, we've scratched the surface of SignalR, but you already should get a sense of the power of thinking differently about how you build your applications by creating your own simple discussion forum. The fact that we just define methods in C# and these are automatically accessible from the client code through the generated proxies makes it really productive to work with. It basically bridges the gap between the client and the server. What you'll notice is that we managed to actually create a forum that works, deploying the latest and greatest of technologies in the ASP.NET space in very little code.

You can find the entire sample code at `https://github.com/dolittle/SignalR_Blueprints/tree/master/Source/Chapter2`.

In the next chapter, we'll dive into how this real-time thinking can go even further and how to deal with scale. By taking another common real-world sample and online newspapers, we'll see how you can deploy SignalR to improve things for newspaper readers and at the same time deal with scaling across multiple servers.

3

Extra! Extra! Read All About It!

This chapter will reiterate some of the concepts from *Chapter 2, Overheating the Discussion*, from a different type of application. It will also show you how SignalR can be used. In this chapter, you will cover the following topics:

- More features of ASP.NET MVC 5 and Razor views
- Securing specific methods
- Using Entity Framework 6 for more advanced querying
- Utilizing a hub
- Bringing in more features to Twitter bootstrap

The goal – how to bring to life an imagined news site

E-newspapers have a great potential to increase the user experience by applying something like SignalR. When doing so, they also accidently make their solution more scalable as they don't have to rely on what a lot of sites do already: a timer that reloads the entire page every so often. Having a number of clients connected to the site, it's much more efficient to just push out any news that gets published, rather than having all of these refresh all the content every so often. The goal is therefore to create a sample of how an e-newspaper could utilize SignalR. With any connected client that receives breaking news, we can improve the user experience by pushing the news to the user. There are obviously quite a few other things one could do, but let's just keep to this. Again, similar to *Chapter 2, Overheating the Discussion*, we will utilize the top-level abstraction called a hub. As a developer, this gives us a far more productive way of working with SignalR. Also, we will start with an ASP.NET MVC 5 template and take it from there.

By the end of this chapter, you'll start to feel a bit more familiar with how SignalR works, and how you should think about your approach.

Let's get started.

Getting started – creating an MVC template

1. Open Visual Studio and create a new project by navigating to **FILE** | **New** | **Project**. The following dialog box will show up:

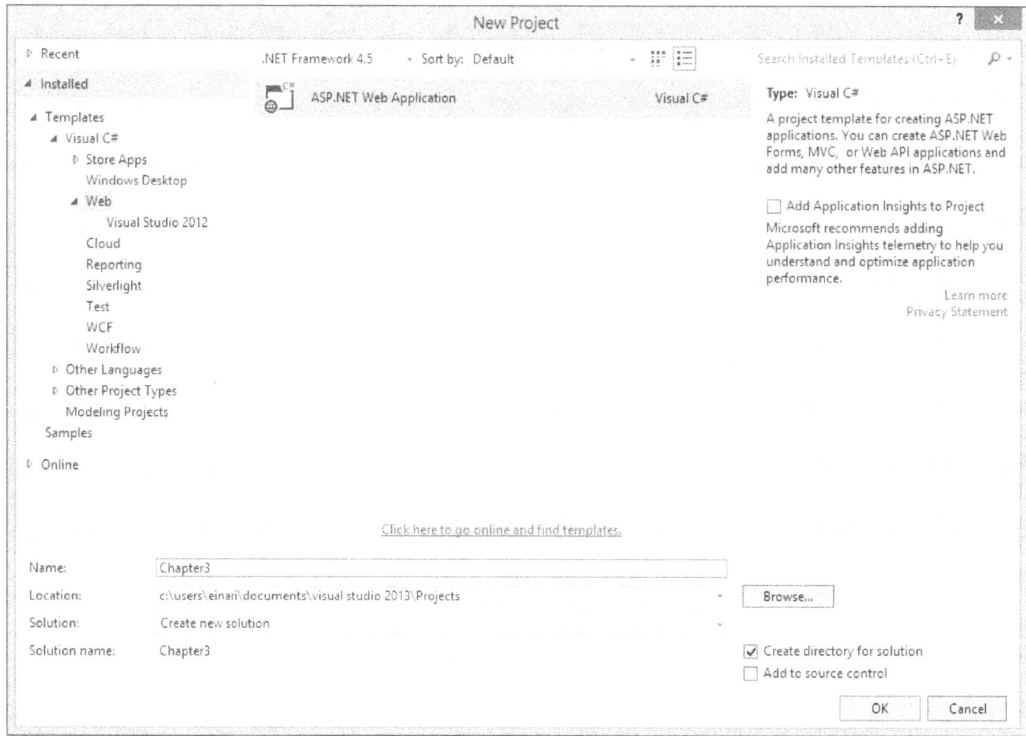

2. From the left-hand side menu, select **Web** and then **ASP.NET Web Application**.
3. Enter `Chapter3` in the **Name** textbox and select your location.
4. Select the **MVC** template from the template selector and make sure you deselect the **Host in the cloud** option.

5. Before we click on **OK**, we want to click on the **Change Authentication** button, as shown in the following screenshot:

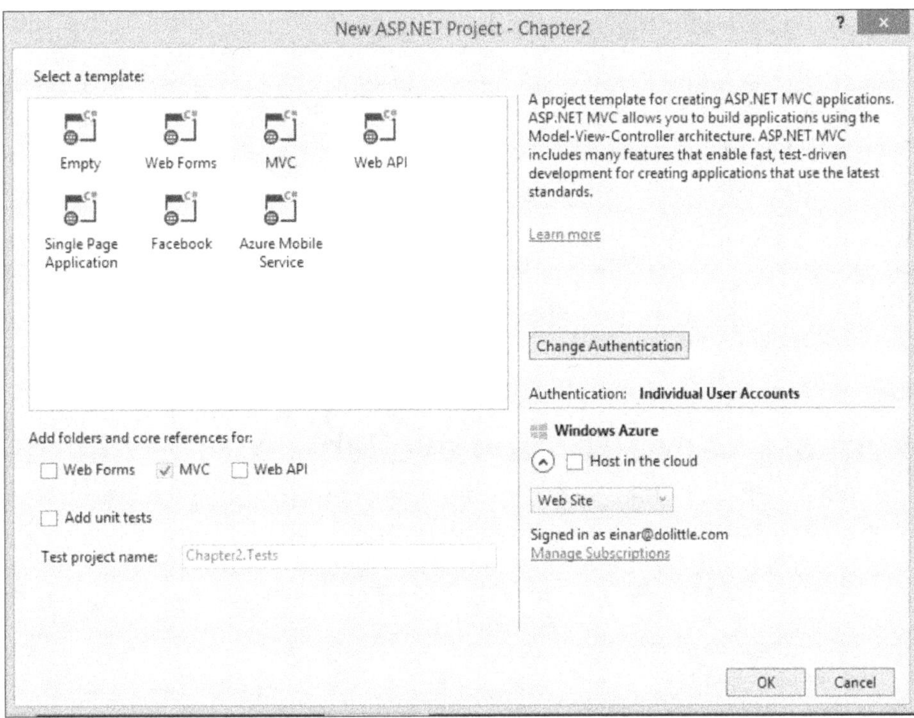

6. Make sure the **Individual User Accounts** option is selected and click on **OK**, followed by **OK** in the template selector dialog box you came from:

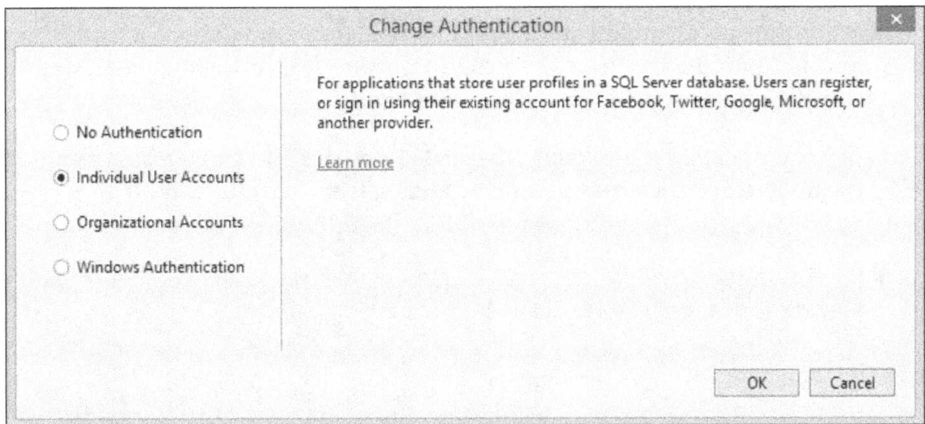

You now have your MVC template created, which enables authentication with its own user database. The foundation has been set!

Setting up the packages

As shown in *Chapter 2, Overheating the Discussion*, we will have to get all the dependencies in order for things to work.

Start by adding the Entity Framework for database access. Download it using NuGet, as described in *Chapter 1, The Primer*. Now, let's right-click on **References** in **Solution Explorer**, select **Manage NuGet Packages**, and type `EntityFramework` in the search dialog box. Select it and click on **Install**.

Continue with SignalR. Add a NuGet package reference, as in the previous step, but this time, type `SignalR` in the search box. Find the package called **Microsoft ASP.NET SignalR**, select it, and click on **Install**. This will download a few other packages that SignalR depends on.

Making any SignalR hubs available for the client

Open up the `Startup.cs` file. At the bottom of the `Configuration` method, we need to add a call to map any SignalR hubs, as follows:

```
public void Configuration(IAppBuilder app)
{
   ConfigureAuth(app);
   app.MapSignalR();
}
```

Creating the models

At the heart of the news domain sits an article. This domain will be a simple one for us, even simpler than the forum we created in *Chapter 2, Overheating the Discussion*. This is the only domain-specific model we will need.

Let's create a folder called `News` inside the `Models` folder and put a class called `Article` inside it (right-click on the `News` folder, select **Class** from **Add**, and name it `Article`). Make the new class look like the following code:

```
using System;
using System.ComponentModel.DataAnnotations.Schema;

namespace Chapter3.Models.News
{
    public class Article
    {
```

```
        [DatabaseGenerated(DatabaseGeneratedOption.Identity)]
        public int ID { get; set; }
        public string ImageUrl { get; set; }
        public string Headline { get; set; }
        public string Byline { get; set; }
        public string Lead { get; set; }
        public string Body { get; set; }
        public DateTime PublishedDate { get; set; }
        public string PublishedBy { get; set; }
    }
}
```

As I mentioned, we only need one model, rather one domain-specific model. However, we will need a second model called ViewModel in which we will use the returning from a controller and utilize it in a view it will refer to. As we're building models right now, let's just build this one while we're at it. Let's create a class called `LandingPage` in the `News` folder and put the following code into the new file:

```
using System.Collections.Generic;

namespace Chapter3.Models.News
{
    public class LandingPageViewModel
    {
        public IEnumerable<Article> TopArticles { get; set; }
        public IEnumerable<Article> OtherArticles { get; set; }
    }
}
```

The two properties in the class represent a particular structure in the page. It will become clearer when we get to using the ViewModel on the page.

Putting in place the Data Access Layer

Let's create a new folder at the root of the project called **Data Access Layer** (**DAL**). As we only have one domain-specific model, we will need only one context that enables us to have access to the database for this type. Add a class to the `DAL` folder called `ArticleContext.cs`.

Let's start by adding the following code into the file:

```
using System;
using System.Collections.Generic;
using System.Data.Entity;
using System.Linq;
```

```
using Chapter3.Models.News;

namespace Chapter3.DAL
{
    public class ArticleContext : DbContext
    {
        public ArticleContext() : base("DefaultConnection") { }
        public DbSet<Article> Articles { get; set; }

        public IEnumerable<Article> GetArticles()
        {
            return Articles.OrderByDescending(a =>
a.PublishedDate);
        }
    }
}
```

As you can see, we expose a public `Articles` property that Entity Framework will ensure gets set up. Secondly, we expose a public way of getting all articles using the LINQ extensions and ordering them by `PublishedDate` in descending order.

Remember the ViewModel we created with the properties called `TopArticles` and `OtherArticles`; we want to create the functionality that can be used to populate these later.

Let's add a constant to the `ArticleContext` class so we have one place to change this, potentially opening up to get this from the configuration file by changing it from a constant to a property:

```
public const int NumberOfTopArticles = 2;
```

Add the following two methods to the `ArticleContext` class:

```
public IEnumerable<Article> GetTopArticles()
{
    return Articles.OrderByDescending(a =>
a.PublishedDate).Take(NumberOfTopArticles).ToArray();
}

public IEnumerable<Article> GetOtherArticles()
{
    return Articles.OrderByDescending(a =>
a.PublishedDate).Skip(NumberOfTopArticles).ToArray();
}
```

As you can see, the methods again not only use the LINQ extension methods for ordering but also utilize the `Take()` and `Skip()` methods (these do exactly what you're expecting). `Take()` only takes the number of items specified, while `Skip()` skips the number of items you specify. These are not run after the data has been retrieved from the database, but run on the database. Therefore, it becomes a highly optimized solution while readability in code is maintained. Here, the `ToArray()` sitting for both queries is just to make sure that we are not returning something that gets executed after the context is possibly collected. Although a queryable is also an enumerable, the implementation will defer and actively dispose of the context, and then using the result of these methods will cause an exception.

Another thing we will need is the ability to get a specific article, typically when one clicks on an article and wants to display it. Add the following method to the `Article` class:

```
public Article GetArticle(int id)
{
    return Articles.Find(id);
}
```

All this does is use the `Find()` method and forward the identifier of the article to it. As we have the `id` property of `Article` that is specified as a primary key for an article, this is what Entity Framework will use to generate the proper data source specific query for finding an article.

An interesting feature of a news site is the ability to search through articles, something we will put in place as well. We therefore need the following method to be added to the class:

```
public IEnumerable<Article> GetArticlesContaining(string phrase)
{
    return Articles.Where(a => a.Headline.Contains(phrase) ||
a.Body.Contains(phrase));
}
```

At this time, we will use the `Where()` extension method from LINQ. In lambda, we specify that we will search for any article with a headline that contains the given phrase or any article with a body containing the phrase.

This is obviously a very naïve implementation; its performance in a large dataset would depend solely on the database and its indexing capability. Out there in the real world, you'd most likely use a search engine, such as Solr, Lucene, or something similar, which would be a more optimal solution.

Lastly, we will need the functionality to actually insert an article. For this, add the following method:

```
public void Insert(Article article)
{
    var currentUser =
System.Threading.Thread.CurrentPrincipal.Identity.Name;
    article.PublishedBy = currentUser;
    article.PublishedDate = DateTime.UtcNow;
    Articles.Add(article);

    SaveChanges();
}
```

The look and feel

We will not use anything from the default layout (we'll change it all around and make it look a bit more like a news site). We will still utilize bootstrap, that is, just some other aspects of it. First, we need a couple of NuGet package references. For the upcoming search capability, we want to have a particular way of typing in the search box and have the result be displayed right underneath the input box while we are typing. We will therefore download something called Twitter typeahead. Add a reference by typing `Twitter.Typeahead` in the search box in the NuGet dialog box. Then, we will need to get it styled properly, add a NuGet reference to its styles by typing `typeahead.js - boostrap.css` in the NuGet search box and then add it.

Templating

Remember the templating engine we created in *Chapter 2, Overheating the Discussion*, we will reuse it in this chapter. Instead of adding the code again over here, use the one from *Chapter 2, Overheating the Discussion* and put it in the `Scripts` folder.

Hubs

The JavaScript client only has one connection from the client to the server at any given time. Its single connection can be shared with many hubs on the page. So, when you have a page composition with more than one hub on it, we need to have a centralized place to initialize this. In addition, out of convenience, we will just expose the hubs that are available for the entire page. Add a file to the `Scripts` folder called `hubsSetup.js` and add the following code inside it:

```
var articleHub = $.connection.articleHub;
var searchHub = $.connection.searchHub;
var hubsConnected = false;
```

```
var hubsConnectedCallbacks = [];

function onHubsConnected(callback) {
    if (hubsConnected == true) {
        callback();
    } else {
        hubsConnectedCallbacks.push(callback);
    }
};

$.connection.hub.start().done(function () {
    hubsConnected = true;

    hubsConnectedCallbacks.forEach(function (callback) {
        callback();
    })
});
```

Notice the `onHubsConnected()` function. It's very important that we don't try calling anything on the server until the general connection for the hubs is started. The mechanism put in place will make sure to call any callbacks when started.

This will be used later on when we start using the hubs.

Layout

We want to start with creating the default layout for the app. Open up the `_Layout.cshtml` file found in the `Views\Shared` folder of your project. Completely replace its content with the following code snippet:

```
<!DOCTYPE html>
<html>
<head>
    <meta charset="utf-8" />
    <meta name="viewport" content="width=device-width, initial-
scale=1.0">
    <title>@ViewBag.Title - My ASP.NET Application</title>
    @Styles.Render("~/Content/css")
    @Scripts.Render("~/bundles/modernizr")

    <link href="~/Content/typeahead.css" rel="stylesheet" />
    <link href="http://getbootstrap.com/examples/jumbotron-narrow/
jumbotron-narrow.css" rel="stylesheet">
```

```
</head>
<body>
    <div class="container">
        <nav class="navbar navbar-default navbar-fixed-top"
role="navigation">
            <div class="container">
                <div class="navbar-header">
                    <button type="button" class="navbar-toggle
collapsed" data-toggle="collapse" data-target="#bs-example-navbar-
collapse-1">
                        <span class="sr-only">Toggle
navigation</span>
                        <span class="icon-bar"></span>
                        <span class="icon-bar"></span>
                        <span class="icon-bar"></span>
                    </button>
                    <a class="navbar-brand" href="/">RNC</a>
                </div>

                <div class="collapse navbar-collapse" id="bs-
example-navbar-collapse-1">
                    <ul class="nav navbar-nav">
                        <li><a href="/Newsroom">Newsroom</a></li>
                        @Html.Partial("_LoginPartial")
                    </ul>
                    <form class="navbar-form navbar-right"
role="search">
                        <div class="form-group">
                            <input type="text" class="form-
control" placeholder="Search" id="searchInput">
                        </div>
                        <button type="submit" class="btn btn-
default">Search</button>
                    </form>
                </div>
            </div>
        </nav>

        <div class="row marketing">
            @RenderBody()
        </div>
```

```
        <div class="footer">
            <p>© Realtime News Company 2014</p>
        </div>
    </div>

    @Scripts.Render("~/bundles/jquery")
    @Scripts.Render("~/bundles/bootstrap")
    <script src="~/Scripts/jquery.signalR-2.1.0.min.js"
type="text/javascript"></script>
    <script src="~/signalr/hubs" type="text/javascript"></script>
    <script src="~/Scripts/typeahead.jquery.min.js"
type="text/javascript"></script>
    <script src="~/Scripts/templating.js"
type="text/javascript"></script>
    <script src="~/Scripts/hubsSetup.js"
type="text/javascript"></script>
    <script src="~/Scripts/_Layout.js"
type="text/javascript"></script>
    @RenderSection("scripts", required: false)
</body>
</html>
```

This will give us a layout that is fixed in width and has a navigation bar that is fixed at the top, which always remains on top. In addition, you'll see that in the `HEAD` element, there are references to two new style sheets; one that exists on the Internet on the bootstrap site itself (it's the one that gives us the fixed width), and the other style sheet is for the search typeahead. Also worth mentioning are the scripts we include; similar to in *Chapter 2, Overheating the Discussion*, we included all the necessary SignalR scripts and the proxy generated hubs. In addition, you'll notice at the end that there is a reference to a file called `_Layout.js`. We need to create this now by adding a new file to the `Scripts` folder called `_Layout.js`. Just let it be empty for now - we will get back to it.

The landing page

Open the `Index.cshtml` file inside the `Views\Home` folder and completely wipe its content so that we have an empty file. It's time to see how far we've come and that we are on the right track. Run the solution by going to the **DEBUG** menu in Visual Studio and select **Run Without Debugging**, or simply hit *Ctrl* + *F5*. You should have something that looks like this:

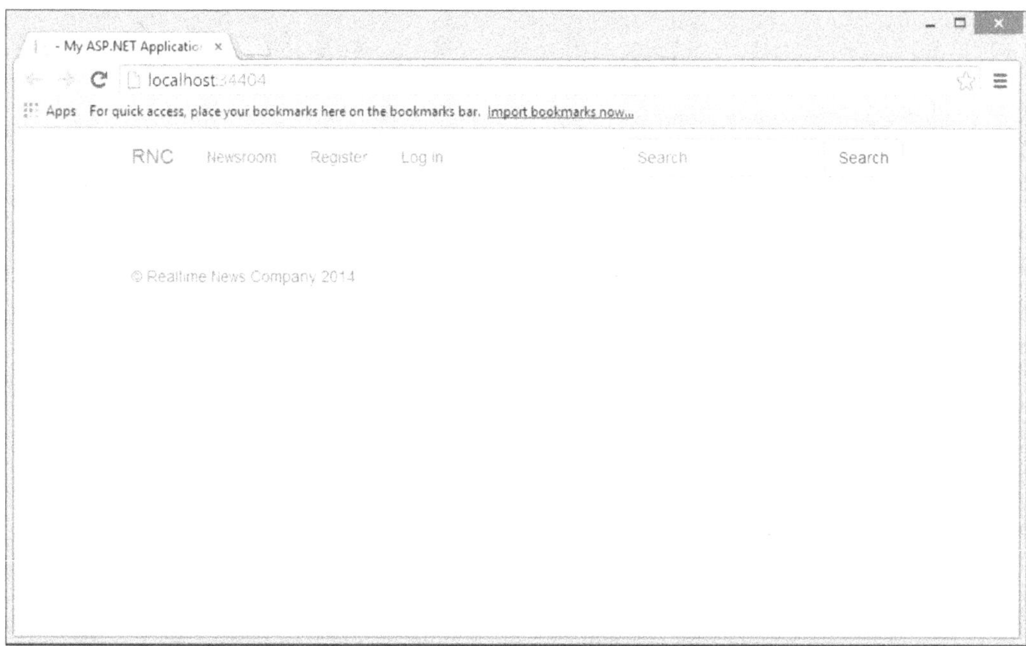

Let's start putting something useful in here. First of all, we need a statement that allows us to use the models we've created without having to refer to the full namespace. Add the following code at the top of the `Index.cshtml` file:

```
@using Chapter3.Models.News
```

Then, we want to specify the model type by adding the following code:

```
@model LandingPageViewModel
```

This tells ASP.NET MVC to render the view and expect to have an instance of the `LandingPageViewModel` as its model. Next, we will give the page a title, as follows:

```
@{
    ViewBag.Title = "RNC";
}
```

We want a JavaScript file associated with the page. Create a new folder called `Home` inside the `Scripts` folder and add a file called `Index.js` to this folder. Leave the file empty for now and go back to the `Index.cshtml` file that we were just in. Now, we will include a reference to this newly created JavaScript file by adding the following code snippet at the end:

```
@section scripts {
    <script type="text/javascript"
src="~/Scripts/Home/Index.js"></script>
}
```

The content

Now, it's time to display some content. The primary goal is to display any articles and also have a live view where we get a live stream of published news articles. Let's start by creating a template for the articles. In ASP.NET MVC, or rather for Razor views, there is a concept of helpers. A helper is basically just a method that can be called as any other method with input arguments, and so on, but it can render HTML directly. Let's create a helper to display an article:

```
@helper DisplayArticle(Article article)
{
    <img src="@article.ImageUrl" style="width:250px;" />
    <h4>@article.Headline</h4>
    <p><a href="/Article/Full/@article.ID">Read more...</a></p>
}
```

As you can see inside the helper, we directly use properties from the article, and in order for them to be rendered, we need to prefix them with `@`.

For the live view, we want a box that is fixed to the right-hand side with scrollable content. So, we will to add a CSS style to do so:

```
<style>
    .livenews {
        height: 460px;
        overflow-y:auto;
        border: 1px solid #428bca;
        -webkit-overflow-scrolling: touch;
    }
</style>
```

Although CSS can be defined directly like this, the best practice is to put it in a separate file, but this is not the focus here right now.

Any article that gets published and that we want to display in the live view needs a template to render. Let's put this in using the following code:

```
<script id="liveNewsItemTemplate" type="text/html">
    <div>
        <p class="bg-primary">%PublishedDateString%</p>
        <p>%Headline%</p>
        <p>%Lead%</p>
        <p><a href="/Article/Full/%ID%">Read more...</a></p>
        <hr />
    </div>
</script>
```

As you'll notice, the syntax for property expansion is slightly different from with regular Razor view syntax as this is something we will perform on the client and not something the server will render for us. It uses the templating engine syntax that we created in *Chapter 2, Overheating the Discussion*.

Now, we want to render the two top articles to the left. Using the bootstrap grid system, we use a fixed size container of six columns in the bootstrap grid system, as shown in the following code, which basically means that we will take up half the width of our viewport:

```
    @foreach( var article in Model.TopArticles )
    {
        @DisplayArticle(article)
    }
</div>
```

Next, we want the `liveview` container to cover the second half. For this, add the following code:

```
<div class="col-xs-6">
    <h4>Live news</h4>
    <div id="livenewsContainer" class="livenews">
    </div>
</div>
```

Now, we want to have the rest of the articles fill the page. We are not limited to any maximum number here; this is something you can experiment with, of course:

```
 
@foreach (var article in Model.OtherArticles)
{
    <div class="col-xs-6">
```

```
        @DisplayArticle(article)
    </div>
}
```

Open `HomeController` as we need to modify it a little bit. The `Index` action needs some work done, as shown here:

```
public ActionResult Index()
{
    using( var articleContext = new ArticleContext() )
    {
        var viewModel = new LandingPageViewModel
        {
            TopArticles = articleContext.GetTopArticles(),
            OtherArticles = articleContext.GetOtherArticles()
        };
        return View(viewModel);
    }
}
```

The magic code

Now we've got the basics of the layout done and we are ready to get some code in here for lighting it all up. Let's start by creating the hub for the article management. Add a folder called `Hubs` in the root of the project, and then create a new class called `ArticleHub` in this folder. Add the following code in the new class:

```
using System;
using System.Collections.Generic;
using Chapter3.DAL;
using Chapter3.Models.News;
using Microsoft.AspNet.SignalR;

namespace Chapter3.Hubs
{
    public class ArticleHub : Hub
    {
        ArticleContext _articleContext;
        public ArticleHub()
        {
            _articleContext = new ArticleContext();
        }
```

```
    protected override void Dispose(bool disposing)
          {
              if (disposing)
              {
                  _articleContext.Dispose();
              }
              base.Dispose(disposing);
          }

          public IEnumerable<Article> GetArticles()
          {
              return _articleContext.GetArticles();
          }
      }
  }
```

Now, this hub just forwards everything to the `ArticleContext` and gets the articles. Let's add a method to publish as we will be needing it when we get to the newsroom where one publishes articles. At the end of the class, add the following method:

```
[Authorize]
public void Publish(Article article)
{
    _articleContext.Insert(article);
    Clients.All.published(article);
}
```

> **Authorization by attribute**
>
> SignalR has an attribute called `Authorize`, much like in ASP.NET MVC, to secure actions in a controller. Remember to use the SignalR one and not the MVC one.

We now have a method that will save the article and also publish it to any connected clients. It's also secured by the `Authorize` attribute so this cannot be invoked without a user being logged in.

> The `Authorize` attribute can authorize specific roles and specific users as well (for example, `[Authorize(Roles="Administrators")]` or `[Authorize(Users="jim")]`). You can have multiple roles or users separated with comma.

Let's go back to the `Index.js` file created in the `Scripts\Home` folder and add the logic that we will need for the landing page, as follows:

```
$(function () {
    var livenewsContainer =
document.getElementById("livenewsContainer");

    function mapArticleAndExpandTemplate(article) {
        article.PublishedDateString = new
Date(article.PublishedDate).toLocaleString();
        var articleElement =
expandTemplateWithData("liveNewsItemTemplate", article);
        return articleElement;
    }

    articleHub.client.published = function (article) {
        var articleElement = mapArticleAndExpandTemplate(article);
        if (livenewsContainer.firstChild) {
            livenewsContainer.insertBefore(articleElement,
livenewsContainer.firstChild);
        } else {
            livenewsContainer.appendChild(articleElement);
        }
    };

    onHubsConnected(function () {
        articleHub.server.getArticles().done(function (articles) {

            articles.forEach(function (article) {
                var articleElement =
mapArticleAndExpandTemplate(article);
                livenewsContainer.appendChild(articleElement);
            });
        });
    });
});
```

At startup, this will connect to the server and can get any articles. It also hooks up the published client function, which gets called from the server after an article is published.

The newsroom

Now that we basically have everything in place to display the news articles up and running, we need to be able to publish them as well, otherwise there won't be anything to show.

Let's start by creating a new controller in the `Controllers` folder called `NewsroomController`; we will only need a default route of `Index`, so make the controller look like the following code snippet:

```
using System.Web.Mvc;

namespace Chapter3.Controllers
{
    [Authorize]
    public class NewsroomController : Controller
    {
        // GET: Content
        public ActionResult Index()
        {
            return View();
        }
    }
}
```

We've also secured the entire newsroom at this point, so we will need a user to be able to publish anything.

Note the `Authorize` attribute (this time, it's the MVC version).

Let's move on by creating the index view for the newsroom. Add a new folder in the `Views` folder called `Newsroom` and add a new empty view called `Index.cshtml` in it.

Let's enter the title and a reference to the JavaScript file for the view, as shown in the following code:

```
@{
    ViewBag.Title = "Newsroom";
}
@section scripts {
    <script type="text/javascript"
src="~/Scripts/Newsroom/Index.js"></script>
}
```

All we want in this file is just a simple form where we can input the details we want for our article. Add the following code:

```
<h1>The Newsroom</h1>
<h2>Publish article</h2>
<form role="form">
    <div class="form-group">
        <label for="imageUrl">ImageUrl</label>
        <input type="text" class="form-control" id="imageUrl"
placeholder="Enter image url">
    </div>
    <div class="form-group">
        <label for="headline">Headline</label>
        <input type="text" class="form-control" id="headline"
placeholder="Enter headline">
    </div>
    <div class="form-group">
        <label for="lead">Lead</label>
        <input type="text" class="form-control" id="lead"
placeholder="Enter lead">
    </div>
    <div class="form-group">
        <label for="byline">Byline</label>
        <input type="text" class="form-control" id="byline"
placeholder="Enter byline">
    </div>
    <div class="form-group">
        <label for="body">Body</label>
        <textarea class="form-control" id="body"
placeholder="Enter body" rows="5"></textarea>
    </div>

    <button id="publishButton" type="button" class="btn btn-
default">Publish</button>
</form>
```

Now, we need the JavaScript file for this view. Add a folder in the `Scripts` folder called `Newsroom` and add a JavaScript file called `Index.js` to it. The code will deal with publishing it to the server:

```
$(function () {
    var imageUrlElement = document.getElementById("imageUrl");
    var headlineElement = document.getElementById("headline");
    var leadElement = document.getElementById("lead");
    var bylineElement = document.getElementById("byline");
    var bodyElement = document.getElementById("body");
```

```
        var publishButton = document.getElementById("publishButton");
        publishButton.addEventListener("click", function () {
            var article = {
                ImageUrl: imageUrlElement.value,
                Headline: headlineElement.value,
                Lead: leadElement.value,
                Byline: bylineElement.value,
                Body: bodyElement.value
            }

            articleHub.server.publish(article).done(function () {
                imageUrlElement.value = "";
                headlineElement.value = "";
                leadElement.value = "";
                bylineElement.value = "";
                bodyElement.value = "";
                alert("Published");
            });
        });
    });
```

The code basically gets all the elements on the page and hooks up the `click` event for the button and from this, we publish to the server.

In fact, we should now be able to actually publish things. Run the solution, register yourself as a user using the register link at the top, log in with the registered user, and then click on the newsroom link at the top. Keep a second window open that points to the landing page, enter all the details for an article, and click on **Publish**. You should now see the newly published article in the live view. If you refresh the page, the article in full should be here.

Finding the needle in the haystack

Finding articles is always nice. This makes it a lot easier for the user to find the right content on your site. We'll put in a really simple yet effective search here.

Let's start by creating a second hub. In the `Hubs` folder, add a class called `SearchHub` and add the following code to it:

```
using System.Collections.Generic;
using Chapter3.DAL;
using Chapter3.Models.News;
using Microsoft.AspNet.SignalR;
```

```
namespace Chapter3.Hubs
{
    public class SearchHub : Hub
    {
        ArticleContext _articleContext;

        public SearchHub()
        {
            _articleContext = new ArticleContext();
        }

        public IEnumerable<Article> GetArticlesContaining(string
phrase)
        {
            return _articleContext.GetArticlesContaining(phrase);
        }
    }
}
```

Remember the `_Layout.js` file we created where we didn't enter anything. Open it and enter the following code:

```
$(function () {
    var searchInput = document.getElementById("searchInput");

    $(searchInput).typeahead({
        hint: true,
        highlight: true,
        minLength: 1
    },
    {
        displayKey: 'Headline',
        source: function (query, callback) {
            searchHub.server.getArticlesContaining(query).
done(function
(articles) {
                callback(articles);
            });
        }
    });

    $(searchInput).bind('typeahead:selected', function (obj,
article) {
        document.location = "/Article/Full/" + article.ID;
    });
});
```

What this code basically does is enable the Twitter typeahead plugin for the search input field. It sets a few options as the first argument and then configures how to provide search results in the drop-down menu. Lastly, we hook up the selected event for typeahead, which will navigate to the article.

Master/detail – navigation

Speaking of which, we haven't put in something that enables us to actually see the article with the full body, and so on. Let's just quickly do this.

Add a new `Controller` class called `ArticleController`. As we only need one action in it, enter the following code:

```
using System.Web.Mvc;
using Chapter3.DAL;

namespace Chapter3.Controllers
{
    public class ArticleController : Controller
    {
        // GET: Article
        public ActionResult Full(int id)
        {
            using( var articleContext = new ArticleContext() )
            {
               var article = articleContext.GetArticle(id);
               return View(article);
            }
        }
    }
}
```

The action takes the identifier as an argument and uses it when calling `GetArticle()` on `ArticleContext`. This gets the specific article that we will use as a ViewModel for the page.

Routing is a concept in ASP.NET MVC that describes allowed URLs and what to do with them. If you navigate to `App_Start\RouteConfig.cs`, you'll see the `RegisterRoutes` method that sets a convention of `{controller}\{action}\{id}`. It sets up default values if the route or URL is incomplete.

Let's create the view for the action. Add a new folder into the `Views` folder called `Article`. Inside this, add a new view called `Full.cshtml` and make it look like this:

```
@model Chapter3.Models.News.Article
@{
    ViewBag.Title = Model.Headline;
}

<img style="width:400px" src="@Model.ImageUrl" />
<h2>@Model.Headline</h2>
<br />
Written by @Model.Byline
<br />
<h4>@Model.Lead</h4>
<br />
@Model.Body
```

Compiling this and running it should now enable you to navigate to an article by clicking on the different links that we have already put in for articles.

Downloading the example code

You can download the example code files for all Packt books you have purchased from your account at `http://www.packtpub.com`. If you purchased this book elsewhere, you can visit `http://www.packtpub.com/support` and register to have the files e-mailed directly to you.

Summary

Building on what we covered in *Chapter 2, Overheating the Discussion*, you should now be familiar with SignalR and its power. We've also seen a bit more of what is possible with the Entity Framework and ASP.NET MVC, although just scratching the surface of these. However, most importantly, the takeaway should be the opportunities of improving the user experience and at the same time meeting technical needs, such as scaling. You can find the entire sample code at `https://github.com/dolittle/SignalR_Blueprints/tree/master/Source/Chapter3`.

In the next chapter, we will focus more on structure, patterns, and practices, and how we can improve the code base and tidy up a bit. At the same time, we will push forward the concept of publish or subscribe, which sits at the heart of SignalR.

4
Can You Measure It?

This chapter will focus on a different programming model for client development: **Model-View-ViewModel** (**MVVM**). It will reiterate what you have already learned about SignalR, but you will also start to see a recurring theme in how you should architect decoupled software that adheres to the SOLID principles. It will also show the benefit of thinking in single page application terms (often referred to as **Single Page Application** (**SPA**)), and how SignalR really fits well with this idea.

In this chapter, we will cover the following topics:

- Introduction to MVVM
- Concrete implementation of MVVM using KnockoutJS
- Brush up against the concept of SPA

The goal – an imagined dashboard

A counterpart to any application is often a part of monitoring its health. Is it running? and are there any failures? Getting this information in real time when the failure occurs is important and also getting some statistics from it is interesting. From a SignalR perspective, we will still use the hub abstraction to do pretty much what we have been doing, but the goal is to give ideas of how and what we can use SignalR for. Another goal is to dive into the architectural patterns, making it ready for larger applications. MVVM allows better separation and is very applicable for client development in general.

By the end of the chapter, you'll have the knowledge about MVVM, how to apply it in JavaScript, and also get the feel of how one can architect SPAs with SignalR at the heart.

A question that you might ask yourself is, why KnockoutJS instead of something like AngularJS? It boils down to personal preference to a certain degree. AngularJS is described as an MVW where **W** stands for **Whatever**. I find AngularJS less focused on the same things I focus on, and I also find it very verbose to get it up and running. I'm in no way an expert in AngularJS, but I have used it on a project and found myself writing a lot to make it work the way I wanted it to in terms of MVVM. However, I don't think it's fair to compare the two. KnockoutJS is very focused in what it's trying to solve, which is just a little piece of the puzzle, while AngularJS is a full client end-to-end framework.

On this note, let's just jump straight to it.

Decoupling it all

MVVM is a pattern for client development that became very popular in the XAML stack, enabled by Microsoft based on Martin Fowler's presentation model (`http://martinfowler.com/eaaDev/PresentationModel.html`). Its principle is that you have a ViewModel that holds the state and exposes behavior that can be utilized from a view. The view observes any changes of the state the ViewModel exposes, making the ViewModel totally unaware that there is a view. The ViewModel is decoupled and can be put in isolation and is perfect for automated testing. As part of the state that the ViewModel typically holds is the model part, which is something it usually gets from the server, and a SignalR hub is the perfect transport to get this. It boils down to recognizing the different concerns that make up the frontend and separating it all. This gives us the following diagram:

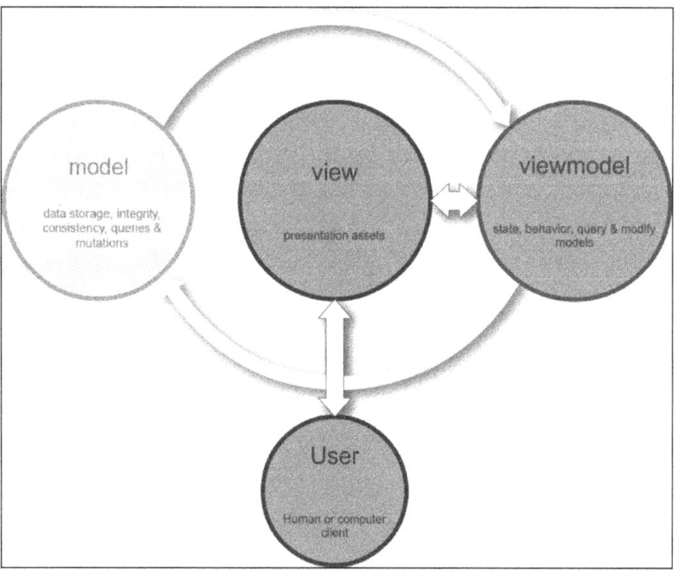

Back to basics

This time we will go back in time, going down what might be considered a more purist path; use the browser elements (HTML, JavaScript, and CSS) and don't rely on any server-side rendering.

Clients today are powerful and very capable and offloading the composition of what the user sees onto the client frees up server resources. You can also rely on the infrastructure of the Web for caching with static HTML files not rendered by the server. In fact, you could actually put these resources on a content delivery network, making the files available as close as possible to the end user. This would result in better load times for the user.

You might have other reasons to perform server-side rendering and not just plain HTML. Leveraging existing infrastructure or third-party tools could be those reasons. It boils down to what's right for you. But this particular sample will focus on things that the client can do. Anyway, let's get started.

1. Open Visual Studio and create a new project by navigating to **FILE** | **New** | **Project**. The following dialog box will show up:

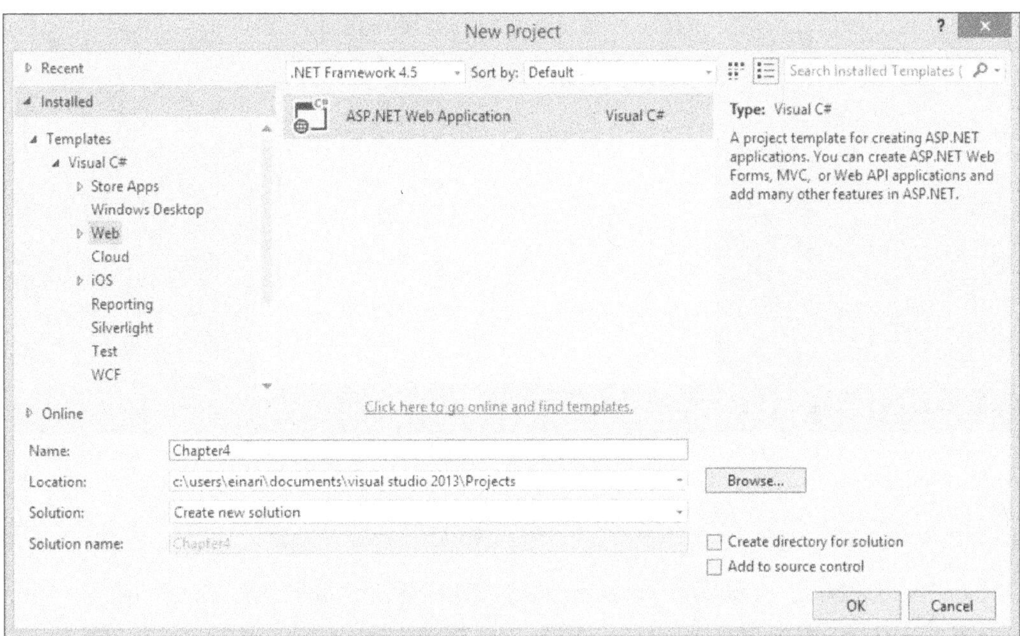

2. From the left-hand side menu, select **Web** and then **ASP.NET Web Application**.
3. Enter `Chapter4` in the **Name** textbox and select your location.
4. Select the **Empty** template from the template selector and make sure you deselect the **Host in the cloud** option. Then, click on **OK**, as shown in the following screenshot:

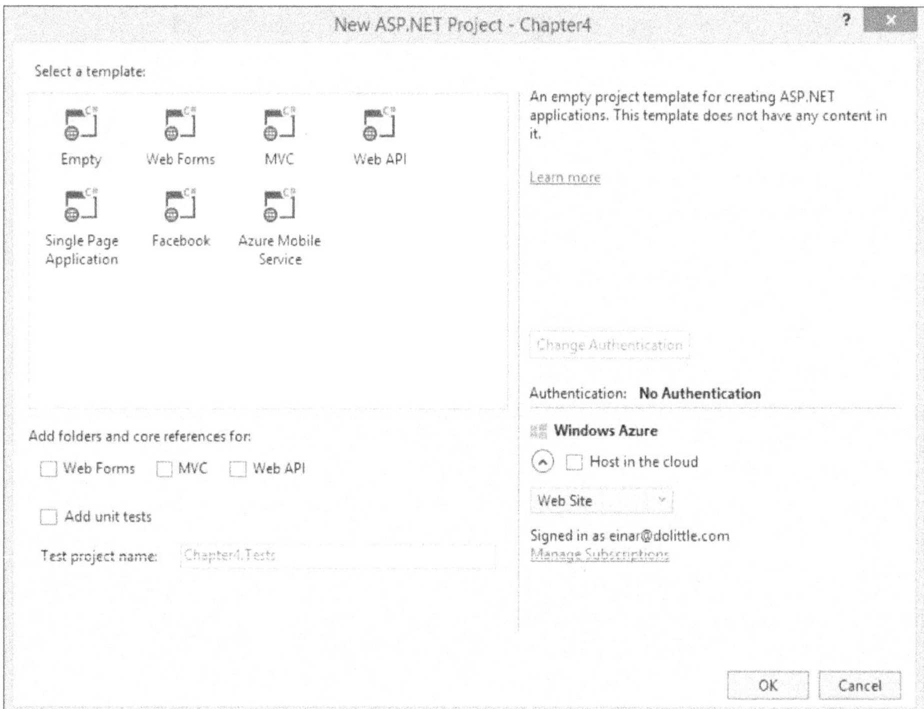

Setting up the packages

As shown in the previous chapters, we are going to download a few dependencies from NuGet.

First, we want Twitter bootstrap. To get this, follow these steps:

1. Add a NuGet package reference, as described in *Chapter 1, The Primer*.
2. Right-click on **References** in **Solution Explorer** and select **Manage NuGet Packages** and type `Bootstrap` in the search dialog box.
3. Select it and then click on **Install**.

We want a slightly different look, so we'll download one of the many bootstrap themes out here. Add a NuGet package reference called **metro-bootstrap**.

As jQuery is still a part of this, let's add a NuGet package reference to it as well.

For the MVVM part, we will use something called KnockoutJS; add it through NuGet as well. Add a NuGet package reference, as in the previous steps, but this time, type `SignalR` in the search dialog box. Find the package called Microsoft ASP.NET SignalR.

Making any SignalR hubs available for the client

Add a file called `Startup.cs` file to the root of the project. Add a `Configuration` method that will expose any SignalR hubs, as follows:

```
public void Configuration(IAppBuilder app)
{
    app.MapSignalR();
}
```

At the top of the `Startup.cs` file, above the namespace declaration, but right below the `using` statements, add the following code:

```
[assembly: OwinStartupAttribute(typeof(Chapter4.Startup))]
```

Knocking it out of the park

KnockoutJS is a framework that implements a lot of the principles found in MVVM and makes it easier to apply. In this chapter, we're going to use the following two features of KnockoutJS, and it's therefore important to understand what they are and what significance they have:

- **Observables**: In order for a view to be able to know when state change in a ViewModel occurs, KnockoutJS has something called an observable for single objects or values and an observable array for arrays.
- **BindingHandlers**: In the view, the counterparts that are able to recognize the observables and know how to deal with its content are known as BindingHandlers. We create binding expression in the view that instructs the view to get its content from the properties found in the binding context. The default binding context will be the ViewModel, but there are more advanced scenarios where this changes. In fact, there is a BindingHandler that enables you to specify the context at any given time called `with`. You can read more about it at `http://knockoutjs.com/documentation/with-binding.html`.

Our single page

Whether one should strive towards having an SPA is widely discussed on the Web these days. My opinion on the subject, in the interest of the user, is that we should really try to push things in this direction. Having not to post back and cause a full reload of the page and all its resources and getting into the correct state gives the user a better experience. Some of the arguments to perform post-backs every now and then go in the direction of fixing potential memory leaks happening in the browser. Although the technique is sound and the result is right, it really just camouflages a problem one has in the system. However, as with everything, it really depends on the situation.

At the core of an SPA is a single page (pun intended), which is usually the `index.html` file sitting at the root of the project. Add the new `index.html` file and edit it as follows:

1. Add a new HTML file (`index.html`) at the root of the project by right-clicking on the `Chapter4` project in **Solution Explorer**. Navigate to **Add** | **New Item** | **Web** from the left-hand side menu, and then select **HTML Page** and name it `index.html`. Finally, click on **Add**.
2. Let's put in the things we've added dependencies to, starting with the style sheets. In the `index.html` file, you'll find the `<head>` tag; add the following code snippet under the `<title></title>` tag:

   ```
   <link href="Content/bootstrap.min.css" rel="stylesheet" />
   <link href="Content/metro-bootstrap.min.css"
   rel="stylesheet" />
   ```

3. Next, add the following code snippet right beneath the preceding code:

   ```
   <script type="text/javascript" src="Scripts/jquery-
   1.9.0.min.js"></script>
   <script type="text/javascript" src="Scripts/jquery.signalR-
   2.1.1.js"></script>
   <script type="text/javascript" src="signalr/hubs"></script>
   <script type="text/javascript" src="Scripts/knockout-
   3.2.0.js"></script>
   ```

4. Another thing we will need in this is something that helps us visualize things; Google has a free, open source charting library that we will use. We will take a dependency to the JavaScript APIs from Google. To do this, add the following script tag after the others:

   ```
   <script type="text/javascript"
   src="https://www.google.com/jsapi"></script>
   ```

5. Now, we can start filling in the view part. Inside the `<body>` tag, we start by putting in a header, as shown here:

   ```
   <div class="navbar navbar-default navbar-static-top
   bsnavbar">
       <div class="container">
           <div class="navbar-header">
               <h1>My Dashboard</h1>
           </div>
       </div>
   </div>
   ```

The server side of things

In this little dashboard thing, we will look at web requests, both successful and failed. We will perform some minor things for us to be able to do this in a very naive way, without having to flesh out a full mechanism to deal with error situations. Let's start by enabling all requests even static resources, such as HTML files, to run through all HTTP modules. A word of warning: there are performance implications of putting all requests through the managed pipeline, so normally you wouldn't necessarily want to do this on a production system, but for this sample, it will be fine to show the concepts. Open `Web.config` in the project and add the following code snippet within the `<configuration>` tag:

```
<system.webServer>
  <modules runAllManagedModulesForAllRequests="true" />
</system.webServer>
```

The hub

In this sample, we will only have one hub, the one that will be responsible for dealing with reporting requests and failed requests. Let's add a new class called `RequestStatisticsHub`. Right-click on the project in **Solution Explorer**, select **Class** from **Add**, name it `RequestStatisticsHub.cs`, and then click on **Add**. The new class should inherit from the hub. Add the following `using` statement at the top:

```
using Microsoft.AspNet.SignalR;
```

We're going to keep track of the count of requests and failed requests per time with a resolution of not more than every 30 seconds in the memory on the server. Obviously, if one wants to scale across multiple servers, this is way too naive and one should choose an out-of-process shared key-value store that goes across servers. However, for our purpose, this will be fine.

Let's add a `using` statement at the top, as shown here:

```
using System.Collections.Generic;
```

At the top of the class, add the two dictionaries that we will use to hold this information:

```
static Dictionary<string, int> _requestsLog = new
Dictionary<string, int>();
static Dictionary<string, int> _failedRequestsLog = new
Dictionary<string, int>();
```

In our client, we want to access these logs at startup. So let's add two methods to do so:

```
public Dictionary<string, int> GetRequests()
{
    return _requestsLog;
}

public Dictionary<string, int> GetFailedRequests()
{
    return _failedRequestsLog;
}
```

Remember the resolution of only keeping track of number of requests per 30 seconds at a time. There is no default mechanism in the .NET Framework to do this, so we need to add a few helper methods to deal with rounding of time. Let's add a class called `DateTimeRounding` at the root of the project. Mark the class as a public `static` class and put the following extension methods in the class:

```
public static DateTime RoundUp(this DateTime dt, TimeSpan d)
{
    var delta = (d.Ticks - (dt.Ticks % d.Ticks)) % d.Ticks;
    return new DateTime(dt.Ticks + delta);
}

public static DateTime RoundDown(this DateTime dt, TimeSpan d)
{
    var delta = dt.Ticks % d.Ticks;
    return new DateTime(dt.Ticks - delta);
}

public static DateTime RoundToNearest(this DateTime dt,
TimeSpan d)
{
```

```
        var delta = dt.Ticks % d.Ticks;
        bool roundUp = delta > d.Ticks / 2;

        return roundUp ? dt.RoundUp(d) : dt.RoundDown(d);
    }
```

Let's go back to the `RequestStatisticsHub` class and add some more functionality now so that we can deal with rounding of time:

```
    static void Register(Dictionary<string, int> log, Action<dynamic,
    string, int> hubCallback)
    {
        var now =
    DateTime.Now.RoundToNearest(TimeSpan.FromSeconds(30));
        var key = now.ToString("HH:mm");

        if (log.ContainsKey(key))
            log[key] = log[key] + 1;
        else
            log[key] = 1;

        var hub =
    GlobalHost.ConnectionManager.GetHubContext<RequestStatisticsHub>()
    ;
        hubCallback(hub.Clients.All, key, log[key]);
    }

    public static void Request()
    {
        Register(_requestsLog, (hub, key, value) =>
    hub.requestCountChanged(key, value));
    }

    public static void FailedRequest()
    {
        Register(_requestsLog, (hub, key, value) =>
    hub.failedRequestCountChanged(key, value));
    }
```

This enables us to have a place to call in order to report requests, and these get published back to any clients connected to this particular hub.

Note the usage of `GlobalHost` and its `ConnectionManager` property. When we want to get a hub instance and when we are not in the hub context of a method being called from a client, we use `ConnectionManager` to get it. It gives us a proxy for the hub and enables us to call methods on any connected client.

Naively dealing with requests

With all this in place, we will be able to easily and naively deal with what we consider correct and failed requests. Let's add a `Global.asax` file by right-clicking on the project in **Solution Explorer** and select the **New** item from the **Add**. Navigate to **Web** and find **Global Application Class**, then click on **Add**. In the new file, we want to replace the `BindingHandlers` method with the following code snippet:

```
protected void Application_AuthenticateRequest(object sender,
EventArgs e)
{
    var path = HttpContext.Current.Request.Path;
    if (path == "/") path = "index.html";

    if (path.ToLowerInvariant().IndexOf(".html") < 0) return;

    var physicalPath = HttpContext.Current.Request.MapPath(path);
    if (File.Exists(physicalPath))
    {
        RequestStatisticsHub.Request();
    }
    else
    {
        RequestStatisticsHub.FailedRequest();
    }
}
```

Basically, with this, we are only measuring requests with `.html` in its path, and if it's only `"/"`, we assume it's `"index.html"`. Any file that does not exist, accordingly, is considered an error; typically a 404 error, and we register it as a failed request.

Bringing it all back to the client

With the server taken care of, we can start consuming all this in the client. We will now be heading down the path of creating a ViewModel and hooking everything up.

ViewModel

Let's start by adding a JavaScript file sitting next to our `index.html` file at the root level of the project, call it `index.js`. This file will represent our ViewModel. Also, this scenario will be responsible for setting up KnockoutJS, so that the ViewModel is in fact activated and applied to the page. As we only have this one page for this sample, this will be fine.

Let's start by hooking up the jQuery document that is ready:

```
$(function() {
});
```

Inside the function created here, we will enter our `viewModel` definition, which will start off being an empty one:

```
var viewModel = function() {
};
```

KnockoutJS has a function to apply a `viewModel` to the document, meaning that the document or body will be associated with the `viewModel` instance given. Right under the definition of `viewModel`, add the following line:

```
ko.applyBindings(new viewModel());
```

Compiling this and running it should at the very least not give you any errors but nothing more than a header saying `My Dashboard`.

So, we need to lighten this up a bit. Inside the `viewModel` function definition, add the following code snippet:

```
var self = this;
this.requests = ko.observableArray();
this.failedRequests = ko.observableArray();
```

We enter a reference to this as a variant called `self`. This will help us with scoping issues later on. The arrays we added are now KnockoutJS's observable arrays that allow the view or any BindingHandler to observe the changes that are coming in.

The `ko.observableArray()` and `ko.observable()` arrays both return a new function. So, if you want to access any values in it, you must unwrap it by calling it something that might seem counterintuitive at first. You might consider your variable as just another property. However, for the `observableArray()`, KnockoutJS adds most of the functions found in the array type in JavaScript and they can be used directly on the function without unwrapping. If you look at a variable that is an `observableArray` in the console of the browser, you'll see that it looks as if it actually is just any array. This is not really true though; to get to the values, you will have to unwrap it by adding `()` after accessing the variable. However, all the functions you're used to having on an array are here.

Let's add a function that will know how to handle an entry into the `viewModel` function. An entry coming in is either an existing one or a new one; the key of the entry is the giveaway to decide:

```
function handleEntry(log, key, value) {
    var result = log().forEach(function (entry) {
        if (entry[0] == key) {
            entry[1](value);
            return true;
        }
    });

    if (result !== true) {
        log.push([key, ko.observable(value)]);
    }
};
```

Let's set up the hub and add the following code to the `viewModel` function:

```
var hub = $.connection.requestStatisticsHub;
var initializedCount = 0;

hub.client.requestCountChanged = function (key, value) {
    if (initializedCount < 2) return;
    handleEntry(self.requests, key, value);
}

hub.client.failedRequestCountChanged = function (key, value) {
    if (initializedCount < 2) return;
    handleEntry(self.failedRequests, key, value);
}
```

You might notice the `initalizedCount` variable. Its purpose is not to deal with requests until completely initialized, which comes next. Add the following code snippet to the `viewModel` function:

```
$.connection.hub.start().done(function () {
    hub.server.getRequests().done(function (requests) {
        for (var property in requests) {
            handleEntry(self.requests, property, 
requests[property]);
        }

        initializedCount++;
    });
    hub.server.getFailedRequests().done(function (requests) {
        for (var property in requests) {
            handleEntry(self.failedRequests, property, 
requests[property]);
        }

        initializedCount++;
    });
});
```

We should now have enough logic in our `viewModel` function to actually be able to get any requests already sitting there and also respond to new ones coming.

BindingHandler

The key element of KnockoutJS is its BindingHandler mechanism. In KnockoutJS, everything starts with a `data-bind=""` attribute on an element in the HTML view. Inside the attribute, one puts binding expressions, and the BindingHandlers are a key to this. Every expression starts with the name of the handler. For instance, if you have an `<input>` tag and you want to get the value from the input into a property on the ViewModel, you would use the BindingHandler value. There are a few BindingHandlers out of the box to deal with common scenarios (text, value for each, and more). All of the BindingHandlers are very well documented on the KnockoutJS site. For this sample, we will actually create our own BindingHandler. KnockoutJS is highly extensible and allows you to do just this amongst other extensibility points.

Let's add a JavaScript file called `googleCharts.js` at the root of the project. Inside it, add the following code:

```
google.load('visualization', '1.0', { 'packages': ['corechart']
});
```

This will tell the Google API to enable the charting package.

The next thing we want to do is to define the BindingHandler. Any handler has the option of setting up an `init` function and an `update` function. The `init` function should only occur once, when it's first initialized. Actually, it's when the binding context is set. If the parent binding context of the element changes, it will be called again. The `update` function will be called whenever there is a change in an observable or more observables that the binding expression is referring to. For our sample, we will use the `init` function only and actually respond to changes manually because we have a more involved scenario than what the default mechanism would provide us with. The `update` function that you can add to a BindingHandler has the exact same signature as the `init` function; hence, it is called an update.

Let's add the following code underneath the load call:

```
ko.bindingHandlers.lineChart = {
    init: function (element, valueAccessor, allValueAccessors,
viewModel, bindingContext) {
    }
};
```

This is the core structure of a BindingHandler. As you can see, we've named the BindingHandler as `lineChart`. This is the name we will use in our view later on.

The signature of `init` and `update` are the same. The first parameter represents the element that holds the binding expression, whereas the second `valueAccessor` parameter holds a function that enables us to access the value, which is a result of the expression. KnockoutJS deals with the expression internally and parses any expression and figures out how to expand any values, and so on. The next three parameters aren't important to us right now, so we skip these, but if you feel an itch and need to learn more about them, it's very well documented at `http://knockoutjs.com/documentation/custom-bindings.html`. Add the following code into the `init` function:

```
optionsInput = valueAccessor();

var options = {
    title: optionsInput.title,
    width: optionsInput.width || 300,
```

```
    height: optionsInput.height || 300,
    backgroundColor: 'transparent',
    animation: {
        duration: 1000,
        easing: 'out'
    }
};

var dataHash = {};

var chart = new google.visualization.LineChart(element);
var data = new google.visualization.DataTable();
data.addColumn('string', 'x');
data.addColumn('number', 'y');

function addRow(row, rowIndex) {
    var value = row[1];
    if (ko.isObservable(value)) {
        value.subscribe(function (newValue) {
            data.setValue(rowIndex, 1, newValue);
            chart.draw(data, options);
        });
    }

    var actualValue = ko.unwrap(value);
    data.addRow([row[0], actualValue]);

    dataHash[row[0]] = actualValue;
};

optionsInput.data().forEach(addRow);

optionsInput.data.subscribe(function (newValue) {
    newValue.forEach(function(row, rowIndex) {
        if( !dataHash.hasOwnProperty(row[0])) {
            addRow(row,rowIndex);
        }
    });

    chart.draw(data, options);
});

chart.draw(data, options);
```

As you can see, observables has a function called `subscribe()`, which is the same for both an observable array and a regular observable. The code adds a subscription to the array itself; if there is any change to the array, we will find the change and add any new row to the chart. In addition, when we create a new row, we subscribe to any change in its value so that we can update the chart. In the ViewModel, the values were converted into observable values to accommodate this.

View

Go back to the `index.html` file; we need the UI for the two charts we're going to have. Plus, we need to get both the new BindingHandler loaded and also the ViewModel. Add the following script references after the last script reference already present, as shown here:

```
<script type="text/javascript" src="googleCharts.js"></script>
<script type="text/javascript" src="index.js"></script>
```

Inside the `<body>` tag below the header, we want to add a bootstrap container and a row to hold two metro styled tiles and utilize our new BindingHandler. Also, we want a footer sitting at the bottom, as shown in the following code:

```
<div class="container">
    <div class="row">
        <div class="col-sm-6 col-md-4">
            <div class="thumbnail tile tile-green-sea tile-large">
                <div data-bind="lineChart: { title: 'Web 
Requests', width: 300, height: 300, data: requests }"></div>
            </div>
        </div>

        <div class="col-sm-6 col-md-4">
            <div class="thumbnail tile tile-pomegranate tile-
large">
                <div data-bind="lineChart: { title: 'Failed Web 
Requests', width: 300, height: 300, data: failedRequests }"></div>
            </div>
        </div>
    </div>

    <hr />
    <footer class="bs-footer" role="contentinfo">
        <div class="container">
            The Dashboard
        </div>
    </footer>
</div>
```

Note the `data: requests` and `data: failedRequests` are a part of the binding expressions. These will be handled and resolved by KnockoutJS internally and pointed to the observable arrays on the ViewModel. The other properties are options that go into the BindingHandler and something it forwards to the Google Charting APIs.

Trying it all out

Running the preceding code (*Ctrl* + *F5*) should yield the following result:

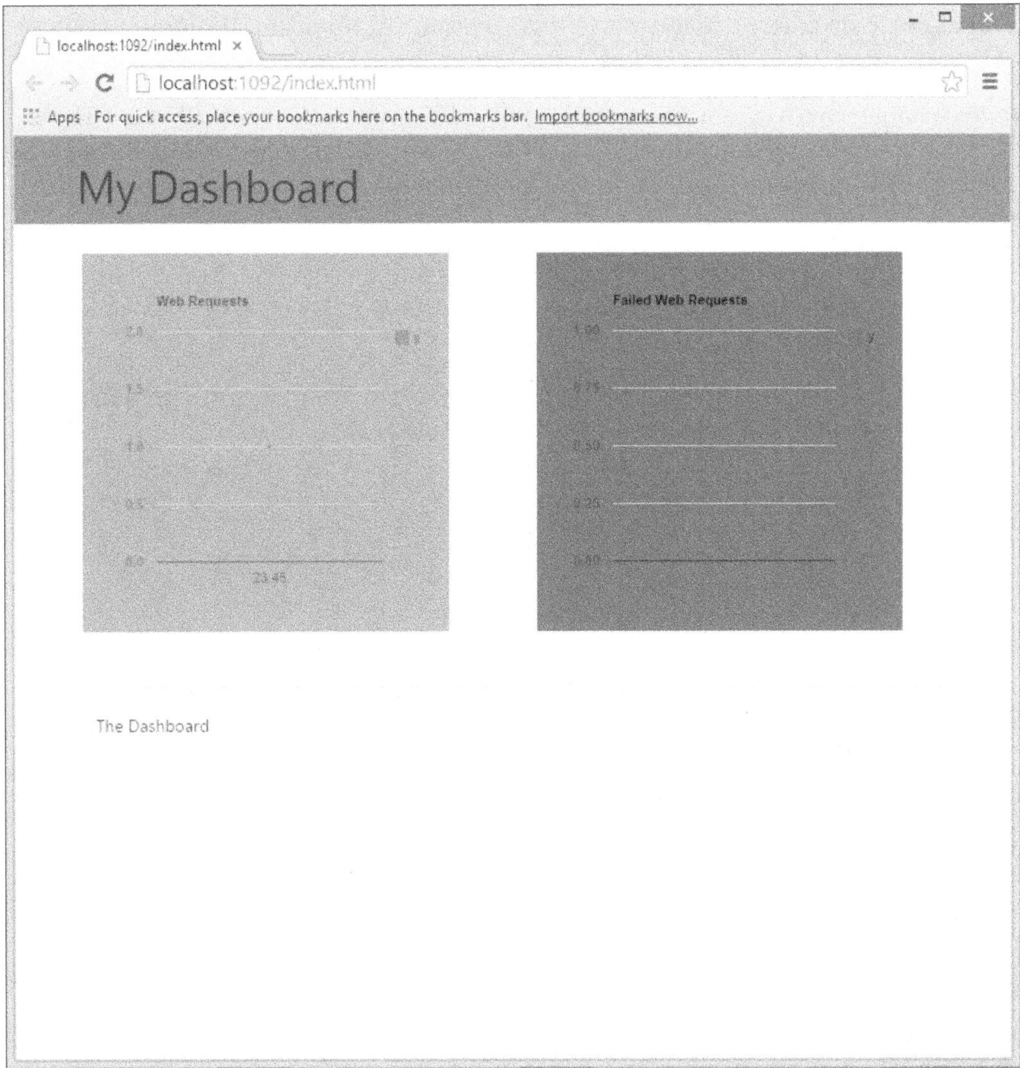

If you open a second browser and go to the same URL, you will see the change in the chart in real time. Waiting approximately for 30 seconds and refreshing the browser should add a second point automatically and also animate the chart accordingly. Typing a URL with a file that does exist should have the same effect on the failed requests chart.

Summary

Building web apps can be really fun, and it does not need to be scary at all if you're not used to it. There are so many techniques and practices out there to really make it a lot easier to do enterprise-level line of business apps, KnockoutJS representing one of these.

In this chapter, we had a brief encounter with MVVM as a pattern with the sole purpose of establishing good practices for your client code. We added this to a single page application setting, sprinkling on top the SignalR to communicate from the server to any connected client.

You should now be familiar with SignalR and its hub mechanism. You can find the entire sample code at `https://github.com/dolittle/SignalR_Blueprints/tree/master/Source/Chapter4`.

In the next chapter, we will take this to the next level, drive forward with what we've seen in this chapter and take it structurally to a new level.

5
What Line of Business Are You In?

In this chapter, you will learn how you can structure a **line of business** (**LOB**) application as a **Single Page Application** (**SPA**) and improve the user experience by adding SignalR. We'll look at how you can make it more maintainable by adding structure and some practices in conjunction with something called Bifrost. Of course, SignalR plays a vital part in it and focuses on how a typical LOB application can benefit from SignalR. It will not only reiterate the concepts of decoupling and MVVM that we've looked at earlier, but also see how things can be more structured and applicable in the real world. We will continue on the same theme in architecting software and bringing more concepts into play.

In this chapter, we will cover the following topics:

- Dive deeper into SPAs
- Dependency Inversion Principle (DIP)
- Make use of Inversion of Control containers to manage our dependencies
- Introduce Bifrost: an open source LOB productivity platform (`http://bifrost.dolittle.com/`) and a framework to build structured applications with good development practices
- Convention over configuration—what does this mean?

The goal – a simple line of business

Anyone who has been working with applications at a certain scale and has to maintain it over years with a team of more than one developer knows the challenges that come with it. Most of the time in projects, we establish a structure and ways of doing things that work for the project and the team that works on it, and often becomes unique for the project. This is fine, but often after a while, one would love to go back and just start rewriting things because of new knowledge and better understanding of how the structure should be. Bifrost brings quite a few things to the table with regards to this, and we will look at how we can get to a project structure that is easier to maintain and establish from day one. All structures are unique to the projects they are on. In small projects, short-lived projects, and unimportant-side projects, your structure doesn't matter that much. In your main project, it does matter and what works at the beginning won't work later as it scales unless you think about it carefully.

In this chapter, we're going to see concrete representations of the SOLID principles (`http://butunclebob.com/ArticleS.UncleBob.PrinciplesOfOod`) defined by Robert C. Martin. They are good principles that are really helpful in creating software that maintains a high level of quality and maintainability.

Decoupling – the next level

In this chapter, one of the things we will brush up is the usage of the Dependency Inversion Principle, that is, the D in SOLID. Let's start with the first principle: the S in SOLID of Single Responsibility Principle, which states that a method or a class should only have one reason to change and only have one responsibility. With this, we can't have our units take on more than one responsibility and need help from collaborators to do the entire job. These collaborators are things we now depend on and we should represent these dependencies clearly to our units so that anyone or anything instantiating it knows what we are depending on.

We have now flipped around the way in which we get dependencies. Instead of the unit trying to instantiate everything itself, we now clearly state what we need as collaborators, opening up for the calling code to decide what implementations of these dependencies you want to pass on. Also, this is an important aspect; typically, you'd want the dependencies expressed in the form of interfaces, yielding flexibility for the calling code. Basically, what this all means is that instead of a unit or system instantiating and managing its dependencies, we decouple and let the **Inversion of Control** (**IOC**) container deal with this.

In the sample, we will use an IOC container called **Ninject** that will deal with this for us. What it basically does is manage the implementations to give to the dependency specified on the constructor. Often, you'll find that the dependencies are interfaces in C#. This means that one is not coupled to a specific implementation and has the flexibility of changing things at runtime based on configuration. Another role of the IOC container is to govern the life cycle of the dependencies. It is responsible for knowing when to create new instances and when to reuse an instance. For instance, in a web application, there are some systems that you want to have a life cycle of per request, meaning that we will get the same instance for the lifetime of a web request. The life cycle is configurable in what is known as a binding. When you explicitly set up the relationship between a contract (interface) and its implementation, you can choose to set up the life cycle behavior as well.

This same concept has been implemented for the client side as well. So, in JavaScript, one can also follow the same pattern and take dependencies into functions using its name.

Proxy generation

In Bifrost, one of the things that have proven very successful is the generation of proxies for JavaScript for artifacts written in C#. This bridges the gap between the two different worlds. We've already seen this with SignalR doing it for hubs. In Bifrost, there also are proxies for hubs. These are slightly different, as we will see, and more consistent with the programming model of Bifrost. In addition to hubs, Bifrost has quite a few other artifacts it generates proxies for. Another aspect of the proxy generation is that it matches the namespaces in C# with JavaScript namespaces. Bifrost has the concept of namespaces for JavaScript, and all the generated code is put into namespaces. You can configure the convention for how it matches the namespaces against each other. We will discuss more on proxies in *Chapter 6, An Architectural Taste.*

Composing the UI

Decoupling should be done at all levels so that the frontend is not excluded from this. Instead of thinking end to end in one view, we divide things and create features in isolation. These features are specialized in doing one thing and one thing only. This makes the individual features experts in their isolated domain instead of trying to fit everything in a wider feature. This creates something that is more decoupled and more maintainable. It's easier to change each of these features so that they become even better at what they do without worrying about breaking other features.

Typically, you could divide a page, as shown in the following figure:

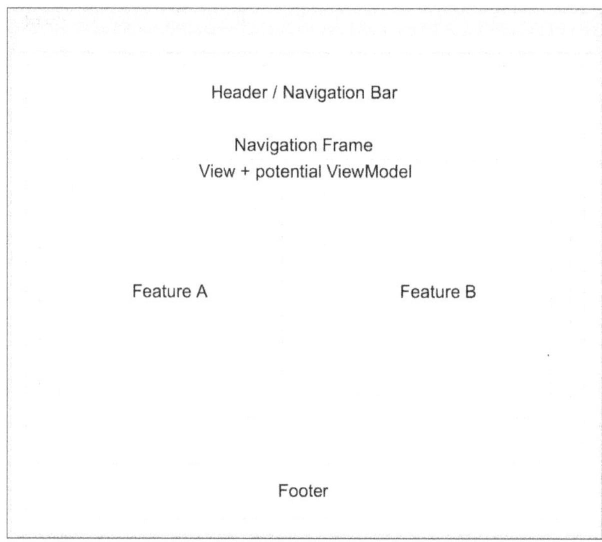

Every box representing a section of the system typically holds a feature. Each individual feature is put together in the larger composition.

One could create the entire preceding composition in one page and one code file, but it would run the risk of being highly coupled together and changing anything could easily break things one didn't mean to touch at all.

Convention over configuration

Often established in projects are ways of doing things, recipes that we follow every time we implement certain aspects of our systems. These can often be automated and put to work as conventions. A good example of this is the configuration of the relationship between an interface and its implementations. One convention that you might find is that the `ISomething` interface has a default implementation called `Something`. The convention here is that the class implementing the interface has the same name without the prefix: `I`. This particular type of convention is something some people consider as anti-pattern, but personally, I don't. There are some discussions that say a better convention would be to drop the `I` prefix for the namespace and instead add the `Impl` postfix on the implementation. In this chapter, we'll see a convention used for views and ViewModels, stating that they go in pairs as long as they have the same name but a different extension (such as `.html` versus `.js`).

Another great example is cross-cutting concerns; things such as transaction management, logging, or similar that can be hooked up by convention in a chain with dynamically created implementations of the interface. This will address the particular concern and then forward it to the real implementation; basically, it will automate things that can be automated.

What about configuration? There are quite a few things we tend to add in the configuration files. Often, I've seen data added in the configuration files that could have been represented as code and really is not dynamic in nature but rather have multiple different implementations. This could be a good time to look at what it is that decides which implementation to use; there might be a convention. Something like the URL could be the deciding factor. This last part is often true for multitenants systems. Instead of having multiple deployments, you could decide code paths based on the URL coming in. Same code base and deployment, which is dynamically self configured based on convention is a powerful way to get a more maintainable solution.

The real beauty of convention over configuration is that you get consistency and developer productivity by default. By doing what is expected, you get all the goodness. If you need or want to go against the convention, you need to do more work. Conventions are just another way of expressing what developers are expecting.

With Bifrost, you'll see conventions being used all over the place for everything. Some of these conventions are hard conventions, defined by Bifrost, and can't be changed. Others are configurable.

Getting assimilated

Bifrost focuses on MVVM; we will therefore start with the bare minimum essentials needed:

1. Open Visual Studio and create a new project by navigating to **FILE** | **New** | **Project**.
2. From the left-hand side menu, select **Web** and then **ASP.NET Web Application**.

3. Enter `Chapter5` in the **Name** textbox and select your location, as shown in the following screenshot:

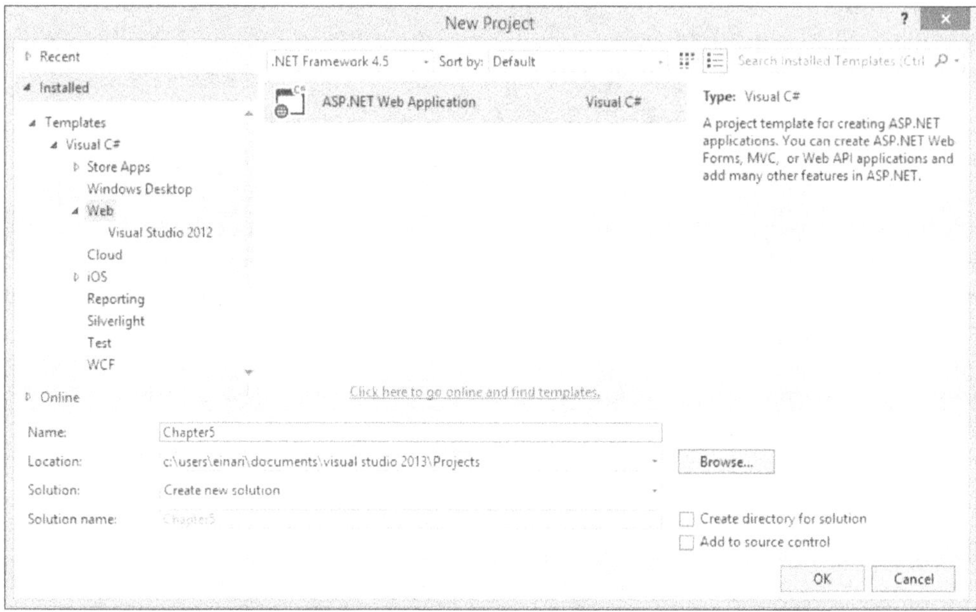

4. Select the **Empty** template from the template selector and make sure you deselect the **Host in the cloud** option, then click on **OK**, as shown here:

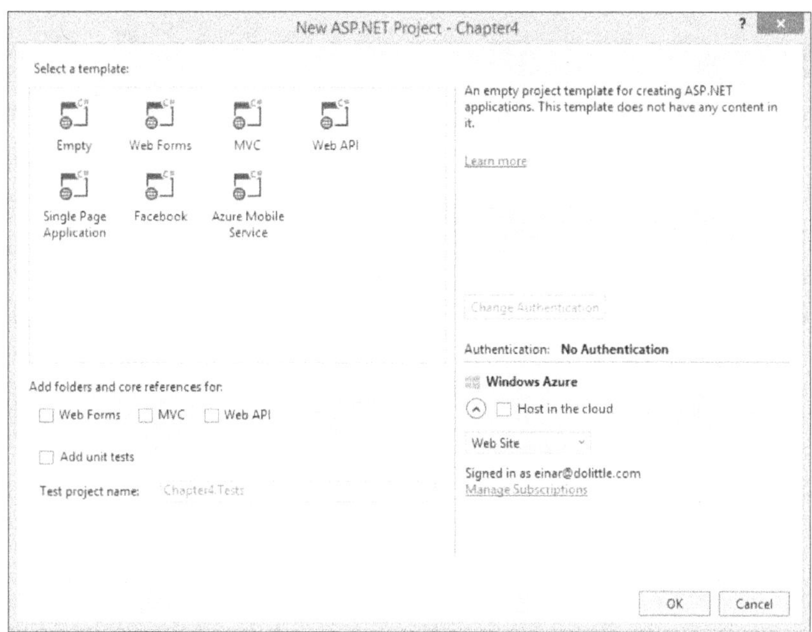

Getting the packages

As shown in the previous chapters, we are going to download a few dependencies from NuGet.

First, we want to get Twitter bootstrap. Add a NuGet package reference, as described in *Chapter 1, The Primer*. Right-click on **References** in **Solution Explorer** and select **Manage NuGet Packages** and type `Bootstrap` in the search dialog box. Select it and then click on **Install**.

We want a slightly different look, so we'll download one of the many bootstrap themes out here. Add a NuGet package reference called `Twitter.Bootstrap.Bootswatch.Flatly`.

Now, we are going to use a package from Bifrost that is meant to get you up and running pretty fast without having to download all the dependencies. Add a NuGet package reference called `Bifrost.Default`. This will download a default setup of Bifrost and some recommended dependencies. Bifrost supports more than the default setup. For instance, if you want to use a different IOC container than Ninject comes with the default one, there are other NuGet packages for this. I recommend going to the NuGet search page and put in Bifrost to see whether there are packages for what you want. If not, get in touch with the `devs` at GitHub. You would be surprised how easy it is to get the dialog box; you can even contribute yourself.

After it has pulled down everything, you should have a few things sitting in your project already. We will not touch these now because we are going to go with the default configuration.

The single page

Bifrost focuses on the notion of SPA; in fact, it provides a few things on the server side that makes it automatically go to the `Index.html` file at root, no matter which URL one enters. This leaves the navigation to be handled in the client instead of the server. Let's open the `Index.html` file, perform a couple of things, and get prepared for the rest of the application.

Let's get the bootstrap style sheets set up. In the head section, add the following code snippet:

```
<link href="Content/bootstrap.min.css" rel="stylesheet" />
<link href="Content/bootstrap.flatly.min.css" rel="stylesheet" />
```

Right below this code, we will reference one script. Bifrost has a route that bundles all the scripts needed. The reason for this is that one of the goals in web applications, especially the ones exposed on the Internet, is to reduce the number of requests. There are ways of disabling specific parts of the bundle. However, for now, we just want the default and let Bifrost manage this for us.

We are now ready to start putting in the code for our application.

Composing

The first thing we want to look at is setting up the composition. Then, we look at the different parts of the page and what should be put into it.

Structure

At the core of the page master, we have a certain structure. We want a header, footer, and main part of the page that holds all the features we will navigate to.

Let's create a new folder called `Structure` in the root of the project. In this folder, we want to add an HTML file called `Header.html`. Put the following code inside the body tag and it will produce a navigation bar:

```
<div class="row">
    <div class="col-lg-12">
        <div class="page-header">
            <h1>Human Resources</h1>
        </div>

        <div class="navbar navbar-default">
            <div class="navbar-header">
                <a class="navbar-brand" href="#">Brand</a>
            </div>

            <ul class="nav navbar-nav">
                <li class="active"><a href="#">Employees</a></li>
            </ul>
        </div>
    </div>
</div>
```

Secondly, we want a footer. Add an HTML file inside the `Structure` folder called `Footer.html`. Put the following code snippet inside the body tag, which will produce a very simple footer:

```
<div class="row">
    <div class="col-lg-12">
        <div class="modal-footer">
            (C)2014 Big Blue Enterprise
        </div>
    </div>
</div>
```

Going back to `Index.html` in the root, we can now start using these new views that we've put in place. Add the following code to the body tag:

```
<div class="container">
    <div data-view="Structure/Header"></div>

    <div data-view="Structure/Footer"></div>
</div>
```

Compiling and running should produce the following result at this stage:

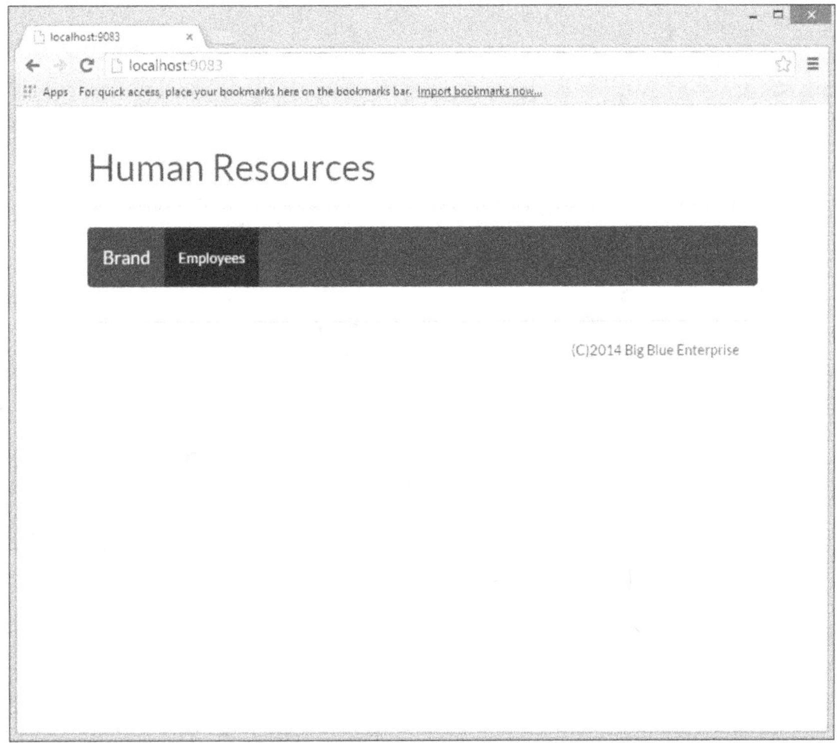

If you right-click on the browser and have a look at the source, you'll notice that it is, in fact, all composed into one valid HTML file, although we're pointing to multiple files and these all carry a full document description. What Bifrost does is to strip away everything except what sits inside the body tag and puts this into the container that is pointing to the particular view. You don't have to have a fully qualified HTML; you could just put what you want for the view and it will be part of a valid HTML page anyway.

Feature

With our structure in place, we can now start putting in a couple of features. We will basically put in place a simple system to register employees. The registration part is isolated in its own feature and the listing of all employees in its own as well. They are completely decoupled from each other, but happen to share a hub.

Let's start by creating a folder called `HumanResources` at the root of the project. Within this folder, add a folder called `Employees`. This will be the folder where we will put our features.

The hub

Before we create any concrete features, we want to get the hub and an object representing an employee in place. In the `Employees` folder inside the `HumanResources` folder, add a class called `Employee.cs`.

At this point, you might ask yourself why we're putting C# files along with HTML files and other artifacts typically used by the frontend. This is the principle of high cohesion. Although we would probably place an object (such as an `Employee`) somewhere else, the concept of high cohesion states that artifacts related to each other need to be kept close to each other. Normally, we separate only in structure by the tier it belongs to. So, back to `Employee.cs`, it should be somewhere else, but in the interest of simplicity for this chapter, we will keep it here. Future chapters will revisit this.

If grouped by its function (for example, controllers, views, models, and so on), you quickly end up with dumping grounds of files. By keeping them close, you can easily see what belongs together at a glance without having to look for it inside these dumping grounds.

In the Employee class, we need a few properties we're going to use. Edit the class to look like the following code snippet:

```
public class Employee
{
    public Guid Id { get; set; }
    public string FirstName { get; set; }
    public string LastName { get; set; }
    public string SocialSecurityNumber { get; set; }
    public string HiredDate { get; set; }
}
```

With this in place, we can move on to the hub. Create a new file inside the Employees folder called EmployeesHub. Start by adding a constructor with a dependency to something called IEntityContext, and we store the instance coming in for methods inside the hub:

```
public class EmployeesHub : Hub
{
    IEntityContext<Employee> _employeesEntityContext;

    public EmployeesHub(IEntityContext<Employee>
employeesEntityContext)
    {
        _employeesEntityContext = employeesEntityContext;
    }
}
```

The next thing we need from the hub is the functionality to get all the employees. Add the following method to the hub:

```
public IEnumerable<Employee>  GetAll()
{
    return _employeesEntityContext.Entities;
}
```

When registering employees, we are, in fact, hiring them so we need functionality to do so. Add the following method to the hub.

```
public void Hire(Employee employee)
{
    employee.Id = Guid.NewGuid();
    _employeesEntityContext.Insert(employee);
    _employeesEntityContext.Commit();

    Clients.All.hired(employee);
}
```

Note that we are taking the `Employee` object instance coming in and passing it directly to other clients. This allows all clients to know about the new hire. At this point, you're probably screaming, what about security? And you're right; one would need to think what is broadcasted and what is not. This is a good example of something you probably don't want to broadcast but rather send to specific groups. However, in the interest of focusing on other things for this chapter, we leave it at this.

This would also be good time to think about conventions and how you could deal with this in a cross-cutting manner. For instance, SignalR has `HubPipeline` that can be extended; you could add your own part. This would make the client part of the right group and also leave the group when needed without all the parts of code having to think about this.

Register

With the hub in place, we can put the actual features. Let's add a view or HTML file called `Register.html` in the `Employees` folder. Leave this for now; we will need a ViewModel for the view. Add the same file but with a `.js` extension: `Register.js`.

Let's populate the `Register.js` file with the following code snippet:

```
Bifrost.namespace("Chapter5.HumanResources.Employees", {
    Register: Bifrost.views.ViewModel.extend(function
(employeesHub) {
        var self = this;

        this.employee = {
            firstName: "",
            lastName: "",
            socialSecurityNumber: "",
            hiredDate: ""
        };

        this.hire = function () {
            employeesHub.server.hire(self.employee);
        };
    })
});
```

Make note of the `employeesHub` parameter for the function used as the definition of the type for `Register`. This is a dependency and there is a client IOC implementation that will start asking dependency resolvers to resolve it. Some of these resolvers have their own conventions. The first resolver being asked will look for an implementation in the same namespace. If it is not found, it tries to load a file. If this does not work, it moves up one level in the namespace and repeats the process. If the resolver fails, it moves on to the next resolver, which can be anyone and also something one can implement oneself.

In the ViewModel, we keep an instance of `Employee` that we can bind to in HTML; we also introduce a function called `hire` that will call the hub to hire.

Go back to the `Register.html` file and add the following code snippet inside the body tag:

```
<div class="well">
    <form class="form-horizontal">
        <fieldset>
            <legend>Register</legend>

            <div class="form-group">
                <label for="firstName" class="col-lg-2 control-
label">F.name</label>
                <div class="col-lg-10">
                    <input type="text" class="form-control"
id="firstName" placeholder="First name" data-bind="value:
employee.firstName">
                </div>
            </div>

            <div class="form-group">
                <label for="lastName" class="col-lg-2 control-
label">L.name</label>
                <div class="col-lg-10">
                    <input type="text" class="form-control"
id="lastName" placeholder="Last name" data-bind="value:
employee.lastName">
                </div>
            </div>

            <div class="form-group">
                <label for="socialSecurityNumber" class="col-lg-2
control-label">SSN</label>
```

```
                <div class="col-lg-10">
                    <input type="text" class="form-control"
id="socialSecurityNumber" placeholder="Social Security Number"
data-bind="value: employee.socialSecurityNumber">
                </div>
            </div>

            <div class="form-group">
                <label for="hiredDate" class="col-lg-2 control-
label">Hired</label>
                <div class="col-lg-10">
                    <input type="date" class="form-control"
id="socialSecurityNumber" placeholder="Hired date" data-
bind="value: employee.hiredDate">
                </div>
            </div>

            <div class="form-group">
                <div class="col-lg-10 col-lg-offset-2">
                    <button type="button" class="btn btn-primary"
data-bind="click:hire">Submit</button>
                </div>
            </div>
        </fieldset>
    </form>
</div>
```

What this does is put in place a form to capture the data needed to register or hire an employee. It uses KnockoutJS binding expressions to do so.

List

In addition to registering, we want to be able to see what we register. Let's go and create an HTML file called `List.html` inside the `Employees` folder and then a JavaScript file called `List.js`.

Let's jump to the `List.js` file first and add the following code:

```
Bifrost.namespace("Chapter5.HumanResources.Employees", {
    List: Bifrost.views.ViewModel.extend(function (employeesHub) {
        var self = this;
        this.employees = ko.observableArray();

        employeesHub.server.getAll().continueWith(function(employees)
{
```

```
                employees.forEach(function (employee) {
                    self.employees.push(employee);
                });
            });

            employeesHub.client(function (client) {
                client.hired = function (employee) {
                    self.employees.push(employee);
                }
            });
        })
    });
```

> Note that all you need to do is make sure that the HTML file and the JavaScript file has the same name and that the namespace is correct in the JavaScript file in order for the system to, by convention, just pick this up and load them together and instantiate the right ViewModel.

The code itself establishes an observable array that the view can subscribe to for changes. Then, we call the server and the `getAll()` method to get the data.

Secondly, we hook up a client function—the one that gets called from the hub on the server.

> Did you see that we are using `.continueWith()` instead of `.done()`, as we have been doing earlier with SignalR when we call functions that we're expecting results from? This is because Bifrost has its own proxies for SignalR that use functionality found in Bifrost, making it more consistent with Bifrost in general.

Let's get into the view: the `List.html` file. Inside the body tag, add the following code:

```
<table class="table table-striped table-bordered table-hover">
    <thead>
        <tr>
            <th>
                SSN
            </th>
            <th>
                First Name
            </th>
            <th>
```

```
                Last Name
            </th>
            <th>
                Employed From
            </th>
        </tr>
    </thead>
    <tbody data-bind="foreach: employees">
        <tr>
            <td data-bind="text: firstName"></td>
            <td data-bind="text: lastName"></td>
            <td data-bind="text: socialSecurityNumber"></td>
            <td data-bind="text: hiredDate"></td>
        </tr>
    </tbody>
</table>
```

This sets up an HTML table as a data grid based on bootstrap. The body of the table holds a template that will be used for each employee in the employees array in the ViewModel.

Completing the composition

We won't see these features yet as we need a couple of things. First of all, we need to add a file called `Index.html` in the `Employees` folder. Add the following code snippet inside the body tag:

```
<div class="row">
    <div class="col-lg-6" data-view="HumanResources/Employees/
Register"></div>
    <div class="col-lg-6" data-view="HumanResources/Employees/List"></
div>
</div>
```

We still have nothing showing up. Open the `Index.html` file in the root of the project. In between the lines referring to header and footer, add the following code:

```
<div data-navigation-
frame="home:HumanResources/Employees/Index"></div>
```

What this line does is to make a container that can respond to URL changes. Although we only have this one feature, you could now go and easily add another feature. Putting in place links that link to the features with relative URLs will be intercepted by Bifrost, so just swap out the content of the navigation frame instead of actually navigating. However, at the same time, update the URL in the browser without doing a full post-back to the server.

Run your app now and you will see the following screenshot:

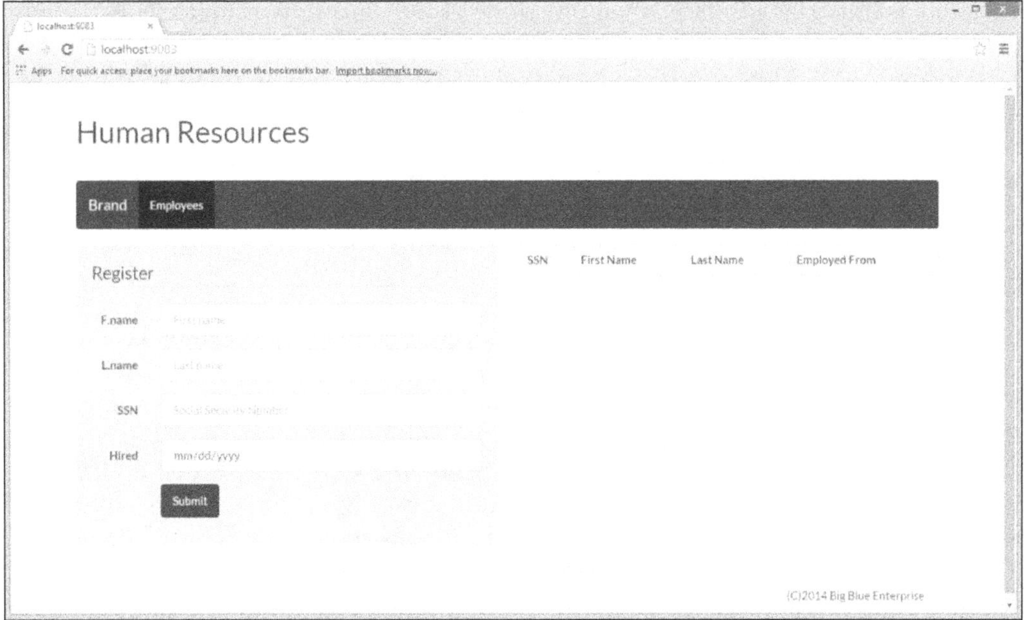

In fact, you should now be able to register an employee and have it automatically appear in the list. You can also refresh the application and your data should be in the list.

Concurrency and staleness

The two issues that often come up when doing development and especially in the LOB application space are concurrency and data staleness. SignalR can be a remedy to this problem. Concurrency is when multiple users update the same thing and is often caused by the fact that the data is stale. If we are currently updating the clients looking at the same data with any changes, this problem pretty much goes away. By saying that this is no longer a problem, the complexity of our solutions can be decreased, creating a more maintainable codebase.

Summary

Structure is important, in fact, it's at times one of the most important aspects of building maintainable applications. In addition to this, it helps one to decide how to apply structure, which can be very valuable. Then, it's all up to your muscle memory when implementing, rather than having to think deep every time for every little feature. Bifrost brings together years of experience in building LOB applications and is not a platform or framework built for itself but built based on real experience. Although, this chapter showed less of SignalR, it's important to see the benefits of putting it together in something that is more structured than simple samples. The benefits are very clear.

SignalR brings a lot to the LOB application development space. It can make a lot of problems go away or simpler, and then also introduce new ways of approaching problem solving for the end user. Bifrost is very committed to taking advantage of SignalR and it's just in its infant stage as far as its usage is concerned. All the security and filtering mentioned is something that Bifrost will tackle in the future and make it seamless for you as a developer and also for the user; you won't even need to think about publishing anything on the SignalR bus. Just by the nature of how Bifrost is architected, we have entry points where we can augment with SignalR and improve performance, user experience, and create new opportunities we never had.

You can find the entire sample code at `https://github.com/dolittle/SignalR_Blueprints/tree/master/Source/Chapter5`.

In the next chapter, we will dive deeper into structure and formalize ways of working with applications with rich domains, which in my opinion applies to most applications.

6
An Architectural Taste

This chapter will focus on bringing forward an alternative to what I would like to refer to as "the default architecture". By this, I mean the classical N-tier architecture with higher focus on data going back and forth from a database mapped through N number of indirections and to a client and then back again. There is nothing inherently wrong or bad with this approach, and it's not an approach that needs to go away, which is being replaced with what this chapter is about. Consider the things in this chapter as another tool in your toolbox.

In this chapter, we will cover the following topics:

- Briefly discuss Domain Driven Design
- Discuss Command Query Responsibility Segregation
- Discuss Event Sourcing
- Show how Bifrost applies the concepts discussed twofold

The goal – banking

With this chapter, we'll have a look at how we can expand the user experience of banking. Having information updated in real time when transferring funds is pretty different from the banking experience I'm having, in fact, it's rather something out of the movies.

Banking is a domain that tends to have lot of data. With its distributed nature, it's not necessarily easy to achieve the goal of real time. By approaching the problem slight differently, it should be possible. **Command Query Responsibility Segregation** (**CQRS**) represents this different approach that allows you to potentially scale at a higher level than more traditional N-tier models.

In addition to CQRS, there is **Domain Driven Design** (**DDD**). With DDD, you reach a higher level of accuracy to model the target. You can establish the vocabulary more accurately and end up with a language that is closer to the domain you're targeting. Combined with CQRS and its concepts, you will get a codebase that is easier to read and understand not only from a technical perspective but also from the perspective of identifying the actual domain.

It's quite an undertaking trying to walk through the full DDD plus CQRS sample in just one chapter but let's try. Big health warnings though; we are running the risk of not modeling things 100 percent perfectly, but the focus is on getting the concepts across and hopefully inspiring us to look more deeply into it. We are going to do a very simple sample where we want to transfer funds from one bank account to another. We will not put in place a full banking site but only deal with this isolated feature. There is definitely the risk of feeling that the approach is quite overkilling when doing something this simple, just imagine the system going further to becoming a full banking experience. Unfortunately, simplifications made undermine the richness and correctness of the domain. Okay! enough with the health warnings, let's get on with it.

Where does it all start?

This might seem a lot for just a single chapter. And yes, to be honest, the topics mentioned are a book per bullet. The idea here is to give a little bit of taste and try to capture its core essence. So, where does it all start then? Well, in this setting, this is really easy. DDD was first coined by Eric Evans in 2003 in his book of the same name. He wrote about how to tackle complexity in software, and from his experience we have found techniques, patterns, and practices that go together and form a mindset that we can use to approach software development with.

In this mindset, it's not only a certain way of working but also a set of core values that are very well-aligned with delivering high quality software that meets the users' requirements. After all, for the most part, we as developers go to work to create something for others to use. It's all about adding business value, and DDD can be the tool to do just that. I would argue that DDD is applicable for most line of business applications; it's always my default approach. This is basically because DDD is a mindset, not a piece of technology or a library one picks up, and it's the way one approaches the problem.

Bounded context

A very important aspect of DDD is recognizing that applications really aren't monolithic. They consist of different parts or contexts and are either put or composed together. However, it goes even further than this; it's about recognizing that domain language is part of each of these contexts and making sure that there is nothing bleeding from one context to the other. Take for instance a domain such as e-commerce; traditionally, we might model something called a product with attributes on it describing it, what price it has, what gross price it has, and also characteristics, such as weight and dimensions. This ends up being part of the "one model to rule them all" concept. This means that we've found all the aspects of a certain object and put them all together, although they're actually never used together. By putting these together, we increase the complexity of the software and end up with technical problems (such as staleness and concurrency issues). The concept of bounded contexts should lead you down the path of describing the different parts specifically for each context with the naming that is right for the concept and only the characteristics needed for the context.

Going back to the product, take the warehouse context, it's probably not referred to as a product but rather a box. They're only interested in a box with a certain dimension, weight, and location in the warehouse. This information is totally irrelevant for the guy that sits in purchasing, who is interested in the gross value of a product and what the retail price would be. For the customer, things such as name of the product, manufacturer, description, technical details, and even customer reviews from others are important aspects. Instead of using them all together, we model the needs in the different contexts, simplifying each context. Martin Fowler has an article about this at `http://martinfowler.com/bliki/BoundedContext.html`.

Core domain

We can divide our system into multiple domains, starting with the core domain. The core domain is what gives you a competitive advantage as a business and is the foundation in which the business is built around. It's most critical and fundamental to your business.

Supporting domain

A supporting domain is the part that provides supporting functionality to the core domain. This could be things such as an internal admin site and tools to assist in achieving the core domain. It's typically where we don't necessarily focus on high code quality and keep things perfectly designed. This is where you have the opportunity of assigning junior developers or even outsourcing.

Generic domain

In the generic domain, you'll find things that can often be fulfilled by off-the-shelf software but perhaps integrated into your system. Things such as dealing with invoicing your client, although critical for the business to survive are not the core domain.

Ubiquitous language

It all starts with recognizing the language of the domain one is trying to create software for. It's vital to recognize that we as developers are most likely not experts in the field we're targeting, unless we're actually making software for developers. This recognition should lead you to talk to the experts in the field and establish the language consisting of the nouns and verbs in that domain. We will use this knowledge together with a set of building blocks to make our code come alive and reflect the business we're targeting. The language is typically unique within each bounded context. It can even be unique when referring to what we traditionally would recognize as one thing.

Entity

This is perhaps the most important building block of them all. An entity is something that has a unique identification attached to it, typically represented with an ID that is either generated by the data source or something such as a GUID that can be created anywhere. However, there is also the notion of natural keys, which can also be unique and make the entity stand on its own. For instance, a natural key can be the bank account number. An entity can be represented differently depending on the state it's in while maintaining the unique identifier. For instance, take the domain of shopping wherein it typically starts as a cart, which turns into a pending order, which then becomes an order leading to a picked order and ultimately a shipped order. They have very different meaning and instead of modeling them all as one single representation, we do it with multiple representations.

Value object

A value object is quite the opposite of an entity; it's not necessarily unique and is rather something the entity relates to. A great example of this is address. More than one person can live at the same address and therefore it holds no value in standing alone. It's dependent on being related back to the entity to actually give meaning. As examples, this might not be correct in the postal domain where the address has higher significance.

Aggregate

Defining the transactional boundaries is a very important aspect of modeling a system. It's often the neglected one. I often see in systems that transaction is `just.BeginTransaction()` at the beginning of a web request and `then.EndTransaction()`, or in a worst case scenario, `.Rollback()` on the end of a web request. This leads to the inclusion of all operations in between, even things that really have nothing to do with each other and a technical worst case scenario of a distributed transaction. This makes the transactional boundaries a technical decision rather than defined from the domain. For instance, by going down the technical path, you might end up with a transaction that includes at the very end an e-mail being sent and it fails and rolls back everything just because the SMTP server was down. Obviously, you're probably thinking, who would do this, and you're right, you would publish it on a queue and let it happen whenever. However, there are quite a few similar scenarios that do not really make sense from the domain perspective and is just a technical decision.

This is what the aggregate is all about: modeling the entities that go together and the operations one can perform on them when they are together. By doing this, we get fewer problems with technical concepts as stale data and a lot of concurrency issues go away as well, and we are in fact modeling the transactions explicitly rather than letting it be arbitrary. It's a very different modeling technique and can be tricky to get right. In entity relationship models, one models the nouns in the domain and the relationships between them, and if you don't have an anemic model, you can add the verbs as methods on these objects. This is very much not the case in this kind of modeling; we are much more interested in each individual business process rather than the nouns and verbs on them. This is a more accurate way of describing the domain as it reflects the processes rather than just state changes on an entity, which leads to code that is often filled with conditionals and ends up being hard to read and hard to maintain.

Repository

Bending spoons in the matrix sense is basically what the repository pattern is representing. The repository represents an abstraction over whatever data source we have and pretends we are all in memory. It's an abstraction over the data source. This is one of the hardest things to model right and get right. Especially, as we all know the lack of functional implementations for something, such as **Language Integrated Query (LINQ)**, for all the different relational databases that typically support something such as **NHibernate** or Entity Framework. There are also a few implementations out here for object-relational mapping that don't even support LINQ. You should try to expose in the interface of the repository what it can do, rather than take a generic approach and run the risk of consuming code performing LINQ statements directly. However, it's a building block that one will have to remember in the DDD setting. We will also see how it's been handled in Bifrost later.

Domain events

As there is behavior in the domain exposed through aggregates, the real-state change of the system happens as a consequence of domain events, instead of changing state directly when calling on behavior in the domain. The aggregates publish an event or more that tells us what has happened. An event is basically just a simple data structure with a name that indicates past tense. On the event sits enough information to describe what has happened, and it shouldn't be complex and keep an object graph of any kind; just model the exact thing that happened. These objects are usually very small and represent the one thing that happened. On the receiving end of this is, typically, a subscriber that knows how to deal with the state change for the system.

Domain services

Some of you might ask, what about domain services? I'm not going to go into detail about them as they are represented through other artifacts. Domain services serve the purpose in DDD of representing domain logic that can be used throughout. This logic will be a part of more focused artifacts in this chapter. In Bifrost, we are yet to find the need to explicitly represent domain services, as we've represented the different aspects into their own artifacts.

Structure

Now that we've covered the basics of DDD, let's take a look at something that can really help save the day, that is, structure. In any project, you'll find structure that is sometimes intentional and sometimes not all that intentional but is structure nevertheless. The concept of high cohesion is one that really makes a lot of sense when you start using it; keep things that are related to each other close in the same folder, except for when they are for totally different layers of your system. You don't keep the domain necessarily in the same folder as the HTML, but keep everything that is related to frontend for the particular feature in one and the same folder. This means that for the frontend, you would keep the HTML, JavaScript, CSS, string resources, any C# services used, all in the same folder and namespace. You don't permit any usage across siblings in the hierarchy. The only usage would be up the hierarchy.

The structure with bounded context at the top module and its specific features is what we promote through Bifrost. It's a structure that helps you focus and lets new developers coming to the project more easily recognize things. Keeping the folder structure intact between the different layers is also very important, providing immediate recognition for the developers and helps with the global understanding in terms of terminology used. Keep it consistent and you'll see huge benefits.

I would also strongly advise you to keep the layers separated out into their own components, that is, in .NET and assemblies. The reason for this is that you won't have everything accessible and don't run the risk of referencing the read side from the domain side. Keep them separate. If you're able to keep them separate by self-discipline or by enforcing it through static code analysis, go for it.

Command Query Responsibility Segregation

To be very clear, the ideas of CQRS have no relation with DDD but are often related to each other with the behavior of the domain being represented by commands. CQRS is decoupling on an architectural level. DDD is complementary in CQRS, and with Bifrost, the building blocks of both go together. CQRS was coined by Greg Young and Udi Dahan a few years ago and was loosely based on **Command Query Separation (CQS)** defined by Bertrand Meyer in 1988. It states that every method should either be a command that performs an action, or a query that returns data to the caller. A method should never do both these things; if put in another way, asking a question should never change the answer.

Let's take a look at the following pseudo sample:

```
public class CustomerService
{
    // Commands
    void MakeCustomerPreferred(CustomerId)
    void ChangeCustomerLocale(CustomerId, NewLocale)
    void CreateCustomer(Customer)
    void EditCustomerDetails(CustomerDefails)

    // Queries
    Customer GetCustomer(CustomerId)
    CustomerSet GetCustomersWithName(Name)
    CustomerSet GetPreferredCustomers()
}
```

As you can see, the commands and the queries are separated out and are very clear about what they are doing. CQRS takes this one step further and says that the separation is even on an object level.

The reason for all this is basically that the use cases for read and write are completely different and have totally different architectural requirements and constraints. It would not be possible to create one representation that was optimal to search, report, and process transactions. Separating reads from writes on an object level, architectural level and, crucially, at a conceptual level opens up endless possibilities. Use the type of data storage or database that is best suited to your concrete scenario.

CQRS is a great representative of the S in the SOLID principles (`http://butunclebob.com/ArticleS.UncleBob.PrinciplesOfOod`).

Bifrost

In this chapter, we will continue to use the platform called Bifrost (`http://bifrost.dolittle.com/`). This platform implements CQRS as well, looking through the glasses of DDD. With this in mind, it's important to explain the artifacts we're going to use.

Command

The definition of a command is to express an action you want. The command is an object that holds the details for the command. It's the instruction to perform a specific action. Basically, a command is nothing but a message. You could easily see it in many ways as a serialized function call. A command represents the user's intent and you can be quite specific in the naming of the command if you please. It will only enrich your domain to be more specific. In fact, you can consider adding reasons as part of the naming as well, not only intent but why. This would give you a great opportunity to measure things later, why are the users doing things that obviously need to capture this in the frontend as well. For instance, say that you have a person and she is changing her address. Instead of just having an `UpdateAddress` command, you could have a `RelocateCustomer` command for a customer that has changed the address. To correct an error in the address, you will have a command called `FixErrorInAddress`. This makes it very clear about what's going on and you lose the woolliness of an `Update` operation on arbitrary fields. It represents opportunity that has the extra information, for instance, statistical information. You'll see that hard technical problems become easier; we don't need all the "what if" code to deal with all kinds of scenarios. We are modeling the exact scenarios.

CommandHandler

In addition to the command, one needs something that knows what to do with the incoming command. The artifact in Bifrost that you will have to implement is called a CommandHandler. Its responsibility is to coordinate what to do when the command comes in. The handler itself does not have to deal with correctness in any way, as reaching this point means that the command is correct. Most of the time, the handler will get an `AggregateRoot` and call a functionality on it.

Validation

Commands need to be confirmed for their correctness in multiple stages. One of these is the validation step that validates the input from the user. Typically, these rules are replicated directly into the client and run there.

Business rules

The next stage for correctness confirmation is business rules. These are typically more complex and run on the server and often require the user to look up things in the database or similar. The result of this gets back to the client.

Security

First and foremost is security. Before we can do anything else, security gets checked and this is done per command. Bifrost has a security system that enables you to configure entire bounded contexts or specific commands and its applications are extensive and can be configured if required.

Events

This is what domain events are. They represent what has happened in the system and sometimes hold the state that represents a change to the system. An event holds information about who produced it, when it occurred, who caused it, by what command it was produced, versioning and other metadata as well. The event can be seen as the counterpart to a command. While the command tells you what the user wants to perform in the system, the event represents what has actually happened. Due to security validation and other things, the event might not happen.

EventSource

Events represent the source of truth, and an EventSource is simply the source of these events. It generates events and represents the source from which the events came. The benefit is that we get the source from where things have happened represented as events, giving us a partitioning for what could also be used as auditing details.

AggregateRoot

A concrete implementation of an EventSource is the AggregateRoot: a very DDD-centric object that represents the transaction boundary. An aggregate is a collection of things that go together. Instead of technical transactions, this is the real transaction of the domain. Being an EventSource, they represent the source of truth and apply events. The AggregateRoot is responsible for maintaining any invariants: all the things that go together. This is what we mean by the transaction boundary. The modeling of these from this perspective is very different from what one might traditionally think of as a domain model object. In fact, most of the time, an AggregateRoot has little or no state.

EventSubscriber

When an event has been applied, the system will deal with finding subscribers that can process the event. These can then do what is best for their scenario and persist, for instance, data in the most optimal way for the feature it represents. One opportunity the subscribers have is to do aggregation and save the result as optimized ready to retrieve value, rather than having to issue a query against the database every time one is reading. For instance, in a banking solution, we could have an overview of what is available in the account for a user instead of issuing a SQL statement to summarize this every time we want to see this overview. We could have a subscriber that does this when events that influence the sum occur and write that optimized to whatever storage makes the most sense.

The purpose of the EventSubscriber is to produce whatever is needed for the feature it represents. You can have multiple subscribers per event for different purposes. For instance, you can store things in a document database for the feature itself, and a second subscriber stores something in a SQL database to do reporting later, and a third subscriber updates the search index; all three in different subscribers not being aware of each other. This is a great opportunity for not necessarily trying to know everything up front and basically, adding functionality as required.

ReadModel

The ReadModel is not the source of truth. It represents the eventual consistent and "cached" state that will be presented to the user. By cached, we mean that it actually does not get updated unless an EventSubscriber has updated it. This is also how it eventually becomes consistent. A ReadModel is typically where things end up at the end of a full round-trip. The ReadModel represents the optimized model that will be used by the specific feature. One should not try to optimize for one model across all features but rather not worry about this and have multiple optimized representations for each feature. How these are stored is a totally different concern; the point is to model what represents the need of the feature. A ReadModel typically won't have relationships and a deep-nested object graph; it will be flattened out for its designated purpose and not try to capture any other features or aspects. In fact, it might make sense for you to model what you need, but due to restrictions, you can't introduce a new source of data, so make projections from whatever data you have today. The projection could be a database view that matches the object. In your app, you could easily mix and match all these different approaches. It's really up to you.

Query

Data is essential for most applications. A specific object representing the ability to query is then needed. With Bifrost, this is a particular object that you implement per query with a good name for the query representing only one query. On this object, you can have parameters that the query uses and gets exposed to the consumer of the query in the frontend. The underlying technology that is used to store data is irrelevant to the consumer and you're free to do whatever is best. Queries return read-models. This approach captures the intent of the queries in the application without being linked to any abstraction that tries to abstract away data storage (NHibernate, Entity Framework, and so on). It also makes optimizing queries very easy as it makes the particular scenario very explicit.

Proxies

Bifrost aims to erase some of the gap between the client and the server. A lot of the APIs exist for both JavaScript and C#, making the developer experience pretty consistent. Another thing that Bifrost provides is generation of JavaScript code from C#. This can then easily be used in JavaScript. Out of the box, Bifrost provides proxy generation of commands, ReadModels, queries, SignalR hubs, and input validation. This is one the most successful aspects of Bifrost and represents true productivity for the developer.

At this point, you might ask yourself, why all these artifacts are involved; let's start by saying that this model is not for all applications. In fact, the beauty of recognizing bounded contexts in your solution enables you to have multiple ways of doing things within the system. Parts of the system might not have any benefit of applying this, and there are even parts of your system that might not even need to think in terms of domain-driven design. This is the purpose of not only thinking in bounded context terms but also the different domains one finds oneself in: core, supporting, or generic. I think the main reason to go down this path is that everything becomes very explicit and you leave woolliness behind. It's in many ways a manifestation of the SOLID principles with high emphasis on single responsibility. It really allows you to change implementations without having to dive into the internals of the app. Bifrost provides the glue that allows you to do these things and focus only on the business value.

With Bifrost, you get a clear manifestation of DDD. There are also scalability benefits for your team that you can harvest from this model. It's easy to start with a query and define the contract in terms of a read-model and then the queries needed. Also, let them just return dummy data before any choice of database has been made. Now, the frontend developer can actually implement the look and feel and model things from the user rather than from a technical perspective, which is the core of DDD. There is another aspect, one is decoupled and future proof, whereas the events that sit here can be replayed for future subscribers and provide new aspects of your system. You can even change storage strategies for your read-models later and replay the subscribers that affect these. Although, events and applying it through an event source really fits well in the full picture, it's not a requirement. Bifrost does support running without events and event sources, it all just really fits well together.

Scalability of your system is important. With everything decoupled in this manner, one can easily scale different parts of the pipeline individually. For instance, with events, one could publish the events on a queue or a bus and have these handled asynchronously. The subscribers that deal with the events could also be out of process running on a completely different server. You can pretty much take any part of the pipeline and scale it out in this manner.

With everything broken down and identified into a well-defined pipeline, it opens up for extensibility. You could easily jump in at any stage of the pipeline and extend it and even extend it cross cuttingly, applying an extension to the entire system at once.

With the event model and subscribers, there is a great opportunity to apply something such as SignalR. The entire model lends itself quite good at this.

Looking at how a system built with Bifrost and all the concepts mentioned, you would get the following figure:

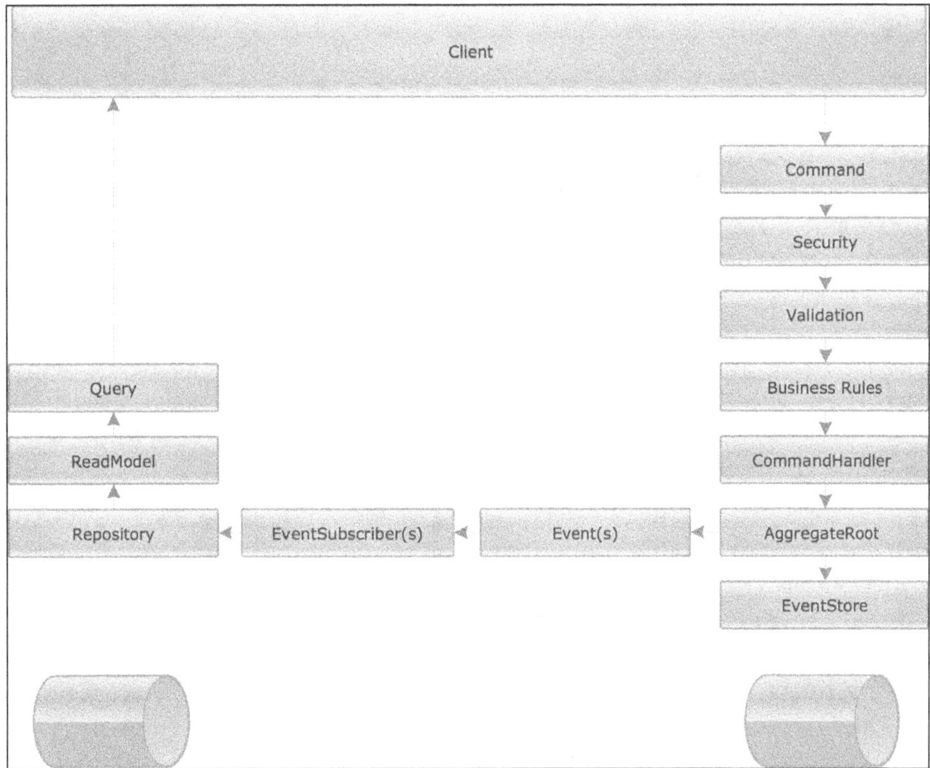

> The events are not published to subscribers unless they are successfully stored. They can't be considered as happened unless we have successfully stored them.

Getting started

To get started, follow these steps:

1. Open Visual Studio and create a new project by clicking on **New** from the **FILE** menu.
2. From the left-hand side menu, select **Web** and then **ASP.NET Web Application**.

3. Enter `Chapter6` in the **Name** textbox and select your location, as shown here:

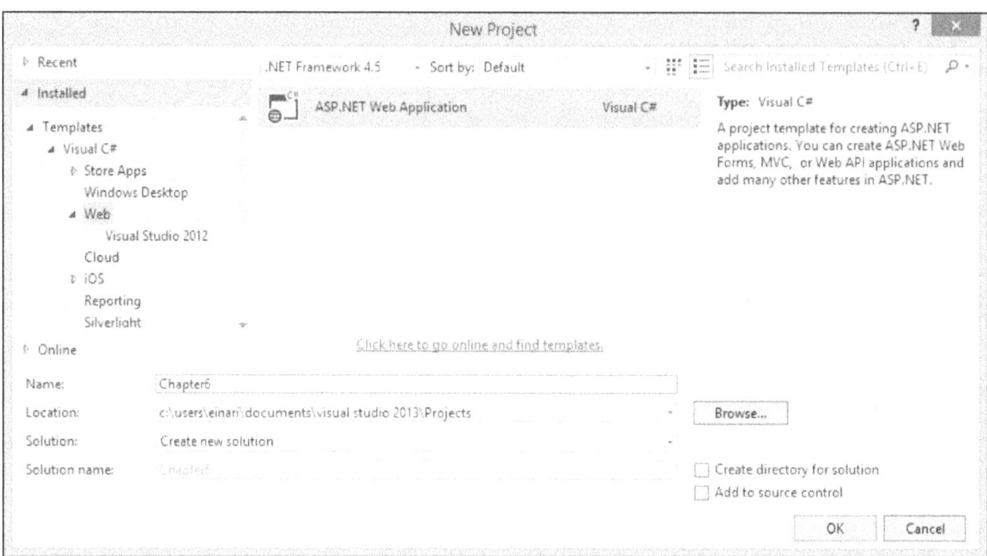

4. Select the **Empty** template from the template selector. We are neither making an **MVC** app nor a **Web Forms** app. This should give us a completely empty web application. Then, make sure you deselect the **Host in the cloud option** and click on **OK**, as shown here:

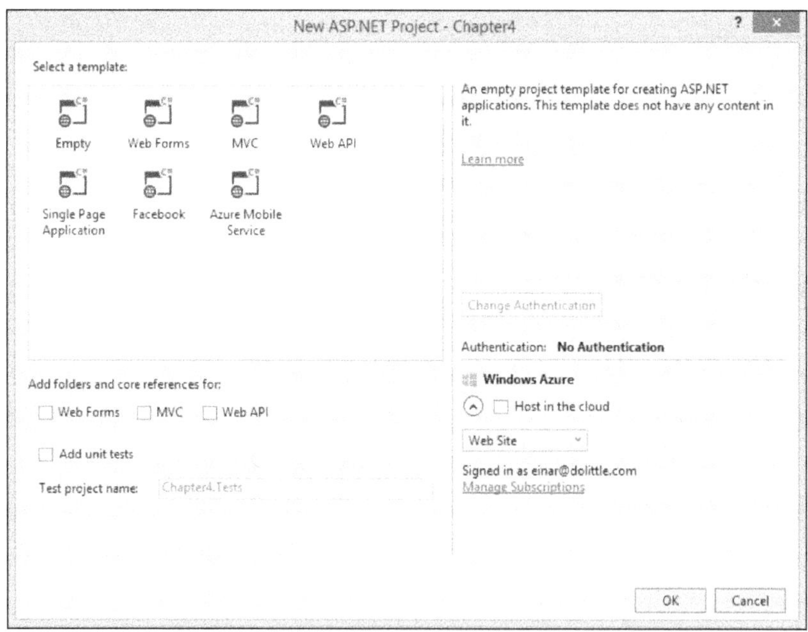

Getting the packages

As in the previous chapters, we are going to pull down a few dependencies from NuGet.

First, we want to get Twitter bootstrap. Add a NuGet package reference, as described in *Chapter 1, The Primer*. Right-click on **References** in **Solution Explorer** and select **Manage NuGet Packages** and type `Bootstrap` in the search dialog box. Select it and click on **Install**.

Now, we are going to use a package from Bifrost that is meant to get you up and running pretty fast without having to pull down all the dependencies. Add a NuGet package reference called `Bifrost.Default`. This will download a default setup of Bifrost and a few recommended dependencies. This is basically what we would consider our default starting point. Bifrost supports more than the default setup, for instance, if you want to use a different IOC container than Ninject that comes with the default one, there are other NuGet packages for this. I recommend going to the NuGet search page and type `Bifrost` to see whether there are packages for what you want. If not, get in touch with the developer at GitHub and you would be surprised how easy it's to get the dialog box going and getting support done; maybe, you can even contribute yourself.

After it has pulled down everything, you should have a few things sitting in your project already. We will not touch these at this time, as we are going to go with the default configuration.

At this time, it would help to change the default namespace and name of the assembly. Right-click on the solution file in the **Solution Explorer** and select **Properties**. In the **Properties** window, set both the **Assembly name** and **Default namespace** as `Web`, as shown in the following screenshot:

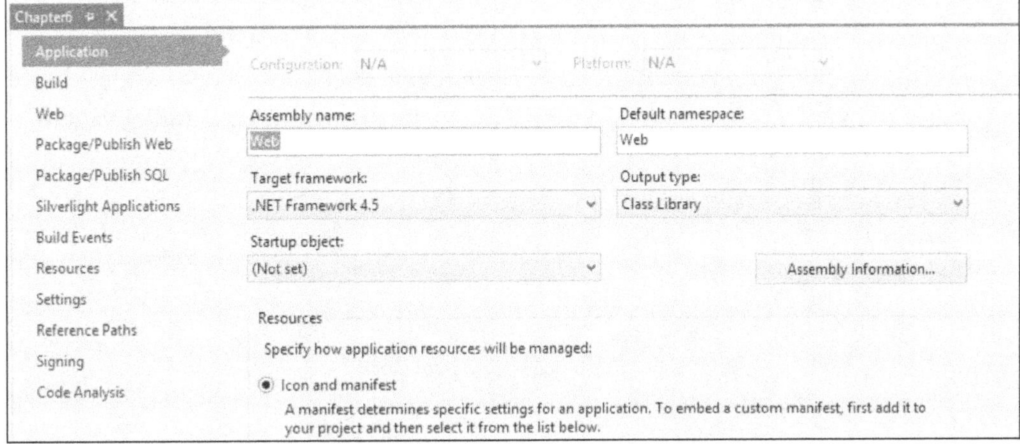

The page

Let's open the `Index.html` file, perform a couple of operations, and get prepared for the rest of the application.

Let's get the bootstrap style sheets set up. In the head section, add the following code:

```
<link href="Content/bootstrap.min.css" rel="stylesheet" />
```

Right below this code, we will reference one script.

Note the script reference for Bifrost/application inside the HTML file. This single script reference loads Bifrost and all its dependencies and all the proxy generated types at the same time. It also holds configuration that is relevant for the client coming from the server. It's a bundled script file.

We are now ready to start putting in the code for our application.

Structure

Let's create a new folder called `Structure` in the root of the project. We want to add an HTML file called `Header.html`:

```
<div class="container">
    <div class="navbar navbar-default navbar-fixed-top">
        <div class="container">
            <div class="navbar-header">
                <a class="navbar-brand" href="#">First Responsive 
Bank</a>
            </div>
        </div>
    </div>
</div>
```

Secondly, we want a footer. Add an HTML file inside the `Structure` folder called `Footer.html`. Put the following code snippet inside the body tag, which will produce a very simple footer:

```
<footer>
    <div class="row">
        <div class="col-lg-12">
            <div class="modal-footer">
                (C)2014 First Responsive Bank
            </div>
```

```
        </div>
    </div>
</footer>
```

Go back to `Index.html` in the root; add the following code snippet to the body tag:

```
<div class="container">
    <div data-view="Structure/Header"></div>

    <div data-view="Structure/Footer"></div>
</div>
```

Compiling and running at this stage will produce the following result:

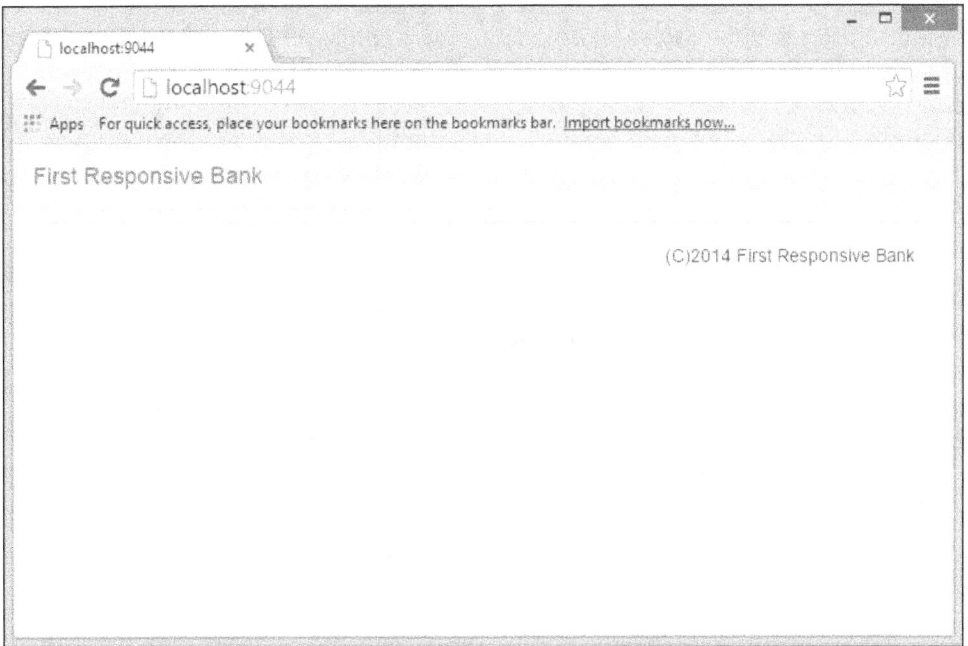

Accounts overview

Now that we have our basic structure in place, we can start creating the first feature: the overview of the accounts in the bank. We're not implementing any user authentication, as this is something that we've covered earlier. This could be reused or, implemented here. So, the accounts are not linked to a user but are considered global. Obviously, you would link these to a user and secure it in a real-world scenario.

Health warning: In this sample, we're going to go against my own advice about how to structure things. We're going to create one project only and not divide things into assemblies. This is due to the interest of saving pages and the division is something you'd do in a real project, but it does not serve a direct purpose here. Every time there is a separate project, I'll mention it.

Concepts

An important part of modeling the domain is finding the concepts you have; the concepts we're talking about at this stage are typically the nouns in your domain. Once found, we model these as something we concretely call a concept. The concept represents just a notion of the real domain noun, a contract of it, and typically, the thing that identifies it uniquely. The reason for modeling these instead of passing around GUIDS, longs, strings, primitives is that we are then expressing them explicitly and making our APIs clearer. In addition to representing the notion of nouns, concepts are also what represent your value objects. They can have more than one property representing a primitive; they do represent the domain concept in your model: a noun with meaning attached to it. By capturing the "concept", we get a more expressive API, a way of applying validation, business rules, or even security for the concepts implicitly and cross cuttingly. It also opens up opportunities to consider the concept type information as metadata at a higher level, for instance, in the frontend. We could make decisions while displaying fields bound to a property of a concept type, making visual decisions on it. Also, the best part is, we don't have to think about these scenarios up front. We can decide later on what we want to do or not.

This is something we would put in our own project (assembly) and reference it by the projects needing them. Typically, concepts are shared between the read and the domain sides.

Let's start by adding a folder in the solution called `Concepts` at the root level of our website. Add another folder within the `Concepts` folder called `Accounts`, which will be the bounded context we're starting off with.

Create a new class called `AccountNumber` within this folder. Add the following using statement:

```
using Bifrost.Concepts;
```

Make class look like the following code snippet:

```
public class AccountNumber : ConceptAs<string>
{
    public static implicit operator AccountNumber (string value)
    {
        return new AccountNumber { Value = value };
    }
}
```

`ConceptAs<>` takes a generic parameter that represents the underlying type; if this type changes, you now have the luxury of being able to change it in one place. Another great thing about modeling the concept like this is that you now get a great opportunity of putting in place cross-cutting concerns. For instance, you could model validation or security for a concept and it would be applied throughout, and the best part is that you can do it later. You're making your code future proof to a certain extent.

The implicit operator will make it possible for us to convert from the underlying primitive to the type; underneath the `ConceptAs` implementation, there is an implicit operator going the other way. This will prove handy later.

Although, we have implicit operators going back and forth, you should not use the underlying type around in your code. We put them there mostly to make our code more readable when dealing with events. In our events, we want to use primitives only. The reason for this is that you can easily run into a couple of issues using complex types on events. Take versioning for instance. Let's say a concept changes characteristics over time when an event is stored and you're replaying it, then the concept would have a different meaning. We'll see the usage of this later.

Read model and queries

Let's start by defining the data, the read aspect of the solution. First, we create a folder called `Read` in the root folder of the project. Within this, we will create `Accounts`, and you should already start to see the pattern. We repeat the name of the bounded context.

Read would typically also be its own project or assembly. It would not know about anything but the concepts and vents. The web project would reference this.

We will now create the read model. Add a file in the `Accounts` folder called `AccountOverview`. We will need a couple of `using` statements, as shown here:

```
using System;
using Bifrost.Read;
using Bifrost.Views;
using Web.Concepts;
using Web.Concepts.Accounts;
```

Then, we need to add a `using` statement for the concepts namespace as well. Now, make the class look like the following code:

```
public class AccountOverview : IReadModel, IHaveId
{
    public Guid Id { get; set; }
    public AccountNumber AccountNumber { get; set; }
    public decimal Balance { get; set; }
}
```

For this particular feature, we only need two interesting properties: `AccountNumber` and `Balance`. These will be what we are going to present in a list of accounts. We don't model anything else, but just what we need.

Note the `IHaveId` interface. This is only being used as we are not really going against a real database, but the default one set up while pulling in the Bifrost default package. This is not a requirement. You could have your own ID in any format. In fact, the `AccountNumber` property on its own probably is more than good enough as the primary key.

Now, we can move on to create a query that we can use to get all the accounts. Let's go and create a class called `AccountsOverview` (note the pluralization) in the same folder.

We will need a `using` statement, as shown here:

```
using System.Linq;
using Bifrost.Read;
```

Then, make the class look like the following code:

```
public class AccountsOverview : IQueryFor<AccountOverview>
{
    IReadModelRepositoryFor<AccountOverview> _repository;
```

```
    public AccountsOverview(IReadModelRepositoryFor<AccountOverview>
repository)
    {
        _repository = repository;
    }

    public IQueryable<AccountOverview> Query
    {
        get
        {
            return _repository.Query;
        }
    }
}
```

Defaults

As we're not creating any features to register accounts, we will need a service that we can call on to get this setup for us. Add a class in the root folder called `Defaults` and add the following `using` statement:

```
using System;
using Bifrost.Read;
using Web.Read.Accounts;
```

Next, add a `using` statement for the `Read.Accounts` namespace that holds the `AccountOverview` read-model. Make the class look like the following code:

```
public class Defaults
{
    IReadModelRepositoryFor<AccountOverview> _repository;

    public Defaults(IReadModelRepositoryFor<AccountOverview>
repository)
    {
        _repository = repository;
    }

    public void Setup()
    {
        _repository.Insert(new AccountOverview
        {
            Id = Guid.NewGuid(),
            AccountNumber = "123456",
            Balance = 1000
        });
```

```
            _repository.Insert(new AccountOverview
            {
                Id = Guid.NewGuid(),
                AccountNumber = "654321",
                Balance = 5000
            });
        }
    }
```

With this in place, we now need to register the service so that we can access it from our browser. Go to the `Configurator` class in the root of the project and add the following line at the bottom of the `Configure` method:

```
RouteTable.Routes.AddService<Defaults>();
```

You should now be able to navigate to this as it's located relative to your site. So, you should be able to access it by navigating to the site and putting in the `/Defaults/Setup` path at the end, such as `http://localhost:9044/Defaults/Setup`, where `:9044` is whatever port your site is running on. Be sure to keep the casing correct, otherwise it won't work. It should just say "null" in your browser. However, we are now ready to put in place a view and a ViewModel to show the result of our work.

View and ViewModel

Go and create a folder in the root of the project called `Accounts`. Let's start by putting in the ViewModel. The feature will be named `Overview`, so add a JavaScript file called `Overview.js`.

This is the frontend, so we will not separate this out in any project or assembly. The web project represents the frontend.

Add the following code:

```
Bifrost.namespace("Web.Accounts", {
    Overview: Bifrost.views.ViewModel.extend(function
(accountsOverview) {
        var self = this;

        this.accounts = accountsOverview.all();
    })
});
```

Note the `accountsOverview` parameter to the constructor of the ViewModel. It's considered a dependency and is automatically resolved by Bifrost. This particular one happens to be a runtime-generated proxy based on the corresponding `accountsOverview` class defined in C#. This is, in fact, the client representation of the query that we can use directly. We call the `.all()` function and get an observable array back that will be populated asynchronously.

We now have enough to get our view up and running. Add an HTML file called `Overview.html` in the same folder. Within the body of the HTML, put the following code snippet:

```
<section>
    <div class="container">
        <div class="row">
            <table class="table table-bordered table-striped">
                <thead>
                    <tr>
                        <th>Account</th>
                        <th>Balance</th>
                        <th>Action</th>
                    </tr>
                </thead>
                <tbody data-bind="foreach: accounts">
                    <tr>
                        <td data-bind="text: accountNumber"></td>
                        <td data-bind="text: '$'+balance"></td>
                        <td>
                            <a class="btn btn-primary" data-
bind="attr: { href: '/Accounts/Transfer?from='+accountNumber
}">Transfer</a>
                        </td>
                    </tr>
                </tbody>
            </table>
        </div>
    </div>
</section>
```

Basically, this is just putting in place a simple table and using KnockoutJS to deal with `foreach` through the `accounts` property that we put in the ViewModel based on the query. In addition, we're putting in a button to transfer funds, which is just a simple anchor. Bifrost will keep this as a single page application, so we won't post it to the server. Even when putting in a URL like this directly, Bifrost will intercept it and make sure we don't post back.

Running the solution now should yield the following result:

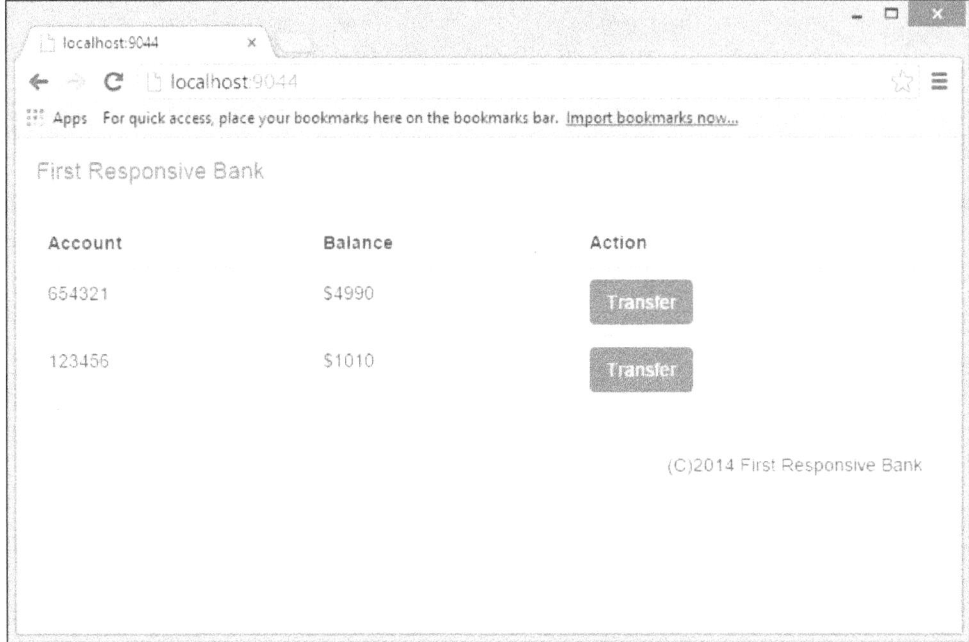

Domain

Before we create the transfer frontend, let's get the domain in place. We are going to need a few artifacts to achieve this. Let's start with creating the `Domain` folder in the root of the project followed by an `Accounts` folder within it. In here, we will start by putting in a command that represents the transfer behavior we want and create a class called `Transfer`.

The domain is something you'd separate out in your own project or assembly; it would only reference concepts and events. The web project would reference this. However, read would not know about it nor would the domain know about read?

Command

Put in place the following `using` statement:

```
using Bifrost.Commands;
```

Then, we need a `using` statement for the concept we put in place. Make the class look like the following code:

```
public class Transfer : Command
{
    public AccountNumber From { get; set; }
    public AccountNumber To { get; set; }
    public decimal Amount { get; set; }
}
```

Events

The command represents what we want to happen, and the counterpart to a command is one or more events that define what is considered as happened. Before we move on, we want to just get these in place as well. Put in place an `Events` folder in the root of the project and again add `Accounts` within it. After analyzing the banking domain and this particular behavior, you'll soon find out that it's all about credit and debit. We will therefore create two events that represent this. Create a class called `Credited` in the new folder. Add the following `using` statement:

```
using Bifrost.Events;
```

Make the class look like the following code:

```
public class Credited : Event
{
    public Credited(Guid eventSourceId) : base(eventSourceId) { }
    public string AccountNumber { get; set; }
    public decimal Amount { get; set; }
}
```

Then, we will need a class called `Debited` look exactly the same, but we won't fall for the temptation of creating a common super class that we can inherit from. This is basically because we don't know if the coupling would be worth it. Besides, **Don't Repeat Yourself** (**DRY**) is all about not repeating logic; properties are not logic. So, with the same `using` statement in place in a file called `Debited.cs`, you should have a class looking like this:

```
public class Debited : Event
{
    public Debited(Guid eventSourceId) : base(eventSourceId) { }
    public string AccountNumber { get; set; }
    public decimal Amount { get; set; }
}
```

We've now modeled what will be considered as the source of truth later.

AggregateRoot

Let's put in place AggregateRoot that represents the behavior from this perspective. In the Accounts folder within the Domain, add a class called Transaction. Put in the following using statement:

```
using Bifrost.Domain;
```

Also, we need to include using statements for the concepts and the events. Add them as well.

Next, we want to make the class look like the following code:

```
public class Transaction : AggregateRoot
{
    public Transaction(Guid id) : base(id) { }

    public void Transfer(AccountNumber from, AccountNumber to,
decimal amount)
    {
        Apply(new Credited(Id) { AccountNumber = from, Amount =
amount });
        Apply(new Debited(Id) { AccountNumber = to, Amount =
amount });
    }
}
```

See the brilliance in naming the AggregateRoot? Not only does it represent the bank transaction between two accounts, it's a very good example of the difference between more technical approach to transactions and this.

Although, being simplified, it proves the difference in modeling. We've not put in an Account aggregate to handle the deposit or the withdrawal. You would normally take this up to a different level and introduce something called a Saga. However, I think it does not really serve a purpose doing this here.

A very important aspect of AggregateRoot in this model is that it does not expose any public state, and this particular type does not need state at all. However, some aggregates do need internal state to perform its operations. If you need to have private state, you simply implement methods called On() with one parameter: the event you want to deal with. When we get an aggregate and there are events and one has implemented On() for the events, it will replay the events on the aggregate. Worth mentioning here is also the Transfer behavior ending up in two events. This is both common and uncommon. The point is that there is no direct correlation between a command and event necessarily.

CommandHandler

We need to move back a bit in order to actually get to the behavior exposed on the aggregate root. Let's add a class called `CommandHandlers` in the same folder as `AggregateRoot`. This will coordinate what to do when the command occur using `Bifrost.Domain`:

```
using Bifrost.Commands;
```

The class should look like the following code:

```
public class CommandHandlers : IHandleCommands
{
    IAggregateRootRepository<Transaction> _repository;

    public CommandHandlers(IAggregateRootRepository<Transaction>
repository)
    {
        _repository = repository;
    }

    public void Handle(Transfer transfer)
    {
        var transferring = _repository.Get(Guid.NewGuid());
        transferring.Transfer(transfer.From, transfer.To,
transfer.Amount);
    }
}
```

This will get the aggregate root and call transfer on it. This particular feature is fairly simple, so one is not going to do much more. However, the handler is where you'd coordinate more complex situations.

Bifrost has really embraced the concept of convention over configuration. For this particular scenario, you'll notice that the `IHandleCommands` is an empty interface with no methods on it. Instead, Bifrost recognizes any methods called `Handle` that takes a command as a parameter and hooks that up.

Back to the frontend

Now that we have a domain to work with, we can implement the transfer frontend for it. Let's navigate back to the `Accounts` folder in the root of the project and add the ViewModel; add a JavaScript file called `Transfer.js` and make it look like the following code:

```
Bifrost.namespace("Web.Accounts", {
    Transfer: Bifrost.views.ViewModel.extend(function (transfer) {
        var self = this;
        var from = ko.observableQueryParameter("from");
        this.transfer = transfer;
        this.transfer.from(from());
        this.transfer.amount(0);

        this.commandResult = ko.observable();

        transfer.failed(function (commandResult) {
            self.commandResult(commandResult);
        });

        transfer.succeeded(function () {
            Bifrost.navigation.navigateTo("/");
        });
    })
});
```

Again, as with the other ViewModel, we're taking advantage of Bifrost's runtime generation of proxies, this time with the command called `Transfer` we wrote. We take it as a dependency to the ViewModel. An extension to KnockoutJS that Bifrost provides is the ability to observable parameters from the query string in the browser. We take the `from` account as a parameter on the query string. If the command fails, we set the command result so that we can show why it failed; if succeeded, we navigate to root again.

Let's add a view for this, add an HTML file called `Transfer.html` in the same folder. Make it look like the following code:

```
<section>
    <div class="container">
        <div class="row">
            <div data-bind="with: commandResult">
                <ul data-bind="foreach: allValidationMessages">
                    <li class="alert-error" data-bind="text:
$data"></li>
```

```
                </ul>
            </div>

            <form role="form" data-bind="with: transfer">
                <div class="form-group">
                    <label for="fromAccount">From</label>
                    <input type="text" class="form-control"
id="fromAccount" data-bind="value: from" disabled>
                    <span data-bind="validationMessageFor:
from"></span>
                </div>
                <div class="form-group">
                    <label for="toAccount">To</label>
                    <input type="text" class="form-control"
id="toAccount" data-bind="value: to">
                    <span data-bind="validationMessageFor:
to"></span>
                </div>
                <div class="form-group">
                    <label for="amount">Amount</label>
                    <input type="number" class="form-control"
id="amount" data-bind="value: amount">
                </div>
            </form>
            <button class="btn btn-primary" data-bind="command:
transfer">Submit</button>
        </div>
    </div>
    <br />
</section>
```

The `with` binding that KnockoutJS provides changes the binding context in any descendant nodes. It's quite handy to avoid having a fully-qualified expression. It is also very handy if the top level has the potential of being null or undefined.

Input validation

As you can see in the view for transfer, there are a few things pointing to validation. For instance, there is a binding handler called `validationMessageFor` being used. So, we're going to need some input validation to guarantee correctness before we reach the CommandHandler. Create a class called `TransferInputHandler` in the `Domain/Accounts` folder.

Add the following using statements:

```
using Bifrost.FluentValidation.Commands;
using FluentValidation;
using FluentValidation.Validators;
```

Then, make the class look like the following code:

```
public class TransferInputValidator :
CommandInputValidator<Transfer>
{
    public TransferInputValidator()
    {
        RuleFor(t => (string)t.From)
            .NotEmpty().WithMessage("You must specify account")
            .Length(6).WithMessage("Account must have 6 digits");
        RuleFor(t => (string)t.To)
            .NotEmpty().WithMessage("You must specify account")
            .Length(6).WithMessage("Account must have 6 digits");
        RuleFor(t => t.Amount)
            .NotEmpty().WithMessage("You must specify an amount")
            .GreaterThan(0).WithMessage("Amount must be more than
0");
    }
}
```

This code sets up rules for each property in the command. The rules should be pretty self-explanatory.

Business rules

The validation rules will run in the client and also be part of the proxies generated as metadata for the commands. We will need some more complex rules; these are called business rules, and typically, only run on the server. In order for us to do these, we're going to explore something that Bifrost has yet to formalize, so we will do something very simple to work around the missing artifact: something called validation queries. Sometimes, one needs to perform a query into a database to verify that everything is correct, for example, it might be linked to a property on the command or the whole of the command. The easiest way for these types of queries is to access read-models already existing, at least without the formalization in Bifrost. However, as we now know, it's not okay for the domain to know about the read side; this is the core principle of CQRS. However, it can know about something that can give the true or false, which then represents a contract. Go and create a folder in the root of the folder called `ValidationQueries`. Create a file called `be_a_valid_account.cs`.

In this, we will only have a delegate that looks like the following code:

```
public delegate bool be_a_valid_account(AccountNumber
accountNumber);
```

Of course, put the usual concept of `using` statement. Then, put a second file, call this `have_sufficient_funds.cs`, which is also a delegate, make it look like the following code:

```
public delegate bool have_sufficient_funds(AccountNumber
accountNumber, decimal amount);
```

The delegate themselves won't do anything, so we need implementations of these that does, and we also need to configure the IOC container to give the right implementation when something has a dependency to it. Go and create a class called `ValidationQuriesModule` in the root of the project. Implement it fully as shown here:

```
using System.Linq;
using Bifrost.Read;
using Ninject;
using Ninject.Modules;
using Web.Concepts.Accounts;
using Web.Read.Accounts;
using Web.ValidationQueries;

namespace Web
{
    public class ValidationQueriesModule : NinjectModule
    {
        public override void Load()
        {
            Bind<be_a_valid_account>().ToMethod(c =>
be_a_valid_account);
            Bind<have_sufficient_funds>().ToMethod(c =>
have_sufficient_funds);
        }

        bool have_sufficient_funds(AccountNumber accountNumber,
decimal amount)
        {
            var repository =
Kernel.Get<IReadModelRepositoryFor<AccountOverview>>();
            var account = repository.Query.Where(a =>
a.AccountNumber == accountNumber).Single();
            return account.Balance >= amount;
        }
```

```
        bool be_a_valid_account(AccountNumber accountNumber)
        {
            var repository = Kernel.Get<IReadModelRepositoryFor<Accoun
tOverview>>();
            var accountExists = repository.Query.Any(a =>
a.AccountNumber == accountNumber);

            var ac = repository.Query.Where(a => a.AccountNumber
== accountNumber);

            return accountExists;
        }

    }
}
```

The code should be fairly self-explanatory. It tells Ninject the IOC to bind the delegates to concrete methods that actually perform the queries based on the concepts coming in.

Now, we need the Ninject module to get hooked up. Open the `ContainerCreator.cs` file and change the kernel instantiation to look like the following code:

```
var kernel = new StandardKernel(new ValidationQueriesModule());
```

With this in place, we can go and create our business rules. Go back to the `Domain/Accounts` folder and create a file called `TransferBusinessValidator`. Make it look like the following code:

```
using Bifrost.Validation;
using FluentValidation;
using Web.ValidationQueries;

namespace Web.Domain.Accounts
{
    public class TransferBusinessValidator :
CommandBusinessValidator<Transfer>
    {
        public TransferBusinessValidator(be_a_valid_account
be_a_valid_account, have_sufficient_funds have_sufficient_funds)
        {
            RuleFor(t => t.From)
                .Must(a =>
be_a_valid_account(a)).WithMessage("Invalid account");
            RuleFor(t => t.To)
                .Must(a =>
be_a_valid_account(a)).WithMessage("Invalid account");
```

```
                ModelRule()
                    .Must(t => have_sufficient_funds(t.From,
t.Amount)).WithMessage("Not enough funds");
            }
        }
    }
```

As you can see, we're taking the validation queries as dependencies and just simply calling these as part of the delegates we give to `FluentValidation`. The nice thing about this approach is that your business rules become very small, clear, and focused. They are also now part of the vocabulary and more reusable.

For now, you can see that there is no direct support in Bifrost to make this as smooth as you'd probably expect. This is something that we are working on and will come out with later. Having said that, there is nothing stopping you in coming up with a convention to hook these up automatically for the IOC, so you don't have to explicitly set up bindings for them all. You could have a convention saying that delegates in the domain should automatically be bound to types found in classes with an `IHaveRules` interface, for instance, and matches the name, limiting it to the same bounded context and structure as they are found in, to make it consistent.

If you run the solution, click on the first transfer button and then try to click on the submit button without entering any input, you will see the following screenshot:

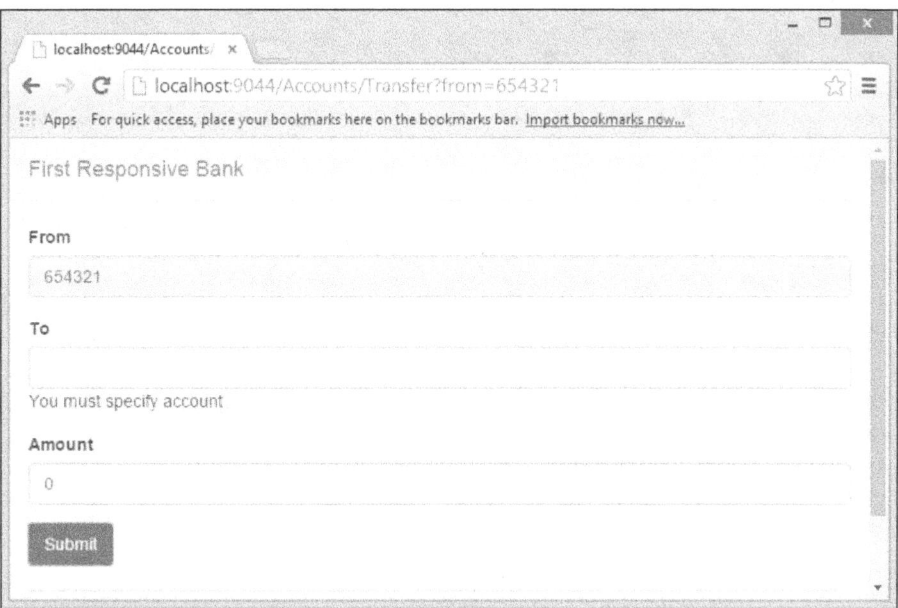

Note the validation message under the **To** input.

EventSubscriber

We still have not changed data in the data source. We will need to subscribe to the events being applied by the `AggregateRoot` in order for us to do this. Navigate back to the `Read/Accounts` folder and enter a class called `EventSubscribers`. Fully implement it as shown here:

```
using System.Linq;
using Bifrost.Entities;
using Bifrost.Events;
using Web.Events.Accounts;

namespace Web.Read.Accounts
{
    public class EventSubscribers : IProcessEvents
    {
        IEntityContext<AccountOverview> _entityContext;

        public EventSubscribers(IEntityContext<AccountOverview>
entityContext)
        {
            _entityContext = entityContext;
        }

        public void Process(Credited @event)
        {
            var accountOverview = _entityContext.Entities.Where(a
=> a.AccountNumber == @event.AccountNumber).Single();
            accountOverview.Balance -= @event.Amount;
            _entityContext.Save(accountOverview);

        }

        public void Process(Debited @event)
        {
            var accountOverview = _entityContext.Entities.Where(a
=> a.AccountNumber == @event.AccountNumber).Single();
            accountOverview.Balance += @event.Amount;
            _entityContext.Save(accountOverview);

        }
    }
}
```

The implementation is very simple. It basically just adds or subtracts depending on the event and saves the result using something called `EntityContext`. Another natural subscriber for these events would be one that maintains the journal for each bank account, showing all the transactions.

Trying things out now should save any transfers. However, we have yet to light it up with some SignalR magic. We have a great opportunity to do this in `EventSubscribers`. So, let's look into how we can do this.

There is no magic in Bifrost yet for this, although it's in the making. For now, we will do something similar to what we did for the business rules to maintain the same level of decoupling, which we've now achieved throughout. Create a new folder called `ClientEvents` in the root of the project. Create a file called `AccountBalanceChanged.cs` and make it look like the following code:

```
using Web.Concepts.Accounts;

namespace Web.ClientEvents
{
    public delegate void AccountBalanceChanged(AccountNumber
accountNumber, decimal balance);
}
```

We will need a Ninject module for this as well, so we add a class called `ClientEventsModule` in the root of the project and implement it as follows:

```
using Microsoft.AspNet.SignalR;
using Ninject.Modules;
using Web.Accounts;
using Web.ClientEvents;
using Web.Concepts.Accounts;

namespace Web
{
    public class ClientEventsModule : NinjectModule
    {
        public override void Load()
        {
            Bind<AccountBalanceChanged>().ToMethod(c=>AccountBalanceC
hanged);
        }

        void AccountBalanceChanged(AccountNumber accountNumber,
decimal balance)
        {
```

```
            GlobalHost.ConnectionManager.GetHubContext<OverviewHub>().
Clients.
All.accountBalanceChanged(accountNumber, balance);
        }
    }
}
```

Now, we go back to the `ContainerCreator` and change the instantiation of the kernel again to look like the following code snippet:

```
var kernel = new StandardKernel(new ValidationQueriesModule(), new
ClientEventsModule());
```

Now, we can take in as a dependency in class with the event subscribers and call whenever the balance changes.

Open the `EventSubscribers` class and make it look like the following code:

```
using System.Linq;
using Bifrost.Entities;
using Bifrost.Events;
using Web.ClientEvents;
using Web.Events.Accounts;

namespace Web.Read.Accounts
{
    public class EventSubscribers : IProcessEvents
    {
        IEntityContext<AccountOverview> _entityContext;
        AccountBalanceChanged _accountBalanceChanged;

        public EventSubscribers(IEntityContext<AccountOverview>
entityContext, AccountBalanceChanged accountBalanceChanged)
        {
            _entityContext = entityContext;
            _accountBalanceChanged = accountBalanceChanged;
        }

        public void Process(Credited @event)
        {
            var accountOverview = _entityContext.Entities.Where(a
=> a.AccountNumber == @event.AccountNumber).Single();
            accountOverview.Balance -= @event.Amount;
            _entityContext.Save(accountOverview);
```

```
            _accountBalanceChanged(accountOverview.AccountNumber,
accountOverview.Balance);
        }

        public void Process(Debited @event)
        {
            var accountOverview = _entityContext.Entities.Where(a
=> a.AccountNumber == @event.AccountNumber).Single();
            accountOverview.Balance += @event.Amount;
            _entityContext.Save(accountOverview);

            _accountBalanceChanged(accountOverview.AccountNumber,
accountOverview.Balance);
        }
    }
}
```

Note the new `using` statement, the dependency, and the private variable holding it. In both these subscribers, you'll see the delegate being called to update any clients.

Go back to the ViewModel called `Overview.js` in the `Accounts` folder in the root of the project. Let's change this substantial to respond to the client event:

```
Bifrost.namespace("Web.Accounts", {
    Overview: Bifrost.views.ViewModel.extend(function
(accountsOverview, overviewHub) {
        var self = this;

        this.accounts = accountsOverview.all();

        overviewHub.client(function (client) {
            client.accountBalanceChanged = function
(accountNumber, balance) {
                var accountOverviewFound;
                self.accounts().forEach(function (accountOverview)
{
                    if (accountOverview.accountNumber ==
accountNumber) {
                        accountOverviewFound = accountOverview;
                    }
                });

                self.accounts.replace(accountOverviewFound, {
```

```
                    id: accountOverviewFound.id,
                    accountNumber: accountNumber,
                    balance: balance
                });
            };
        });

    })
});
```

Note that we again have a proxy that we can take a dependency to: the hub. As we've seen in the earlier chapters, this is nothing new. However, it's kind of, the proxy coming in here is not the one SignalR would produce; Bifrost creates its own to fit the model of Bifrost better and reuse concepts from Bifrost. So, you'll see, for instance, the use of the promise pattern implemented in Bifrost.

Run this and keep the two browsers open: one pointing to the landing page and the other doing transfers; you should now see the account information being updated in real time.

Summary

DDD and CQRS are not necessary for all types of applications; it might not even be for all bounded contexts of your application. However, I highly recommend looking deeper into this. It's probably a good idea to go down the path of looking at the SOLID principles, if you haven't already done this before. Also, it's worth looking at Behavior Driven Design, as it's close in mindset. Bifrost has been created to provide a full experience when implementing on top of these concepts and principles. It should give you a great opportunity for productivity and help you stay on the narrow path of being SOLID.

You can find the entire sample code at `https://github.com/dolittle/SignalR_Blueprints/tree/master/Source/Chapter6`.

In the next chapter, we will move on to how we can hook a Windows Phone client into this bank.

7
The Three Screens – Mobile First

In this chapter, we're going to move away from the web sphere and focus on the mobile space. After all, SignalR knows no boundaries. The team has been great at providing support not only for JavaScript but all types of clients (Windows Phone is the one among these). There are multiple programming models and versions; this chapter will focus on the model for the future: Windows Phone 8.1 RT-based. This is a converged model that blends with Windows 8.x store apps and will also be the one that Windows 10 is based on, which takes this convergence across all Microsoft's platforms. In this chapter, we'll cover the following topics:

- Briefly discuss XAML and binding
- MVVM in XAML
- Using SignalR .NET Client
- Using Bifrost Client
- Using Yggdrasil as an IOC container

XAML

Microsoft introduced XAML as a part of **Windows Presentation Foundation** (**WPF**), which saw the light of day back in 2006. XAML is basically a declarative model to define UIs with an object model, among other things, that represent the objects put in the XAML. This is what represents the view in the MVVM setting.

Binding

XAML puts a lot of effort into binding declaratively from the view to what is called the datacontext. The model is hierarchical, meaning that one can set a context at a higher level and it inherits the context deeper within the hierarchy, but at any given place in the hierarchy, a node can redefine what the context is and everything is now relatively bound to the context unless an explicit source is specified. Binding is done through something called markup extensions; these are basically expressions expressed through curly brackets ({ }). Bindings have the ability to observe changes in the object they are bound to; it does this by recognizing interfaces that allow you to hook up events that get triggered when there are changes made. The most familiar of these interfaces are `INotifyPropertyChanged` and `INotifyCollectionChanged`. Triggering these events is vital to be done on the UI thread. You can ensure this using a dispatcher that allows you to schedule an operation on the UI thread if your code happens to run in a different thread; for instance, if you're calling the server that needs to happen asynchronously.

Binding is only possible for properties that are on objects, such as `DependencyObject`, and on properties, such as `DependencyProperty`.

The goal – mobile banking

We are now going to expand on what we did in *Chapter 6, An Architectural Taste*, and provide a mobile app to perform the same things. Unfortunately, Bifrost Client doesn't have all the facilities in place for the CQRS and DDD stack yet but we will manage. This is something that will get a lot more attention and you will love moving forward.

Getting started

Before you start, make sure that you have installed the Windows Phone 8.1 extensions to Visual Studio, and make sure you have everything up to date. If you haven't installed the prerequisites, refer to `http://dev.windows.com/en-us/develop/download-phone-sdk`. To install the Windows Phone 8.1 extensions, follow these steps:

1. Open Visual Studio and create a new project by clicking on **New** from the **FILE** menu.
2. From the left-hand side menu, open **Store Apps** and select **Windows Phone Apps**. For simplicity, we will only build a phone version, but you can also use the universal and targeted version rather than just the phone version.

3. Enter `Chapter7` in the **Name** textbox and select your location, as shown in the following screenshot:

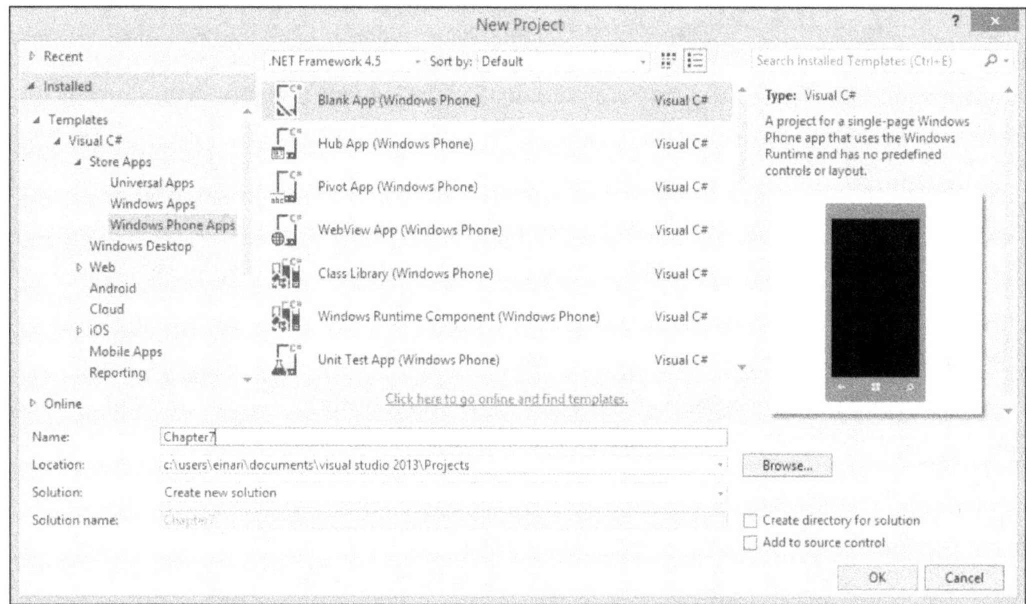

Getting the packages

As shown in the previous chapters, we are going to download a few dependencies from NuGet. To do this, follow these steps:

1. First, we want to get a Bifrost Client. Add a NuGet package reference, as described in *Chapter 1, The Primer*.
2. Right-click on **References** in **Solution Explorer** and select **Manage NuGet packages** and type `Bifrost.Client` in the search dialog box.
3. Finally, select it and click on **Install**.

Now, we will need an IOC container. Normally, I would use **Ninject**. However, it just happens that IOC containers were introduced at a later stage to the Windows 8 and Windows Phone 8 platforms, and although Ninject is now here, it lacks conventions, which is something I'm really fond of. So, instead of Ninject, we will use **Yggdrasil**, which is a simple IOC container that does what we want and suits our needs right now. Add a NuGet package reference called Yggdrasil. Then, we will need SignalR; the NuGet package we want for this is called `Microsoft.AspNet.SignalR.Client`.

Lastly, we want to get rid of some pain prior to experiencing it firsthand. Remember the `INotifyPropertyChanged` interface mentioned earlier. Although it makes it possible for the view to observe any changes in your ViewModel, it's also the source of a lot of meaningless repetition. For every property one exposes, one has to implement it with a backing field and remember to call the `PropertyChanged` event every time the value gets set. There are a few ways to deal with this. For instance, a commonly used pattern is to make the properties virtual and just generate proxies at runtime that overrides the property and does this plumbing for you. Reflection and emitting code is limited to the Windows runtime model, so we are going to do the same thing at compile time. To do this, we will include something called **Fody** and, in particular, a NuGet package called `PropertyChanged.Fody`; go and add this as a reference now.

Plumbing

Now that we have all the packages we need, we must initialize a few of them so that these work and become helpful. Open the `App.xaml.cs` file in your project.

Add the following `using` statements at the top of the code:

```
using Bifrost.Execution;
using Bifrost.Messaging;
using Bifrost.ViewModels;
using Yggdrasil;
```

Introduce a private variable for the IOC container at the top of the `App` class, as shown here:

```
static readonly IContainer _container;
```

Now, we will need a static constructor for the `App` class to initialize the container and something called a `ViewModelService`, which we will use later. Add the following `static` constructor to the `App` class:

```
static App()
{
    _container = ContainerContext.Current;
    _container.Register<IMessenger>(new Messenger());
    ViewModelService.TypeFinder = (name) => {
        var typeDiscoverer = _container.Get<ITypeDiscoverer>();
        var types = typeDiscoverer.FindAnyByName(name);
        if (types.Length > 1) throw new
ArgumentException("Ambiguous viewModel name");
        return types[0];
    };
    ViewModelService.InstanceCreator = (t) => _container.Get(t);
}
```

Then, a final piece of the configuration puzzle needs to fall into place. The spot to perform this is very specific. Find the method override called `OnLaunched`, and then find a line saying `if( rootFrame.Content == null );` we will add the following code right before this line:

```
var dispatcher = rootFrame.Dispatcher;
DispatcherManager.Current = new Bifrost.Execution.
Dispatcher(dispatcher);
_container.Register<Bifrost.Execution.IDispatcher>(DispatcherManag
er.Current);
```

This code basically configures the Bifrost Client library with the dispatcher for it to use. In addition we're also telling the IOC container that whenever something is asking for the `IDispatcher` interface from Bifrost, use the implementation that we set up before. This might seem like something one should expect not to have to do, and you're right as Bifrost Client is not as mature as the JavaScript counterpart, which hides these kinds of things. Eventually, it will be.

Bringing back the Web

This chapter is an expansion of *Chapter 6, An Architectural Taste*, which means that we will need the code from it as well. We will put the project from *Chapter 6, An Architectural Taste*, together with this project so that we can run the website and have the mobile app interact with it. Right-click on the solution in **Solution Explorer**, select **Existing Project** from the **Add** menu, navigate to the code of *Chapter 6, An Architectural Taste* is placed, and then add `.csproj` for this project, as shown in the following screenshot:

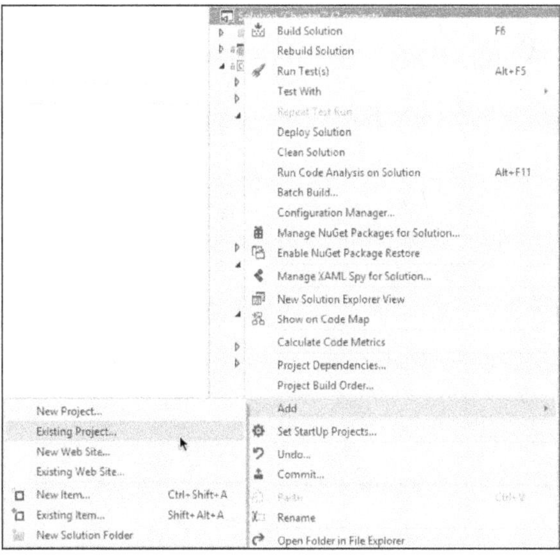

Extending the hub

As mentioned earlier, Bifrost Client is not as mature as the JavaScript counterpart. The concepts of command, query, and ReadModel is lacking for now, so we will need to expand on the OverviewHub, which we created in *Chapter 6, An Architectural Taste*, to provide functionality that we can call on.

Open the `OverviewHub.cs` file found in the `Accounts` folder of the code bundle of *Chapter 6, An Architectural Taste*. This class should be empty at this stage.

Let's start by adding a few `using` statements at the top of the file:

```
using System.Collections.Generic
using Bifrost.Commands;
using Web.Domain.Accounts;
using Web.Read.Accounts;
```

Now, we need a couple of dependencies that we will use to provide data to our new client that we're building and to be able to fire off commands in Bifrost. At the top of the class, let's add the following code:

```
AccountsOverview _accountsOverview;
ICommandCoordinator _commandCoordinator;
public OverviewHub(AccountsOverview accountsOverview,
ICommandCoordinator commandCoordinator)
{
    _accountsOverview = accountsOverview;
    _commandCoordinator = commandCoordinator;
}
```

This pulls in the `AccountsOverview` query, which we consumed in the JavaScript client code, and something called `commandcoordinator` that we will use to send off commands to. We want to reuse the entire application code we wrote before; just provide an interface through the hub to use it. Exposing the query is up next, enter the following method:

```
public IEnumerable<AccountOverview> GetAccountsOverview()
{
    return _accountsOverview.Query;
}
```

Next, we will need a method to perform the transfer, as shown in *Chapter 6, An Architectural Taste*:

```
public void Transfer(string from, string to, decimal amount)
{
    var command = new Transfer
    {
        From = from,
        To = to,
        Amount = amount
    };
    _commandCoordinator.Handle(command);
}
```

This will then expose a `Transfer` method that can be called on directly in a client proxy, which will turn itself into a command that will be passed on to Bifrost.

That's it. For additions needed in the code of *Chapter 6, An Architectural Taste,* let's move back to the mobile app code.

Pivoting

Windows Phone enables you to pretty much create things as you see fit, but there are paradigms in the UX that are pretty consistently implemented by apps these days. Pivot is one of these. Open the `MainPage.xaml` file and let's enter a pivot control and some transition settings to make it smooth.

Right after the opening tag called `Page` and before the opening tag of `Grid`, enter the following code:

```
<Page.Transitions>
    <TransitionCollection>
        <NavigationThemeTransition>
            <NavigationThemeTransition.
DefaultNavigationTransitionInfo>
                <CommonNavigationTransitionInfo
IsStaggeringEnabled="True"/>
            </NavigationThemeTransition.
DefaultNavigationTransitionInfo>
        </NavigationThemeTransition>
    </TransitionCollection>
</Page.Transitions>
```

This ensures we get smooth animations for transitions while navigating. Now, let's add the pivot itself inside the `Grid` element:

```
<Pivot Title="FIRST RESPONSIVE BANK"
        CommonNavigationTransitionInfo.IsStaggerElement="True">

    <PivotItem
        Margin="19,14.5,0,0"
        Header="overview"
        CommonNavigationTransitionInfo.IsStaggerElement="True">


    </PivotItem>

    <PivotItem
        Margin="19,14.5,0,0"
        Header="transfer"
        CommonNavigationTransitionInfo.IsStaggerElement="True">

    </PivotItem>

</Pivot>
```

Under production circumstances, you might want to have the string resources in a localizable resource file. Windows Phone does, of course, support this, but in the interest of time, we don't go and do this here.

Let's build the application and start it. Note the device dropdown in the menu bar. By default, it should be set to run in an emulator, but you can choose your device if you have it connected, as shown in the following screenshot:

When you run your app now, you should be seeing something like this:

You should now be able to navigate the pivot either by swiping across or clicking on the header for the pivot items we put in.

Our first ViewModel

Let's set up a ViewModel for the `MainPage`. Add a class to the root of the Windows Phone project called `MainPageViewModel.cs`. Let's add a property called `SelectedPageIndex`. Your class should look like this:

```
public class MainPageViewModel
{
    public int SelectedPageIndex { get; set; }
}
```

Nothing special yet, the property we put here will be used later; we'll return to it. However now, let's make sure that the `INotifyPropertyChanged` interface gets implemented at build time. Add the following `using` statement at the top of the file:

```
using PropertyChanged;
```

Now, adorn the class with the following attribute:

```
[ImplementPropertyChanged]
```

Make the class look like this:

```
[ImplementPropertyChanged]
public class MainPageViewModel
{
    public int SelectedPageIndex { get; set; }
}
```

This should now make it possible for the view to observe changes to the property.

Now, we need to hook up the ViewModel in the view. Open the `MainPage.xaml` file and add the following XML namespace reference in the `Page` tag along with the others:

```
xmlns:vm="using:Bifrost.ViewModels"
```

This now gives us an XML namespace called `vm` that points to the `Bifrost.ViewModels` CLR namespace. We can then start using whatever sits in this namespace declaratively. We will now hook up something called `ViewModelService` that allows us to specify a ViewModel to be associated by name. It will then resolve this using the `TypeFinder` delegate, which we configured at the beginning of the project, and instantiate it using the `InstanceCreator` delegate that we configured:

```
vm:ViewModelService.ViewModel="MainPageViewModel"
```

With this hooked up, we can start binding the view. We created a property that we want to bind for the pivot. Go to the `Pivot` tag and add the following attribute with a binding expression:

```
SelectedIndex="{Binding SelectedPageIndex, Mode=OneWay}"
```

Note the `Mode` property in the binding expression. By default, it's set to `OneWay`, which means that it will only take values from the ViewModel and if it's observable, it will take any subsequent changes, but not put values back. There are two other modes. The first mode is called `OneTime`, which gets it the first time, but no subsequent changes are made other than what we have set now, and `TwoWay`, which enables changes in the `SelectedIndex` property on the pivot control to go back to the `SelectedPageIndex` property.

This won't do much, but at least, we are now ready for what is coming.

Accounts

Let's create a new folder called `Accounts` in the root of the project. We are now just following the established structure of *Chapter 6, An Architectural Taste*. In this folder, we will put all the artifacts related to the accounts. Let's start by putting in what we need to be able to connect with the server.

The `AccountOverview` read model that we have on the server does not exist here. So let's start by creating a class called `AccountOverview` in the `Accounts` folder; add the following `using` statement:

```
using PropertyChanged;
```

Then, we want to make it look like the following code:

```
[ImplementPropertyChanged]
public class AccountOverview
{
    public Guid Id { get; set; }
    public string AccountNumber { get; set; }
    public decimal Balance { get; set; }
}
```

As you can see, we've added the `ImplementPropertyChanged` attribute for this as well. We will be receiving updates for the accounts as transfers occur; we want this to be seamlessly updated in the view without having to think about it.

Add an interface called `IAccountsOverview` to the `Accounts` folder and then add the following `using` statement at the top of the file:

```
using System.Collections.Generic;
```

Then, enter the following code inside the namespace declaration:

```
public delegate void AccountBalanceChanged(string accountNumber,
decimal balance);

public interface IAccountsOverview
{
    IEnumerable<AccountOverview> GetAccountsOverview();
    void OnAccountBalanceChanged(AccountBalanceChanged callback);

    void Transfer(string from, string to, decimal amount);
}
```

This will now represent our hub that lives on the server (it's the interface for it). Let's leave the concrete implementation for now, as we now have what we need for the rest of the features.

Overview

As in the web solution, we want to have the overview of all the accounts and the details of each account. One of the things that XAML is really good at is the compositional part, which we briefly discussed in the two chapters prior to this one. Our features: overview and transfer will be encapsulated in something called User Control, which gives us a self-contained XAML and we add a ViewModel to go with each of them. Right-click on the `Accounts` folder and then select **New Item** from the **Add** menu. Select the **User Control** option, as shown in the following screenshot, and name it `Overview.xaml`, then click on **Add**:

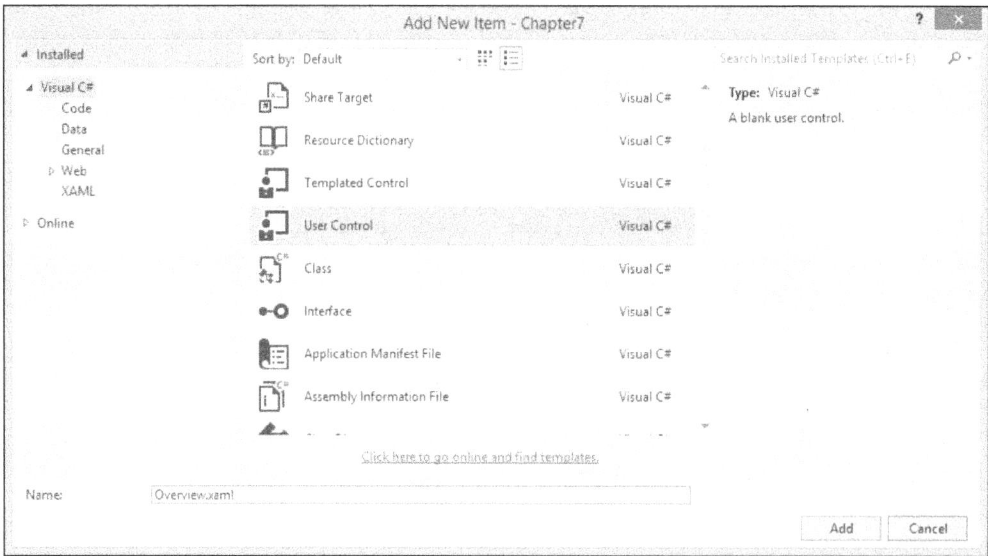

In this project, we will insert the necessary declarations to get the view we want for the feature. Let's start by giving a name to the grid in the new User Control. Make the `Grid` tag look like this:

```
<Grid x:Name="TopLevel">
```

The reason we do this is to make it accessible to bind expressions later. The XAML dialects differ between the different platforms; one of the nuances is the ability to navigate in the hierarchy during binding expressions. On the Windows runtime-side, there are fewer capabilities, and we will therefore need to find a particular element by its name when we find ourselves deep in the hierarchy. Normally, name is not needed when applying MVVM, as we won't need them in the code-behind but name is useful for these scenarios and also when performing visual state management.

Inside the grid element, insert the following code:

```
<StackPanel Orientation="Vertical">
    <GridView ItemsSource="{Binding Accounts}">
        <GridView.ItemTemplate>
            <DataTemplate>
                <StackPanel Margin="20">
                    <TextBlock Text="{Binding AccountNumber}"
FontWeight="Bold" Style="{StaticResource BaseTextBlockStyle}"/>
                    <TextBlock Text="{Binding Balance}"
Style="{StaticResource BodyTextBlockStyle}" />
                    <Button Command="{Binding DataContext.
TransferCommand, ElementName=TopLevel}"
CommandParameter="{Binding AccountNumber}">Transfer</Button>
                </StackPanel>
            </DataTemplate>
        </GridView.ItemTemplate>
        <GridView.ItemsPanel>
            <ItemsPanelTemplate>
                <ItemsWrapGrid MaximumRowsOrColumns="2"/>
            </ItemsPanelTemplate>
        </GridView.ItemsPanel>
    </GridView>
</StackPanel>
```

This creates a simple `GridView` that will display our accounts.

> As you can see, there is something that refers to a `DataContext.TransferCommand` and uses `ElementName` to get to it. What this basically says is that we want to use an element as the source to bind, and we are accessing the `DataContext` property on the element and the `TransferCommand` on whatever is in the `DataContext` of the element.

Now, we have binding expressions that point to properties on an imagined ViewModel. Let's create the ViewModel now. We will need to refer to the ViewModel that we will create, as we did in the `MainPageViewModel`. Add the following code snippet to the `Page` tag:

```
xmlns:vm="using:Bifrost.ViewModels"
vm:ViewModelService.ViewModel="OverviewViewModel"
```

Add a class called `OverviewViewModel.cs` to the `Accounts` folder and add the following `using` statements at the top of the file:

```
using System.Collections.Generic;
using System.Windows.Input;
using Bifrost.Interaction;
using Bifrost.Messaging;
using PropertyChanged;
```

Let's start by exposing the properties that the view is assuming:

```
public IEnumerable<AccountOverview> Accounts { get; private set; }
public ICommand TransferCommand { get; private set; }
```

This will be null at this point, so we need a constructor that deals with it. Insert the following code at the top of the class:

```
IMessenger _messenger;
public OverviewViewModel(IMessenger messenger, IAccountsOverview
accountsOverview)
{
    _messenger = messenger;
    Accounts = accountsOverview.GetAccountsOverview();

    accountsOverview.OnAccountBalanceChanged((accountNumber,
balance) =>
    {
        foreach (var accountOverview in Accounts)
        {
            if (accountOverview.AccountNumber == accountNumber)
            {
                accountOverview.Balance = balance;
            }
        }

    });

    TransferCommand = DelegateCommand.Create<string>(Transfer);
}
```

The code does a few things. It takes dependencies on two systems: `IMessenger` and `IAccountsOverview` that we just created. The messenger sits as publish or subscribe system, just as everything else we've done in this book. We will use it to decouple our systems. In addition, it sets up a callback to be called when the `OnAccountBalanceChanged` event occurs from the server. Lastly, we set up the command using something called `DelegateCommand`. This command has no relation to the Bifrost commands; it's something that XAML supports. There is an interface called `ICommand` that encapsulates the operations one wants to perform. This can be tedious to implement; therefore, Bifrost exposes a way of creating commands that just points to methods on your ViewModel. However, we have yet to implement the actual method. So, let's do this:

```
public void Transfer(string accountNumber)
{
    _messenger.Publish(new TransferMessage { AccountNumber =
accountNumber });
}
```

The implementation is fairly simple. It just publishes a message saying that we should transfer. It does not say anything about what is expected to happen. Something else will deal with it. However, it refers to a message type we have not created, so let's go and create it. Add a class called `TransferMessage.cs` at the root of the project. Make it look this:

```
public class TransferMessage
{
    public string AccountNumber { get; set; }
}
```

Now, we can go back and react to the message in our `MainPageViewModel`. Let's insert a constructor that does this:

```
public MainPageViewModel(IMessenger messenger)
{
    messenger.SubscribeTo<TransferMessage>(t =>
    {
        SelectedPageIndex = 1;
    });

    messenger.SubscribeTo<NavigateHomeMessage>(t =>
SelectedPageIndex = 0);
}
```

What this does is set the selected page index that we introduced whenever the `TransferMessage` comes, navigating us to pivot item number `1`.

The solution won't run just yet, so let's just continue and create the second feature.

Transfer

Add another `UserControl` in the `Accounts` folder as with the overview User Control and call it `Transfer.xaml`. Again, in the `Page` tag, we need to specify the ViewModel by adding the following code snippet in the tag as attributes:

```
xmlns:vm="using:Bifrost.ViewModels"
vm:ViewModelService.ViewModel="TransferViewModel"
```

Then, let's create the ViewModel, add a class called `TransferViewModel.cs`. Also, add the following `using` statements at the top of the file:

```
using System.Windows.Input;
using Bifrost.Interaction;
using Bifrost.Messaging;
using PropertyChanged;
```

Make the class look like the following code:

```
[ImplementPropertyChanged]
public class TransferViewModel
{
    IMessenger _messenger;
    IAccountsOverview _accountsOverview;
    public TransferViewModel(IMessenger messenger,
IAccountsOverview accountsOverview)
    {
        _messenger = messenger;
        Amount = "0";
        messenger.SubscribeTo<TransferMessage>(t =>
        {
            From = t.AccountNumber;
            To = string.Empty;
            Amount = "0";
        });
        _accountsOverview = accountsOverview;

        TransferCommand = DelegateCommand.Create(Transfer);
    }

    public string From { get; set; }
    public string To { get; set; }
    public string Amount { get; set; }

    public ICommand TransferCommand { get; private set; }
    public void Transfer()
```

```
        {
            decimal amount = 0;
            decimal.TryParse(Amount, out amount);
            _accountsOverview.Transfer(From, To, amount);

            _messenger.Publish(new NavigateHomeMessage());

            From = string.Empty;
            To = string.Empty;
            Amount = "0";
        }
    }
```

Most of this code looks like something that we've already done: subscribing to a message, setting up a command, exposing properties for binding, and also setting up the property changed attribute. For the `Transfer()` method, we are publishing a message at the end. Then, we want to navigate back to home.

Create an empty class in the root of the project called `NavigateHomeMessate.cs`. We don't need any properties or anything on it, so just leave it.

Let's go back the `Transfer.xaml` view. We need to get a UI for the behavior and state we expose through the ViewModel. Within the grid element, insert the following code:

```
<StackPanel Orientation="Vertical">

    <TextBlock Text="From"/>
    <TextBox Text="{Binding From, Mode=TwoWay}"/>

    <TextBlock Text="To"/>
    <TextBox Text="{Binding To, Mode=TwoWay}"/>

    <TextBlock Text="Amount"/>
    <TextBox Text="{Binding Amount, Mode=TwoWay}"/>

    <Button Command="{Binding TransferCommand}">Transfer</Button>

</StackPanel>
```

This should be the full UI needed to input the account information and the amount to transfer. We won't get any validation errors in the UI at this point, as Bifrost Client has not been built for it yet. This is something that will be there in the future.

XAML is not like HTML and has no flowing layout by default. In fact, everything put into XAML is positioned absolutely by default. There are a few containers that can used to create a flowing layout, StackPanel is one of these. It supports the flow of the content either horizontally or vertically.

Putting it all into the composition

Now that we have our two features, we need these in the pivot. Open the `MainPage.xaml` file again. On the `Page` element, add the following XML namespace declaration:

```
xmlns:accounts="using:Chapter7.Accounts"
```

Within the first `PivotItem` tag, insert the following code:

```
<accounts:Overview/>
```

Then, within the second `PivotItem` tag, insert the following code:

```
<accounts:Transfer/>
```

Your composition is now done. The UI is considered complete at this stage. However still, we need something more in order for the application to work.

What about that SignalR?

The only thing missing right now is the actual SignalR bit. The entire app should work, except for a tiny fact: the app wouldn't run because of SignalR, but this is the only thing missing. Let's put an implementation for this.

The `IAccountsOverview` interface needs an implementation. If we add a class in the same namespace that it exists with the exact same name, just dropping the `I` prefix and making it implement the interface should connect these together in the Yggdrasil IOC, by default, and make this the implementation that gets used. So, create a class called `AccountsOverview.cs` in the `Accounts` folder. Add the following `using` statements at the top of the file:

```
using System.Collections.Generic;
using System.Collections.ObjectModel;
using Bifrost.Execution;
using Microsoft.AspNet.SignalR.Client;
using Microsoft.AspNet.SignalR.Client.Transports;
```

We're going to need a couple of variables and a constructor. Insert the following code at the top of the class:

```
IHubProxy _proxy;
IDispatcher _dispatcher;

List<AccountBalanceChanged> _accountBalanceChangedCallbacks;

public AccountsOverview(IDispatcher dispatcher)
{
    _dispatcher = dispatcher;
    _accountBalanceChangedCallbacks = new
List<AccountBalanceChanged>();

    var hubConnection = new HubConnection("http://localhost:9044/");

    _proxy = hubConnection.CreateHubProxy("OverviewHub");
    _proxy.On("accountBalanceChanged", (string accountNumber,
decimal amount) =>
    {
        _dispatcher.BeginInvoke(() =>
        {
            foreach (var callback in
_accountBalanceChangedCallbacks)
            {
                callback(accountNumber, amount);
            }
        });
    });

    hubConnection.Start(new LongPollingTransport()).Wait();
}
```

The constructor takes a dependency on the dispatcher, which we discussed earlier. This is the Bifrost dispatcher that wraps the system dispatcher. It adds a list of callbacks that we can register for when the `accountBalanceChanged` event occurs. The first SignalR thing we need to do is to create an instance of the `HubConnection` and point it back to the website. Right-click on the `Chapter6` project and go to **Properties**.

Under the **Web** section, you'll find the **Project Url** that you will use when instantiating the `HubConnection`, as shown in the following screenshot:

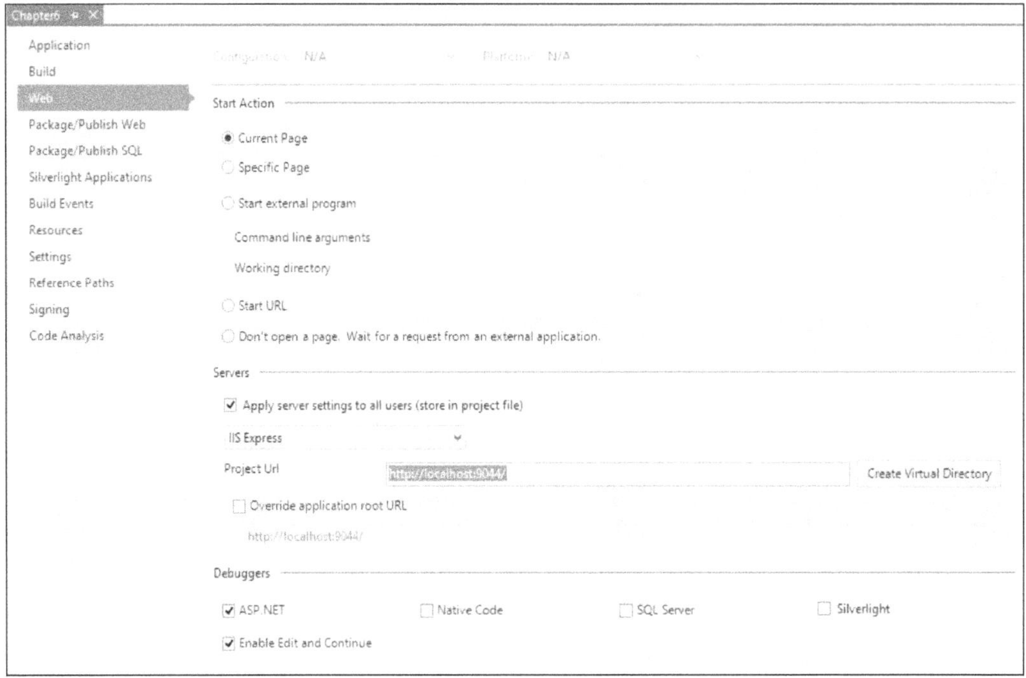

As you can see, the `.On()` method call allows us to hook up events that gets fired from the server. Last but not least, we need to start the hub connection. There have been known issues with letting SignalR negotiate the right transport, resulting in poor performance. The safest bet is always long polling, that's why it has been hardcoded to this.

Now, we need to implement the `IAccountsOverview` interface and add it to the class definition, as follows:

```
public class AccountsOverview : IAccountsOverview
```

Then, start with the method to get accounts overviews:

```
public IEnumerable<AccountOverview> GetAccountsOverview()
{
    var accounts = new ObservableCollection<AccountOverview>();
    _proxy.Invoke<IEnumerable<AccountOverview>>("GetAccountsOvervi
ew").ContinueWith(t =>
    {
        foreach (var accountOverview in t.Result)
```

```
        {
            _dispatcher.BeginInvoke(() =>
accounts.Add(accountOverview));
        }
    });
    return accounts;
}
```

This code uses the `Invoke()` method on the proxy to call the server by passing a string literal. The particular overload that is being used allows us to specify what we expect as a return type from calling it, which will then be what's available in the task in the delegate given to `ContinueWith()`. The API exposes an enumerable of `AccountOverview`, and instead of specifying in the interface that it's async, it uses the C# 5.0 pattern of async or await: we return in the implementation something that can be observed instead. The nature of being async is not necessary in most cases to bleed out to calling code, as it is a concern it has to deal with and is an implementation detail. This also enables easier testing scenarios for us to unit test. As you can see, we use the dispatcher to add the items when they are coming back from the server. This is because the call is happening on a separate thread and not the UI thread, something XAML won't allow on any of the platforms.

The next method we want to implement is the `OnAccountBalanceChanged()` method. The purpose of this method is to register delegates that get called when the `accountBalanceChanged` event occurs on the server:

```
public void OnAccountBalanceChanged(AccountBalanceChanged
callback)
{
    _accountBalanceChangedCallbacks.Add(callback);
}
```

With this in place, the only thing we're missing now is the actual `Transfer()` method. Let's add it, as shown here:

```
public void Transfer(string from, string to, decimal amount)
{
    _proxy.Invoke("Transfer", from, to, amount);
}
```

Again, this just uses the `Invoke()` method on the proxy. This time, we're not expecting anything to come back. The `Invoke()` methods allow a `params` array of parameters of any type. They will just be serialized and sent to the server.

Making it a bit more useable

The onscreen soft keyboard can easily get in the way. We're going to do something to make it easier to use. Open the `MainPage.xaml.cs` code-behind file. At the bottom of the constructor, add the following code:

```
this.KeyUp += (s,e) =>
{
    if (e.Key == Windows.System.VirtualKey.Enter)
    {
        this.Focus(FocusState.Programmatic);
    }
};
```

This will get the focus back to the page whenever the *Enter* key is pressed, making it easier to hit enter in any of the textboxes and make the keyboard go away.

Grand finale – running it all

Now that we have it all implemented, it's time to run it all. Start by building and running the *Chapter 6, An Architectural Taste*, web project. Once this is up and running and working, run the Windows Phone project. You should now be able to navigate around this and perform transfers; try to perform a transfer on the web solution and see if it gets updated in real-time in the mobile app and vice versa. Your app should look like the following screenshot:

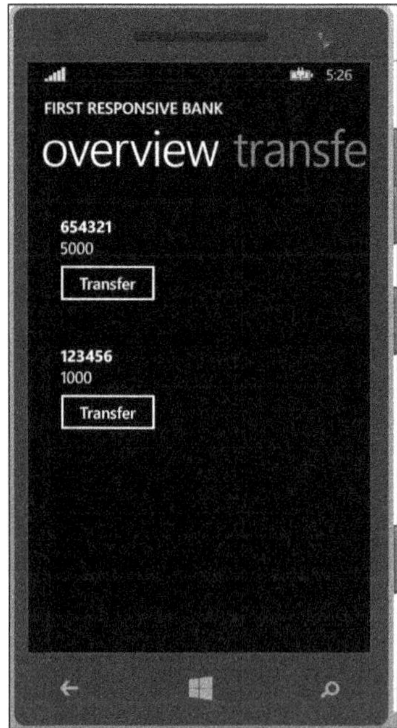

Summary

XAML and Windows Phone development can be a lot of fun. Personally, I love the XAML platform and sprinkling the sweetness of MVVM on top. It really feels like a place where I can apply my SOLIDs and be happy. As we've seen, the API for Windows Phone has a certain consistency with the APIs found for web development and it's almost just as easy to work with, although a bit more verbose. You could achieve the same abstraction level, as in JavaScript, using dynamic in C# as well and implement your own dynamic object that would simplify the code and less "stringified". As we've seen, the same principles still applies (you can bring the same mindset of MVVM, SOLID and all into it and create highly maintainable code).

> You can find the entire sample code at `https://github.com/dolittle/SignalR_Blueprints/tree/master/Source/Chapter7`.

In the next chapter, we will take on more platforms than just Windows Phone.

8

Putting the X in .NET – Xamarin

Ever since the release of Microsoft .NET 1.0 back in 2002, it has grown to more and more platforms, not only on Microsoft's own platforms but also others. Already in 2003, we saw an open source implementation for BSD variants called **DotGNU** and its Portable.NET. In 2004, the initial release of Mono came out, whereas a second open source implementation aimed at Linux and Mac OS X. In 2007, with Silverlight, all of a sudden, we saw Microsoft targeting multiple platforms themselves with Windows and Mac OS X with an implementation of the CLI and a subset of .NET Framework.

Over the years, we've seen Silverlight come and go, and then Windows Phone 7 came along, which kind of picked up Silverlight and bought it in the future. Back in 2006, before Silverlight came, Microsoft launched **Windows Presentation Foundation (WPF)**—a new way to perform client development on the Windows stack. This is what Silverlight was built around; a subset of and also what Windows Phone 7 brought with it further as well. With Windows 8 and the store applications, Microsoft invested even more in XAML but again for a new implementation. The people behind Mono did implement a Silverlight version to run on Linux, as Microsoft only provided OS X, which was called Moonlight. It never quite matured before being abandoned and was sitting in a hybrid state of supporting some of the features in Silverlight version 1 and some of version 2 and 3, even some of version 4 sneaking in.

Xamarin is a company that is leading the development of Mono. The company provides professional services for Mono and also branded editions of the IDE used for Mono called MonoDevelop (its branded version is called Xamarin Studio). Fast forwarding to 2014, Xamarin launched something called as Xamarin Forms: a set of commercial tools to rapidly build mobile applications, targeting the most popular mobile platforms out there with a "write once, run many" philosophy. Xamarin Forms is yet another XAML dialect, not as fully matured as the ones found in Microsoft, but nevertheless really powerful and fully capable of delivering very rich applications. It's already built on top of Xamarin's MonoTouch and MonoDroid, which are the .NET binding implementations for iOS and Android.

The goal – rinse and repeat

This time around, we are not going to do any heavy lifting. We will basically repeat what we did in *Chapter 7, The Three Screens - Mobile First*, with some adjustments. In this chapter, we will walk through only one platform; although the Visual Studio template that is being used will make sure that it runs on other platforms as well. We will focus on doing this for iOS. The reason for this is basically to avoid having to set up a Mac environment, when there is a big chance of you as a reader not even having access to a Mac. From a Xamarin perspective, the code is for the most reusable. There are some differences and things you need to explicitly implement for each platform, but for most applications, I wouldn't be surprised if this is not the case.

Xamarin provides a core library that is the same and represents Xamarin's abstractions over the underlying platforms. These abstractions will look the same for your code but have different DLLs that implement the abstractions specifically for each platform. On platforms, such as the Windows Phone, which already have a lot of the concepts Xamarin has embraced, the abstractions are thinner. However, most importantly, why use Xamarin? There are a few approaches one could pick to perform a "write once and run many approaches to developing when targeting multiple platforms. For instance, you have something called PhoneGap that allows standard HTML, CSS, and JavaScript development with their abstractions on the different platforms.

This is then would be embedded in a browser view, making it look as if it was a native app but having a few disadvantages over native apps when it comes to its look and feel. Also, it was a bit harder to get it to really feel native in general. Some have had great success with this, but from my experience, this is harder. In fact, there are a few of these platforms out there, another one being Apache Cordova that allows the same thing. Also, Microsoft is bringing full support for this in Visual Studio as well.

Again, from my experience, it's harder to get it to feel native. Obviously, you could just go native and write things the number of times you have platform that you want to support, which is a completely legitimate approach; there is absolutely nothing wrong with this. In fact, I would encourage you to do this if you have the resources and budget to do so. True native will always feel right. Having said that, Xamarin represents a middle ground that promises both: the native feel on the performance-side and the joy of writing things for the most part only once in one programming language.

Getting started

Before you start, you might want to run down to your local Apple Store and pick up a Mac, if you haven't already got one. Just kidding! The code is the same no matter which platform you choose, but as the iOS one is the hardest with most moving parts, we'll focus on this. In fact, this is a lot cheaper than buying a Mac. There are, in fact, cloud providers that will give you a virtual Mac in the cloud (for instance, the commercial provider: `http://www.macincloud.com`). The reason you need a Mac is because of the way Xamarin actually gets compiled. When you're writing code in C#, it will not run inside a runtime on iOS, but it will be compiled down to a native language for iOS.

In order for Xamarin to be able to do this, it relies on tools found in Xcode, which is only available on Mac. The same approach is for Android. It does not have a **Common Language Runtime** (**CLR**). So, it compiles down to what is right for Android and runs it. Any references you have will be included, but it's really smart and does not include things you're not using. Therefore, if you have a reference to an assembly from the base class library, it will extract the functionality that is used and natively compiles it down and only includes this. This way, you don't have a full copy of the .NET Framework embedded in your application on the devices but only the stuff your application consists of. When you install Xamarin, it will download the necessary prerequisites too. So, if you install it on Mac, it will download whatever it needs to be able to do the things it needs. Likewise for Android; it will download the environment and emulators so that you can get started. Microsoft has also built an emulator themselves for Android that integrates even better in Visual Studio for a better developer experience. When doing this, read more about it at `http://blogs.msdn.com/b/visualstudioalm/archive/2014/11/12/introducing-visual-studio-s-emulator-for-android.aspx`.

I am a Mac user myself and my setup consists of OS X as my host operating system and then I run Windows in a virtualized environment; I prefer using parallels for virtualization. In order for us to get things working, you will have to switch from Shared Networking to Bridged Networking, as we will access the virtual computer through its IP address.

Once your OS X environment is good to go, you will need software (this is where it might sting a bit). Xamarin Forms is not free and the cheapest you can get is the Indie license. Once you've decided which way to go with licensing, you will need the software, which can all be found at `http://xamarin.com/forms`. You have the option of working with Visual Studio or Xamarin Studio. I've chosen to use Visual Studio, as everything, so far, has been based on it in this book. In addition to this, you will have to get Xcode installed on your OS X host. This can be done through the OS X app store. In addition, you'll have to read the documentation from Xamarin to see how to connect your Visual Studio to Xcode through its build host, as this book can't cover the entire environment setup.

A slight health warning; there are typically things you'd need to do like keep configuration in a clever way and also deal with errors that can occur. The code is naive in this way. Anyways, let's get started:

1. Open Visual Studio and create a new project by clicking on **New** from the **FILE** menu.
2. From the left-hand side menu, open **Mobile Apps** and select **Blank App (Xamarin.Forms Portable)**. For simplicity, we will only build a phone version, but you can use the universal and targeted version rather than just the phone version.
3. Enter `Chapter8` in the **Name** textbox and select your location, as shown in the following screenshot:

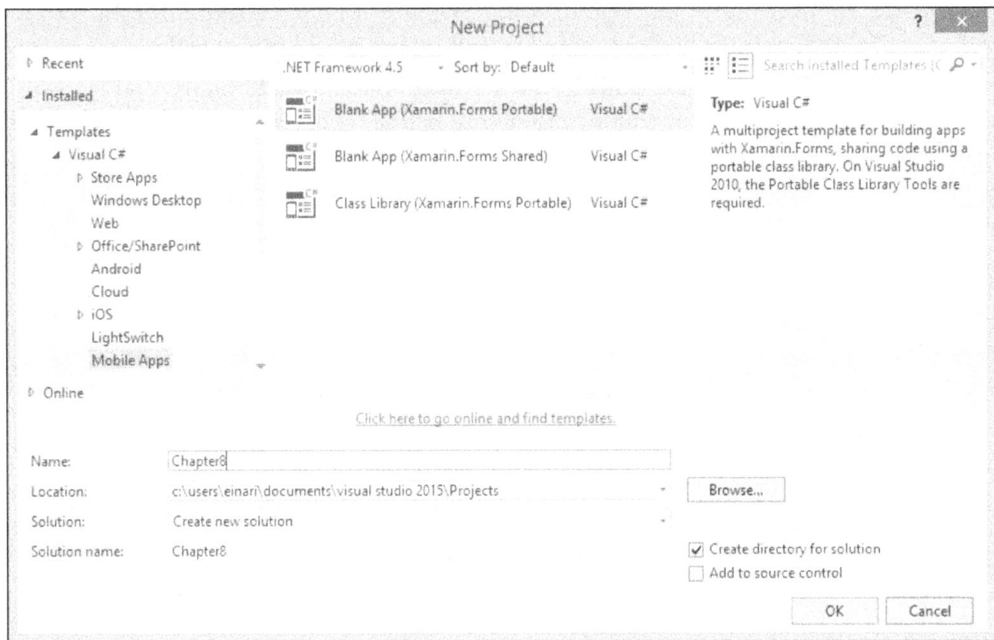

Getting the packages

As shown in the previous chapters, we will download a few dependencies from NuGet. First, we want to get the pain reliever we used in *Chapter 7, The Three Screens – Mobile First*: `PropertyChanged.Fody`. To do this, follow these steps:

1. Add a NuGet package reference, as described in *Chapter 1, The Primer*.
2. Right-click on **References** in **Solution Explorer** and select **Manage NuGet Packages**, and enter `PropertyChanged.Fody` in the search dialog box.
3. Select it and then click on **Install**.

Now we will need SignalR; the NuGet package we want for this is called `Microsoft.AspNet.SignalR.Client`.

Features

There will not be any plumbing in this project. Basically, I've decided not to use any IOC container, as we proved that in the previous chapter. I would normally never go into a project without it but it serves no added learning value in reiterating it again. However, if you are interested; for Ninject, there is an implementation called `Portable.Ninject` that should give "joy" in Xamarin projects.

As a result of creating the project, you should have four different projects in your solution file. One for each of the different platforms and then a shared project for what is commonly shared among the other three. Typically, one will try to get as much code as possible into the shared one, but on some occasions, one has to create something platform-specific. For this project, we will only be in the shared one, which should be called `Chapter8 (Portable)`. The portable in the name refers to a project type for portable class libraries. This is a type of class library that lets you target multiple platforms and will give you compiler errors if you try to use things that aren't on all the targeted platforms.

Overview

Let's start by creating the `Accounts` folder at the root of the portable project, as we did in the previous project. Inside this, we'll need an XAML file for our first view. To do this, follow these steps:

1. Add a new item of the **Forms Xaml Page** type and call it `Overview`, as shown in the following screenshot:

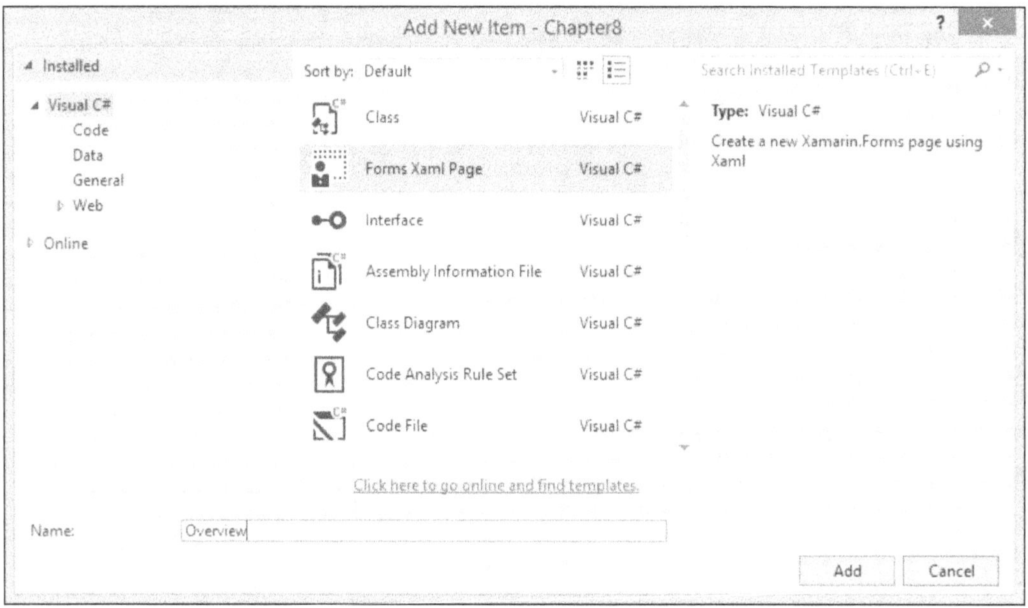

   Now that we have this page, let's go and hook it up so that we see this page.

2. Open the `App.cs` file. Put a static variable at the top of the file that will expose navigation to the rest of the app:

   ```
   public static INavigation Navigation { get; private set; }
   ```

   Then, replace the implementation of the `GetMainPage()` method, as shown here:

   ```
   public static Page GetMainPage()
   {
       Navigation = navigationPage.Navigation;
       var navigationPage = new NavigationPage(new Overview());
       return navigationPage;
   }
   ```

This will create a navigation frame that will have a native look and feel and make our overview page as the first page it will be on.

3. The `AccountOverview` read model that we have on the server does not exist here, so let's start by creating a class called `AccountOverview` in the `Accounts` folder, and then enter the following `using` statements:

```
using System;
using System.Windows.Input;
using PropertyChanged;
```

Then, we want to make it look as follows:

```
[ImplementPropertyChanged]
public class AccountOverview
{
    public Guid Id { get; set; }
    public string AccountNumber { get; set; }
    public string Balance { get; set; }

    public ICommand TransferCommand { get; set; }
}
```

> You might ask yourself, what the command is doing on the ViewModel. This is a bit of a workaround. Xamarin Forms does not have relative source binding, and in general, there are limitations to sourcing to bind expressions. One could use something called Xamarin Behaviors: a project one can find on GitHub to enable binding to things outside the current binding context, but in the interest of keeping moving parts to a minimum, we're doing a bit of a hack by exposing the command on the `AccountOverview`.

As you can see, we've added the `ImplementPropertyChanged` attribute for this as well. We will receive updates for the accounts as transfers occur; we just want this to be seamlessly updated in the view without having to think about it.

4. Now, we will implement the class that will act as our client hub representation. This time, we don't represent it with an interface. However, note one thing: the implementation is pretty much exactly the same as in *Chapter 7, The Three Screens – Mobile First*. Create a file called `AccountsOverview.cs` inside the `Accounts` folder and insert the following `using` statements:

```
using System;
using System.Collections.Generic;
using System.Collections.ObjectModel;
```

```
using Microsoft.AspNet.SignalR.Client;
using Microsoft.AspNet.SignalR.Client.Transports;
using Xamarin.Forms;
```

5. Next, inside the namespace declaration, we will define a delegate that we will use when the server calls clients:

```
public delegate void AccountBalanceChanged(string accountNumber,
decimal balance);
```

6. Then, make the entire class look like the following code, as we did in *Chapter 7, The Three Screens - Mobile First*; I don't think it's necessary to break it down. Don't worry about the hardcoded connection strings. Obviously, you'd put this in a helper object that gave you the configuration:

```
public class AccountsOverview
{
    IHubProxy _proxy;

    List<AccountBalanceChanged>
_accountBalanceChangedCallbacks;

    public AccountsOverview()
    {
        _accountBalanceChangedCallbacks = new
List<AccountBalanceChanged>();

        var hubConnection = new
HubConnection("http://10.0.1.101:9044/");

        _proxy = hubConnection.CreateHubProxy("OverviewHub");
        _proxy.On("accountBalanceChanged", (string
accountNumber, decimal amount) =>
        {
            Device.BeginInvokeOnMainThread(() =>
            {
                foreach (var callback in
_accountBalanceChangedCallbacks)
                {
                    callback(accountNumber, amount);
                }
            });
        });

        hubConnection.Start(new
LongPollingTransport()).Wait();
    }
```

```
    public IEnumerable<AccountOverview>
GetAccountsOverview(Action<AccountOverview> itemCallback)
    {
        var accounts = new
ObservableCollection<AccountOverview>();
        _proxy.Invoke<IEnumerable<AccountOverview>>("GetAccountsO
ve
rview").ContinueWith(t =>
        {
            foreach (var accountOverview in t.Result)


            {
                Device.BeginInvokeOnMainThread(() => {
                    itemCallback(accountOverview);
                    accounts.Add(accountOverview);
                });
            }
        });
        return accounts;
    }

    public void OnAccountBalanceChanged(AccountBalanceChanged
callback)
    {
        _accountBalanceChangedCallbacks.Add(callback);
    }


    public void Transfer(string from, string to, decimal
amount)
    {
        _proxy.Invoke("Transfer", from, to, amount);
    }
}
```

7. Now that we have this in place, let's create the ViewModel for the `Overview` view. In the `Accounts` folder, create a file called `OverviewViewModel.cs` and enter the following `using` statements:

```
using System.Collections.Generic;
using System.Windows.Input;
using PropertyChanged;
using Xamarin.Forms;
```

8. Again, as with the `AccountsOverview` class, this ViewModel and the one found in *Chapter 7, The Three Screens - Mobile First*, are almost exactly the same, so no point in breaking it down. Go ahead and make the class look like the following code:

```
[ImplementPropertyChanged]
public class OverviewViewModel
{
    public OverviewViewModel()
    {
        TransferCommand = new
Command<AccountOverview>(Transfer);

        var accountsOverview = new AccountsOverview();
        Accounts =
accountsOverview.GetAccountsOverview(a=>a.TransferCommand =
TransferCommand);

   accountsOverview.OnAccountBalanceChanged((accountNumber,
balance) =>
        {
            foreach (var accountOverview in Accounts)
            {
                if (accountOverview.AccountNumber ==
accountNumber)
                {
                    accountOverview.Balance =
balance.ToString();
                }
            }
        });
    }

    public IEnumerable<AccountOverview>    Accounts { get;
private set; }

    public ICommand TransferCommand { get; private set; }

    public void Transfer(AccountOverview account)
    {
        var transfer = new Transfer();
        transfer.ViewModel.From = account.AccountNumber;
        App.Navigation.PushAsync(transfer);
    }
}
```

Open the `Overview.xaml` file and add the following XML namespace declaration in the `ContentPage` tag:

```
xmlns:local="clr-
namespace:Chapter8.Accounts;assembly=Chapter8"
```

9. Then, we add a title to the `ContentPage` tag as well:

   ```
   Title="Accounts"
   ```

   The title will be visible in the navigation frame.

10. Now, add the following XAML inside the `ContentPage` tag:

    ```
    <ContentPage.BindingContext>
      <local:OverviewViewModel/>
    </ContentPage.BindingContext>

    <ListView ItemsSource="{Binding Accounts}">
      <ListView.ItemTemplate>
        <DataTemplate>
          <ViewCell>
            <StackLayout Orientation="Horizontal"
    Padding="16,0">
              <Label Text="{Binding AccountNumber}"
                     HorizontalOptions="StartAndExpand"
                     VerticalOptions="Center" />
              <Label Text="{Binding Balance}"
                     HorizontalOptions="StartAndExpand"
                     VerticalOptions="Center" />

              <Button Text="Transfer" Command="{Binding
    TransferCommand}" CommandParameter="{Binding}"/>
            </StackLayout>
          </ViewCell>
        </DataTemplate>
      </ListView.ItemTemplate>
    </ListView>
    ```

11. You'll notice small nuances with the XAML used in *Chapter 7, The Three Screens – Mobile First*. For instance, `StackLayout` instead of `StackPanel`, but for the most part, it's very similar.

The ViewModel is instantiated directly in the XAML in this view and is set to be the binding context. This is different from what we did in *Chapter 7, The Three Screens – Mobile First*, where we had something that resolved it for us. As we are not using an IOC container, we can do this. Another thing you might notice here is something that is called `BindingContext` and not `DataContext`, which is a slight nuance in the XAML.

12. Now, let's add the second feature: the actual transfer page. Let's start by creating the ViewModel; add a class called `TransferViewModel.cs` to the `Accounts` folder. Add the following `using` statements:

```
using System.Windows.Input;
using PropertyChanged;
using Xamarin.Forms;
```

13. Make the class look like this:

```
[ImplementPropertyChanged]
public class TransferViewModel
{
    AccountsOverview _accountsOverview;

    public TransferViewModel()
    {
        TransferCommand = new Command(Transfer);
        _accountsOverview = new AccountsOverview();
    }

    public string From { get; set; }
    public string To { get; set; }
    public string Amount { get; set; }

    public ICommand TransferCommand { get; private set; }

    void Transfer()
    {
        decimal amount = 0;
        decimal.TryParse(Amount, out amount);
        _accountsOverview.Transfer(From, To, amount);

        From = string.Empty;
        To = string.Empty;
        Amount = "0";

        App.Navigation.PopAsync();
    }
}
```

14. Add an XAML file as before. This time, let's call it `Transfer`. Add the following XML namespace declaration in the `ContentPage` tag:

    ```
    xmlns:local="clr-
    namespace:Chapter8.Accounts;assembly=Chapter8"
    ```

15. Then, we add a title to the `ContentPage` tag as well:

    ```
    Title="Transfer"
    ```

16. Now, add the following XAML inside the `ContentPage` tag:

    ```
    <ContentPage.BindingContext>
      <local:TransferViewModel/>
    </ContentPage.BindingContext>

    <StackLayout Orientation="Vertical">

      <Label Text="From"/>
      <Entry Text="{Binding From, Mode=TwoWay}"/>

      <Label Text="To"/>
      <Entry Text="{Binding To, Mode=TwoWay}"/>

      <Label Text="Amount"/>
      <Entry Text="{Binding Amount, Mode=TwoWay}"/>

      <Button Command="{Binding TransferCommand}"
    Text="Transfer"/>

    </StackLayout>
    ```

Bringing back the Web

This chapter expands on *Chapter 6, An Architectural Taste*, which means that we will need the code from it. We will put the *Chapter 6, An Architectural Taste*, project together with this project so that we can run the website and have the mobile app interact with it.

Right-click on the solution in **Solution Explorer**, select **Existing Project** in the **Add** menu, navigate to where the code of *Chapter 6, An Architectural Taste,* is placed, and then add `.csproj` for that project, as shown here:

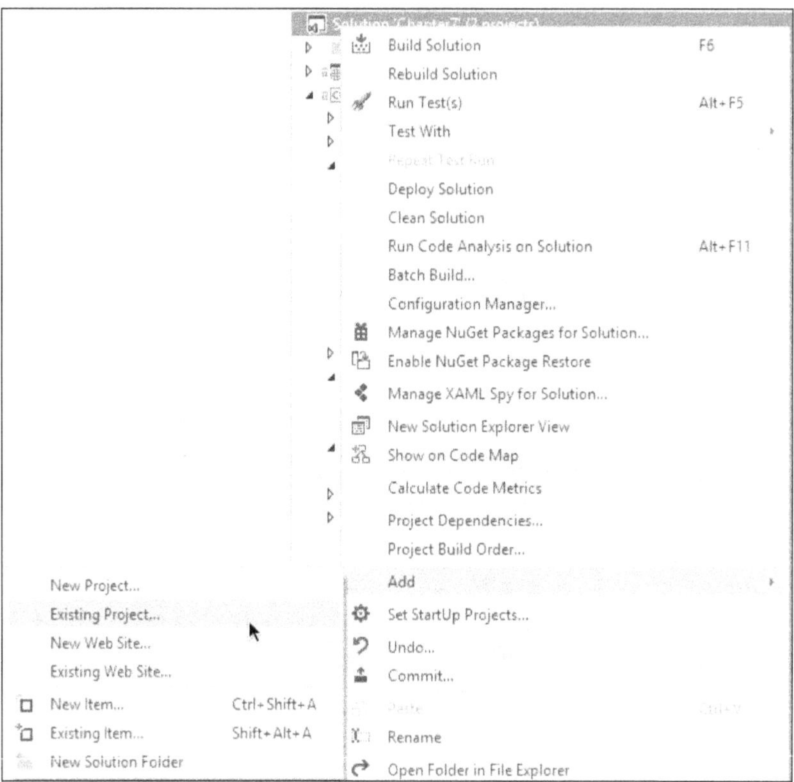

Running things

This should be all the code needed to make this work. However, there is a slight problem when running with IIS Express, as it only binds to the localhost and not the public IP address. First of all, let's start by making sure that you're running Visual Studio as an administrator. If you are, it should say **Administrator** in the title bar of Visual Studio. If you're not, restart it by running it as administrator. Then, run the web project of `Chapter8`; this will make sure that IIS Express is running. Find IIS Express in your notification area, right-click on it and select **Show All Applications**, as shown here:

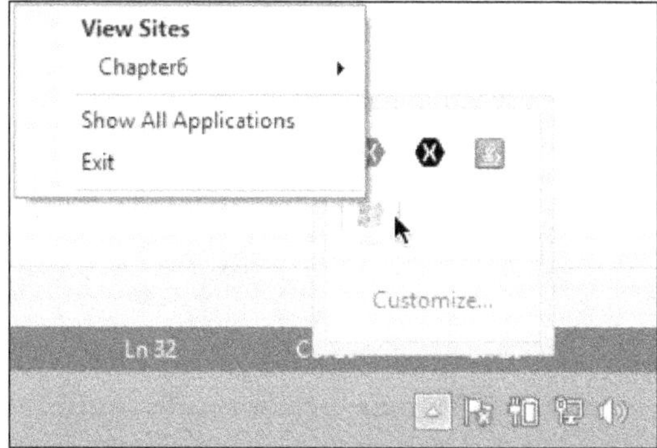

Click on the **Chapter6** site and open the `applicationhost.config` file, as shown in the following screenshot:

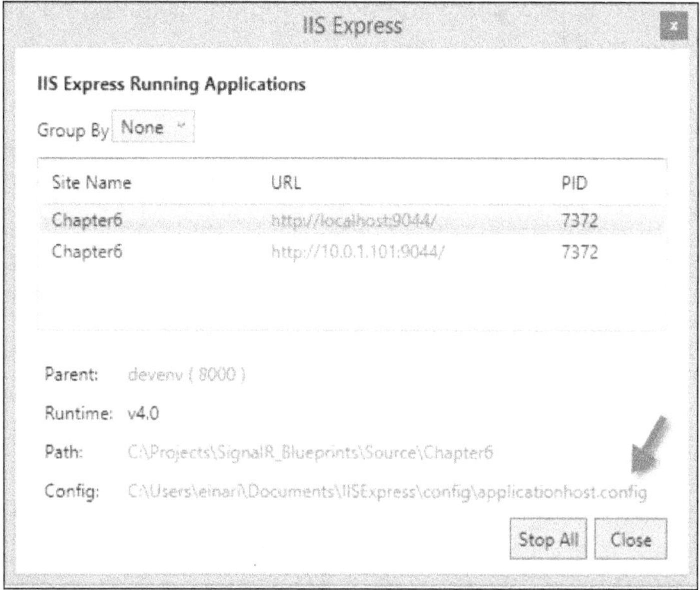

Find the site tag that represents **Chapter6** and let's add a second binding to it, but before we do this, let's figure out what the IP address of your Windows machine is: the IPv4 address. This is what we'll be using in the binding.

Make sure that the `site` tag with binding looks something like the following code:

```
<site name="Chapter6" id="5">
    <application path="/" applicationPool="Clr4IntegratedAppPool">
        <virtualDirectory path="/"
physicalPath="C:\Projects\SignalR_Blueprints\Source\Chapter6" />
    </application>
    <bindings>
        <binding protocol="http"
bindingInformation="*:9044:localhost" />
        <binding protocol="http" bindingInformation="*:9044:YOUR
IP ADDRESS HERE" />
    </bindings>
</site>
```

Go back to the `AccountsOverview.cs` file and update the IP address for the `HubConnection` as well. Compiling all this and running it should give you something like this on iOS:

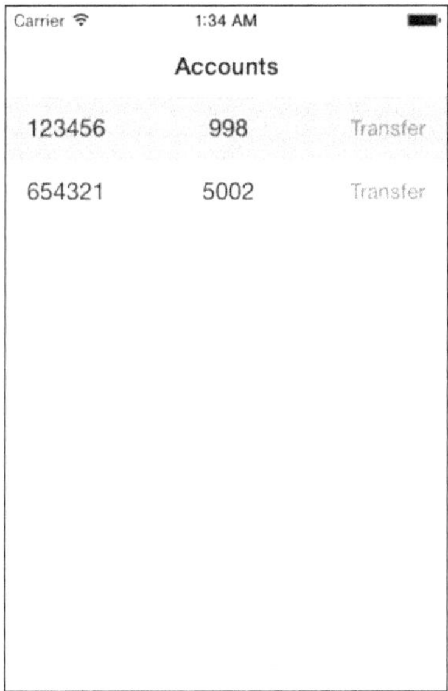

Summary

Xamarin has come a long way in making things feel great from a developer's perspective. With XAML, one gets the familiarity with other XAML platforms, and one can get up and running pretty fast. The platform is maturing every day and through the tight cooperation with Microsoft, Xamarin is getting the love it needs to be a first class citizen in the ecosystem. With Microsoft's move to open source the .NET Framework completely and, in fact, create a fully installable package on Mac OS X and Linux eventually is a massive move forward for the .NET platform that one has to keep an eye on. This means that we do have an environment now that is truly becoming cross-platform, which is not only cross-platform in the old Microsoft sense of Windows and Windows Phone.

The opening of the platform and the change of the license model to an open one means that the Mono project in which Xamarin is built on top of can take the parts that are missing from the base class library and move them in Mono. Also, looking at the other way around as well, one can take things that are in Mono and bring them back to .NET, in fact, they are accepting pull requests from anyone; something we witnessed on stage when they announced that .NET was becoming open source. This gives us a reassurance that Xamarin and this approach is not something that is going away any time soon. It's no longer just a pet project for someone but something that is being backed up by companies and becoming widely used as well.

You can find the entire sample code at `https://github.com/dolittle/SignalR_Blueprints/tree/master/Source/Chapter8`.

In the next chapter, we will see how you can debug things and figure out when there are problems in a good way.

9
Debugging or Troubleshooting

This chapter will show the tools that exist to help you know what is going on in your SignalR-enabled system. Sometimes, what causes a problem moving into single page applications is not that obvious; this shift of looking at postbacks looks at the traffic between the server and the client. With the right tools and know-how, this shouldn't be a problem.

In this chapter, we will cover the following topics:

- Enabling tracing or logging
- Using Fiddler
- Enabling performance counters
- Getting debug info into Visual Studio
- Chrome Developer Tools

Logging

Perhaps, one of the most efficient debugging tools is logging; just get the text out that says what is going on in your system. SignalR has a great support for this in all tiers.

Server

You simply enable logging on the server by adding configuration to the application configuration file (`App.config` or `Web.config`) depending on the project type. In the configuration, you specify what events you are interested in seeing. You can also specify where you want it to log to, such as a text file, the Windows event log or a custom log, using an implementation of `TraceListener`. The following table shows what trace sources are available and a description of what they represent:

Source	Messages
`SignalR.SqlMessageBus`	This scales out the setup, database operation, error, and timeout events
`SignalR.ServiceBusMessageBus`	This scales out provider topic creation and subscription, error, and messaging events
`SignalR.RedisMessageBus`	This scales out provider connection, disconnection, and error events
`SignalR.ScaleoutMessageBus`	This scales out messaging events
`SignalR.Transports.WebSocketTransport`	This transports connection, disconnection, messaging, and error events
`SignalR.Transports.ServerSentEventsTransport`	This transports connection, disconnection, messaging, and error events
`SignalR.Transports.ForeverFrameTransport`	This transports connection, disconnection, messaging, and error events
`SignalR.Transports.LongPollingTransport`	This transports connection, disconnection, messaging, and error events
`SignalR.Transports.TransportHeartBeat`	This transports connection, disconnection, messaging, and error events
`SignalR.ReflectedHubDescriptorProvider`	This reflects the hub discovery events

To enable this, you can add the following code to your application `config` file (`App.config` or `Web.config`) within the configuration tag of one of these files:

```
<system.diagnostics>
    <sources>
      <source name="SignalR.SqlMessageBus">
        <listeners>
          <add name="SignalR-Bus" />
        </listeners>
      </source>
      <source name="SignalR.ServiceBusMessageBus">
        <listeners>
          <add name="SignalR-Bus" />
        </listeners>
      </source>
      <source name="SignalR.RedisMessageBus">
        <listeners>
          <add name="SignalR-Bus" />
        </listeners>
      </source>
      <source name="SignalR.ScaleoutMessageBus">
        <listeners>
          <add name="SignalR-Bus" />
        </listeners>
      </source>
      <source name="SignalR.Transports.WebSocketTransport">
        <listeners>
          <add name="SignalR-Transports" />
        </listeners>
      </source>
      <source name="SignalR.Transports.ServerSentEventsTransport">
        <listeners>
          <add name="SignalR-Transports" />
        </listeners>
      </source>
      <source name="SignalR.Transports.ForeverFrameTransport">
        <listeners>
          <add name="SignalR-Transports" />
        </listeners>
      </source>
      <source name="SignalR.Transports.LongPollingTransport">
        <listeners>
          <add name="SignalR-Transports" />
        </listeners>
      </source>
      <source name="SignalR.Transports.TransportHeartBeat">
```

```
          <listeners>
            <add name="SignalR-Transports" />
          </listeners>
        </source>
        <source name="SignalR.ReflectedHubDescriptorProvider">
          <listeners>
            <add name="SignalR-Init" />
          </listeners>
        </source>
      </sources>
      <!-- Sets the trace verbosity level -->
      <switches>
        <add name="SignalRSwitch" value="Verbose" />
      </switches>
      <!-- Specifies the trace writer for output -->
      <sharedListeners>
        <!-- Listener for transport events -->
        <add name="SignalR-Transports" type="System.Diagnostics.
TextWriterTraceListener"
initializeData="transports.log.txt" />
        <!-- Listener for scaleout provider events -->
        <add name="SignalR-Bus"
type="System.Diagnostics.TextWriterTraceListener"
initializeData="bus.log.txt" />
        <!-- Listener for hub discovery events -->
        <add name="SignalR-Init" type="System.Diagnostics.
TextWriterTraceListener"
initializeData="init.log.txt" />
      </sharedListeners>
      <trace autoflush="true" />
    </system.diagnostics>
```

Running an application with this should yield something similar in the `transports.log.txt` file. Typically, this file is located in your application `bin` output folder, whereas for a web application, it's located in the root of the web application:

transports.log.txt

```
SignalR.Transports.TransportHeartBeat Information: 0 : Connection 9aa62c9b-09b3-416c-b367-06520e24f780 is New.
SignalR.Transports.TransportHeartBeat Verbose: 0 : KeepAlive(9aa62c9b-09b3-416c-b367-06520e24f780)
SignalR.Transports.TransportHeartBeat Verbose: 0 : KeepAlive(9aa62c9b-09b3-416c-b367-06520e24f780)
SignalR.Transports.TransportHeartBeat Verbose: 0 : KeepAlive(9aa62c9b-09b3-416c-b367-06520e24f780)
SignalR.Transports.WebSocketTransport Information: 0 : CloseSocket(9aa62c9b-09b3-416c-b367-06520e24f780)
SignalR.Transports.WebSocketTransport Information: 0 : Abort(9aa62c9b-09b3-416c-b367-06520e24f780)
SignalR.Transports.TransportHeartBeat Information: 0 : Removing connection 9aa62c9b-09b3-416c-b367-06520e24f780
SignalR.Transports.WebSocketTransport Information: 0 : End(9aa62c9b-09b3-416c-b367-06520e24f780)
SignalR.Transports.WebSocketTransport Verbose: 0 : DrainWrites(9aa62c9b-09b3-416c-b367-06520e24f780)
SignalR.Transports.WebSocketTransport Information: 0 : CompleteRequest (9aa62c9b-09b3-416c-b367-06520e24f780)
```

Windows has what is called the Windows event log: a log in which the system itself registers events that occur, but it's also a place in which applications can post to. This is often used by IT to monitor what goes on. Popular toolsets out here can use this to alert IT when something happens. To get the same logging in the Windows event log, you simply need to change the listeners as follows:

```
<sharedListeners>
  <!-- Listener for transport events -->
  <add name="SignalR-Transports" type="System.Diagnostics.
EventLogTraceListener"
initializeData="SignalRScaleoutLog" />
  <!-- Listener for scaleout provider events -->
  <add name="SignalR-Bus"
type="System.Diagnostics.EventLogTraceListener"
initializeData="SignalRTransportLog" />
  <!-- Listener for hub discovery events -->
  <add name="SignalR-Init"
type="System.Diagnostics.EventLogTraceListener"
initializeData="SignalRInitLog" />
</sharedListeners>
```

To see the result, the easiest way is to open the event viewer in Windows. This is accessible by pressing Windows key + *R* and entering `eventvwr` in it, as shown here:

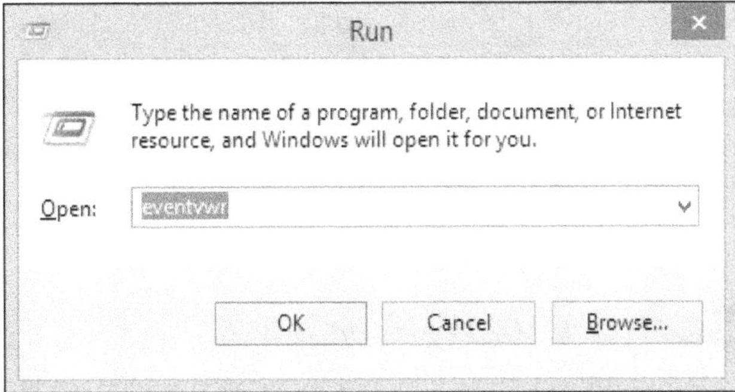

Once it's opened, you should then see the events, as shown in the following screenshot:

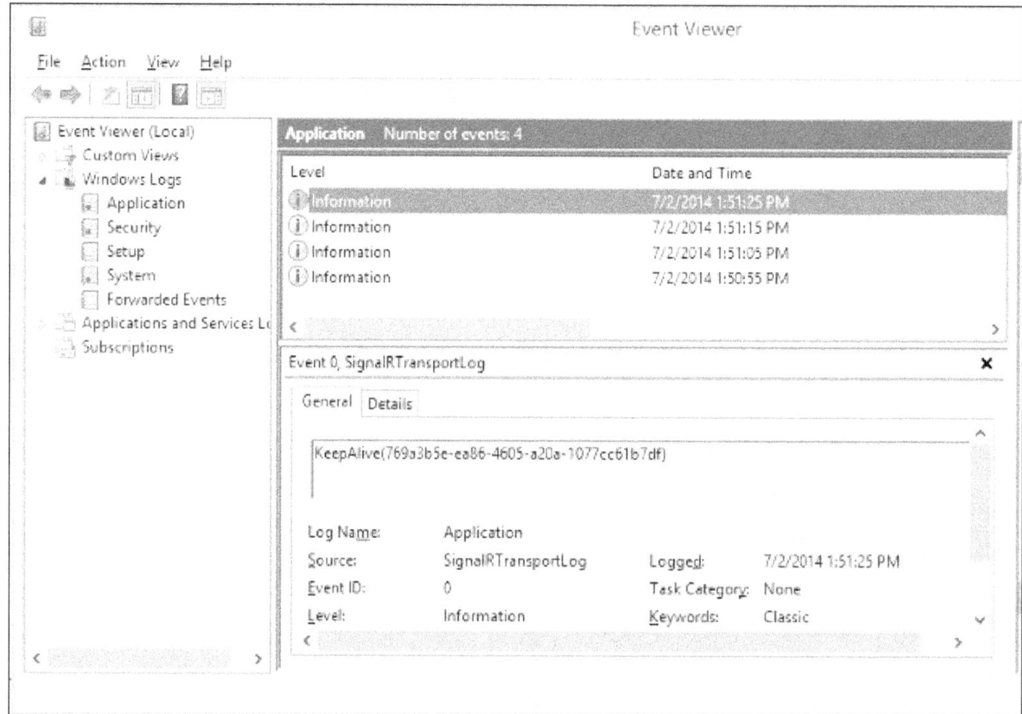

To keep the level of events in the event log to a manageable level, you should set **TraceLevel** to `Error`.

The JavaScript client

The server side will only tell you parts of the truth; you might run into issues in the client as well. Enabling this is very simple.

If you are using the generated proxies for the hubs, you can simply enable it with the following code:

```
$.connection.hub.logging = true;
$.connection.hub.start();
```

If you're not using the proxies, you can enable it as follows:

```
var connection = $.hubConnection();
connection.logging = true;
connection.start();
```

In the browser's developer tools in the console output, you should see something similar to the following screenshot. The developer tools are typically available by pressing the *F12* button on your keyboard. For some browsers, you might need to enable it in the settings of the browser.

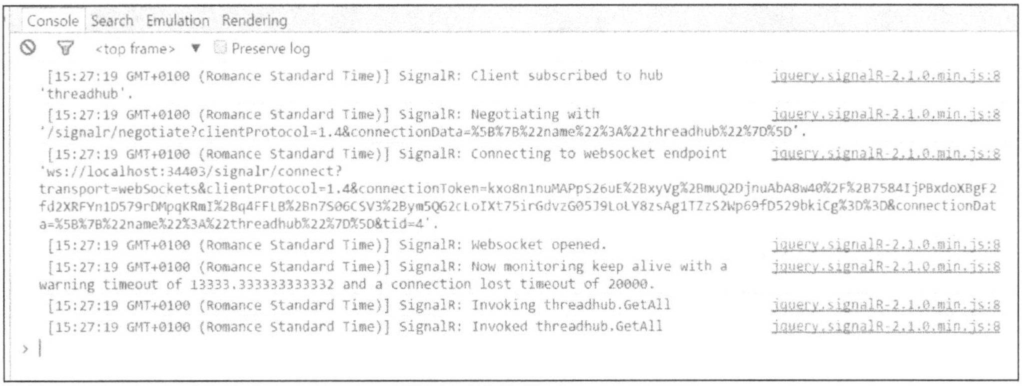

```
Console  Search  Emulation  Rendering
<top frame> ▼  Preserve log
[15:27:19 GMT+0100 (Romance Standard Time)] SignalR: Client subscribed to hub      jquery.signalR-2.1.0.min.js:8
'threadhub'.
[15:27:19 GMT+0100 (Romance Standard Time)] SignalR: Negotiating with      jquery.signalR-2.1.0.min.js:8
'/signalr/negotiate?clientProtocol=1.4&connectionData=%5B%7B%22name%22%3A%22threadhub%22%7D%5D'.
[15:27:19 GMT+0100 (Romance Standard Time)] SignalR: Connecting to websocket endpoint      jquery.signalR-2.1.0.min.js:8
'ws://localhost:34403/signalr/connect?
transport=webSockets&clientProtocol=1.4&connectionToken=kxo8n1nuMAPpS26uE%2BxyVg%2BmuQ2DjnuAbA8w40%2F%2B7584IjPBxdoXBgF2
fd2XRFYn1D579rDMpqKRmI%2Bq4FFLB%2Bn7S06CSV3%2Bym5QG2cLoIXt75irGdvzG05J9LoLY8zsAg1TZzS2Wp69fD529bkiCg%3D%3D&connectionDat
a=%5B%7B%22name%22%3A%22threadhub%22%7D%5D&tid=4'.
[15:27:19 GMT+0100 (Romance Standard Time)] SignalR: Websocket opened.      jquery.signalR-2.1.0.min.js:8
[15:27:19 GMT+0100 (Romance Standard Time)] SignalR: Now monitoring keep alive with a      jquery.signalR-2.1.0.min.js:8
warning timeout of 13333.333333333332 and a connection lost timeout of 20000.
[15:27:19 GMT+0100 (Romance Standard Time)] SignalR: Invoking threadhub.GetAll      jquery.signalR-2.1.0.min.js:8
[15:27:19 GMT+0100 (Romance Standard Time)] SignalR: Invoked threadhub.GetAll      jquery.signalR-2.1.0.min.js:8
>
```

The .NET client

In a regular .NET client, this is just as simple, as shown in the following code:

```
var hubConnection = new HubConnection("http://localhost:9044/");
hubConnection.TraceLevel = TraceLevels.All;
hubConnection.TraceWriter = Console.Out;
await hubConnection.Start();
```

The `TraceWriter` property is set to output to the console; this can be customized to be outputting to a file instead if you want, as shown here:

```
var hubConnection = new HubConnection("http://localhost:9044/");
var writer = new StreamWriter("client.log.txt");
writer.AutoFlush = true;
hubConnection.TraceLevel = TraceLevels.All;
hubConnection.TraceWriter = writer;
await hubConnection.Start();
```

The file would then be written to the place it runs from. By default, this is the binary output folder of the project. Once you run this, you should see the following output:

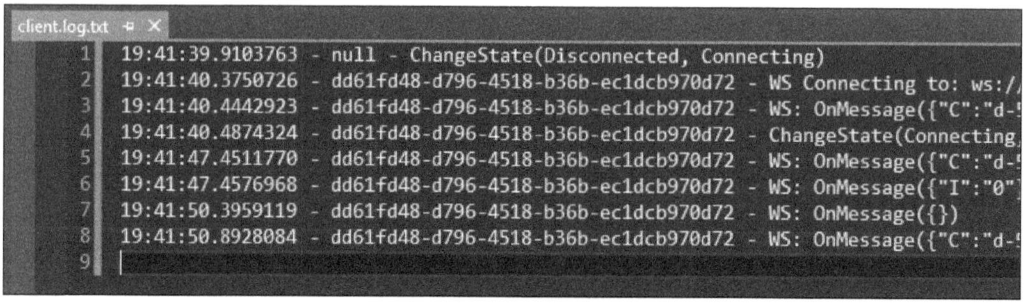

```
client.log.txt
19:41:39.9103763 - null - ChangeState(Disconnected, Connecting)
19:41:40.3750726 - dd61fd48-d796-4518-b36b-ec1dcb970d72 - WS Connecting to: ws:/
19:41:40.4442923 - dd61fd48-d796-4518-b36b-ec1dcb970d72 - WS: OnMessage({"C":"d-
19:41:40.4874324 - dd61fd48-d796-4518-b36b-ec1dcb970d72 - ChangeState(Connecting
19:41:47.4511770 - dd61fd48-d796-4518-b36b-ec1dcb970d72 - WS: OnMessage({"C":"d-
19:41:47.4576968 - dd61fd48-d796-4518-b36b-ec1dcb970d72 - WS: OnMessage({"I":"0"
19:41:50.3959119 - dd61fd48-d796-4518-b36b-ec1dcb970d72 - WS: OnMessage({})
19:41:50.8928084 - dd61fd48-d796-4518-b36b-ec1dcb970d72 - WS: OnMessage({"C":"d-
```

Windows Phone 8.x client

The API for the Windows Phone is pretty much exactly the same as for the .NET client, so enabling it is also very similar. However, there is no regular console, so we need a different writer; you basically give it the current synchronization context, which enables threads to communicate with other threads (in this case, the UI thread). Secondly, we give it `StackPanel` in which it can output to, as shown here:

```
var hubConnection = new HubConnection("http://localhost:9044/");
var writer = new TextBlockWriter(SynchronizationContext.Current,
TheStackPanelYouWantOutput);
hubConnection.TraceLevel = TraceLevels.All;
hubConnection.TraceWriter = writer;
await hubConnection.Start();
```

This might be inconvenient as you have limited screen real estate to begin with, so getting it into Visual Studio would probably be a better solution. All we need then is to implement `TextWriter` that can actually do this, as shown in the following code:

```
public class DebugTextWriter : TextWriter
{
    StringBuilder _messageBuilder;

    public DebugTextWriter()
    {
        _messageBuilder = new StringBuilder();
    }

    public override void Write(char value)
    {
        switch (value)
```

```
            {
                case '\n':
                    return;
                case '\r':
                    Debug.WriteLine(_messageBuilder.ToString());
                    _messageBuilder.Clear();
                    return;
                default:
                    _messageBuilder.Append(value);
                    break;
            }
        }

        public override void Write(string value)
        {
            Debug.WriteLine(value);

        }
        #region implemented abstract members of TextWriter
        public override Encoding Encoding
        {
            get { throw new NotImplementedException(); }
        }
        #endregion
    }
```

This should yield an output similar to the following screenshot:

```
Output
Show output from: Debug
21:28:31.2304978 - 6a814351-d98b-40d0-93fc-e5c80ddbc0da - Connection Timeout Warning : Notifying user
21:28:31.2332513 - 6a814351-d98b-40d0-93fc-e5c80ddbc0da - OnConnectionSlow
The thread 0x344 has exited with code 259 (0x103).
21:28:37.9333602 - 6a814351-d98b-40d0-93fc-e5c80ddbc0da - Connection Timed-out : Transport Lost Connection
21:28:40.3468824 - 6a814351-d98b-40d0-93fc-e5c80ddbc0da - ChangeState(Connected, Reconnecting)
21:28:40.3493533 - 6a814351-d98b-40d0-93fc-e5c80ddbc0da - SSE: GET http://localhost:8080/signalr/signalr/recon
The thread 0x624c has exited with code 259 (0x103).
21:28:47.0880453 - 6a814351-d98b-40d0-93fc-e5c80ddbc0da - ChangeState(Reconnecting, Connected)
21:28:47.0900522 - 6a814351-d98b-40d0-93fc-e5c80ddbc0da - SSE: OnMessage(Data: initialized)
21:28:47.0920523 - 6a814351-d98b-40d0-93fc-e5c80ddbc0da - SSE: OnMessage(Data: {})
The thread 0x2668 has exited with code 259 (0x103).
21:29:02.4985668 - 6a814351-d98b-40d0-93fc-e5c80ddbc0da - Connection Timeout Warning : Notifying user
21:29:02.5005628 - 6a814351-d98b-40d0-93fc-e5c80ddbc0da - OnConnectionSlow
The thread 0x78 has exited with code 259 (0x103).
The thread 0xe5c has exited with code 259 (0x103).
21:29:09.1994472 - 6a814351-d98b-40d0-93fc-e5c80ddbc0da - Connection Timed-out : Transport Lost Connection
21:29:11.5268651 - 6a814351-d98b-40d0-93fc-e5c80ddbc0da - ChangeState(Connected, Reconnecting)
21:29:11.5288482 - 6a814351-d98b-40d0-93fc-e5c80ddbc0da - SSE: GET http://localhost:8080/signalr/signalr/recon
Client dbc01994-6aff-4073-aa5b-07d8df2a3fbc explicitly closed the connection.
```

The same writer could be used in a regular .NET application as well. For a developer, this is a great way to see things while working.

Going deeper

Logging is really helpful and can really save you a lot of time to figure out what is going on. However, sometimes, you need to go even deeper. At times, you need to look at the raw traffic. There are a few ways to do this.

Fiddler

A popular, free, and very good debugging tool to debug HTTP traffic is **Fiddler**. You can download it for free at `http://www.telerik.com/fiddler`. It gives you the opportunity to monitor all HTTP requests happening on your computer.

Fiddler sets itself as a proxy between all traffic and in order to get the best experience from it, you need to enable streams, otherwise SignalR will fall back to long-polling, but not immediately (typically, after 3-5 seconds), as shown in the following screenshot:

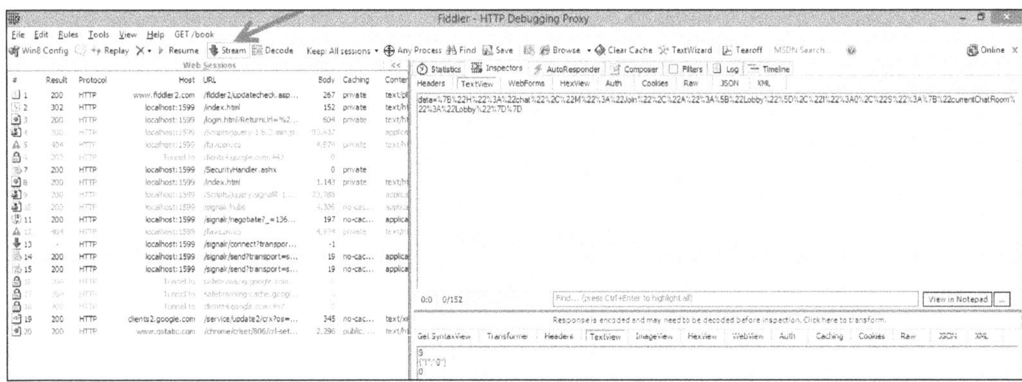

Long-polling in SignalR

If the browser and server support web sockets, SignalR might choose to use this as its preferred transport. In this case, you want to open the **Log** tab, as shown here:

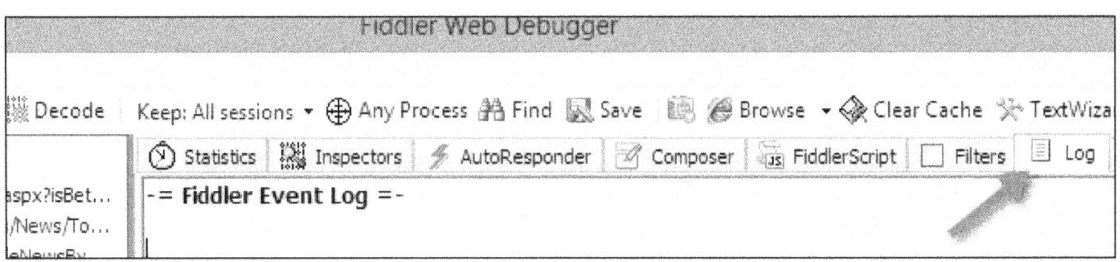

Performance counters

Monitor messages on a higher level to see the throughput of your application and the number of failing messages; this is vital when putting a system into production. SignalR has a utilities project that gives you performance counters that can be installed on the server(s) that host your application.

The utility is available through NuGet as a package. So, right-click on **References** in any of the projects, select **Manage NuGet Packages**, find the package called **Microsoft ASP.NET SignalR Utilities**, and then click on **Install**, as shown in the following screenshot:

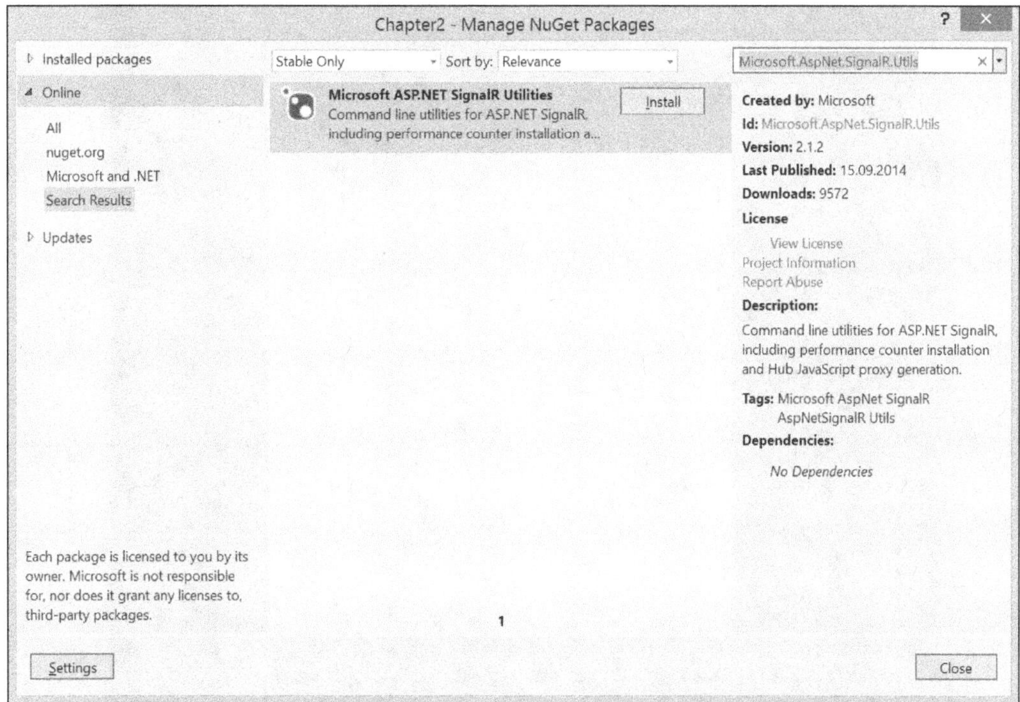

In order to install the performance counters, we need to open Command Prompt in **Administrator** mode.

Navigate yourself to the path of your solution. Inside this, you will find a folder called `packages` and, inside it, a folder called `Microsoft.AspNet.SignalR.Utils.2.1.2` or similar, depending on the version you installed. Within this, you'll find a folder called `tools`.

Now that you've navigated to all these, enter `signalr.exe ipc` and press *Enter*. This will install all the performance counters, as shown in the following screenshot:

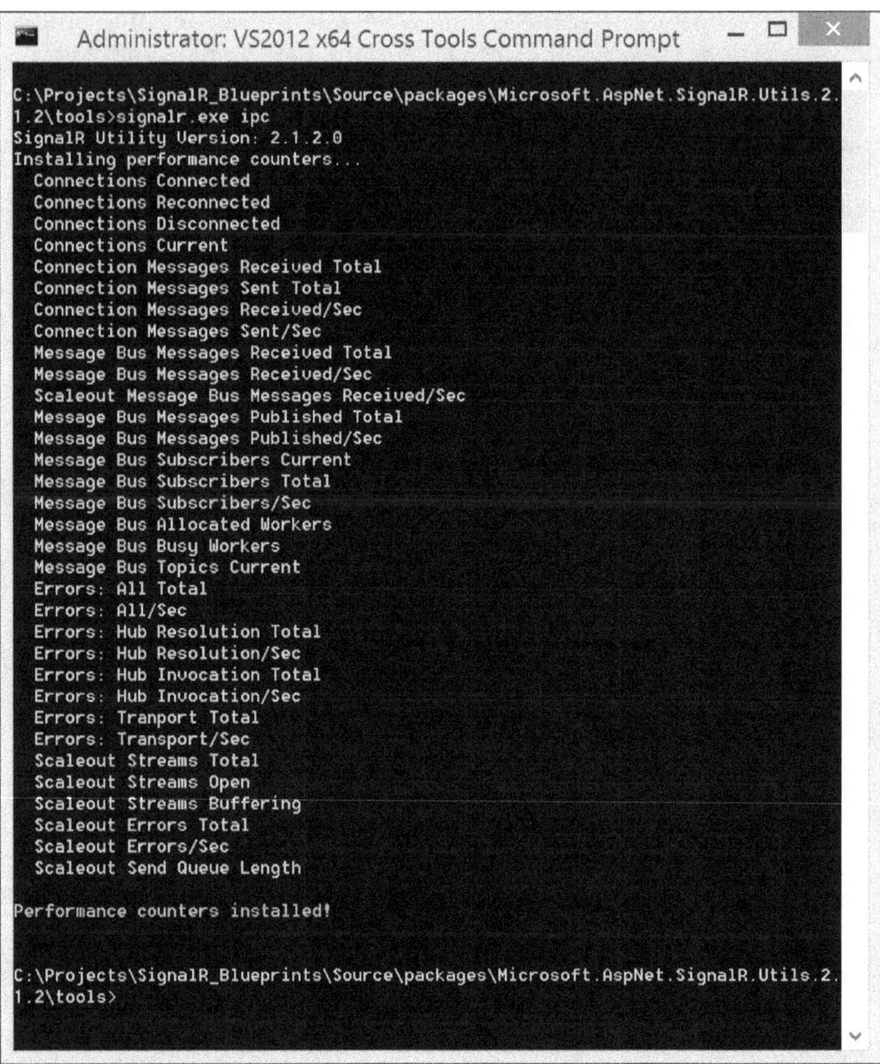

To see the performance counters, we need to open `perfmon` (Windows key + *R*); type `perfmon` and then press *Enter*, as shown here:

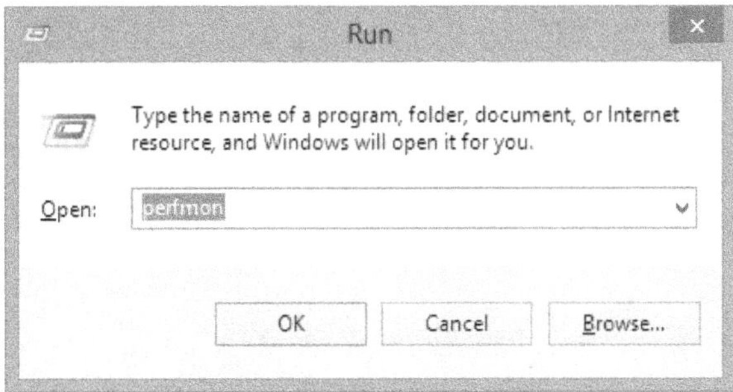

Inside `perfmon`, you expand the monitoring tools; click on the **Performance Monitor** node, and you will see a graph. Click on the big **+** button at the top, so we can add the SignalR counters you want to look at. If you have your application running, you should see it in the **Instances of selected object filter** list, as shown in the following screenshot:

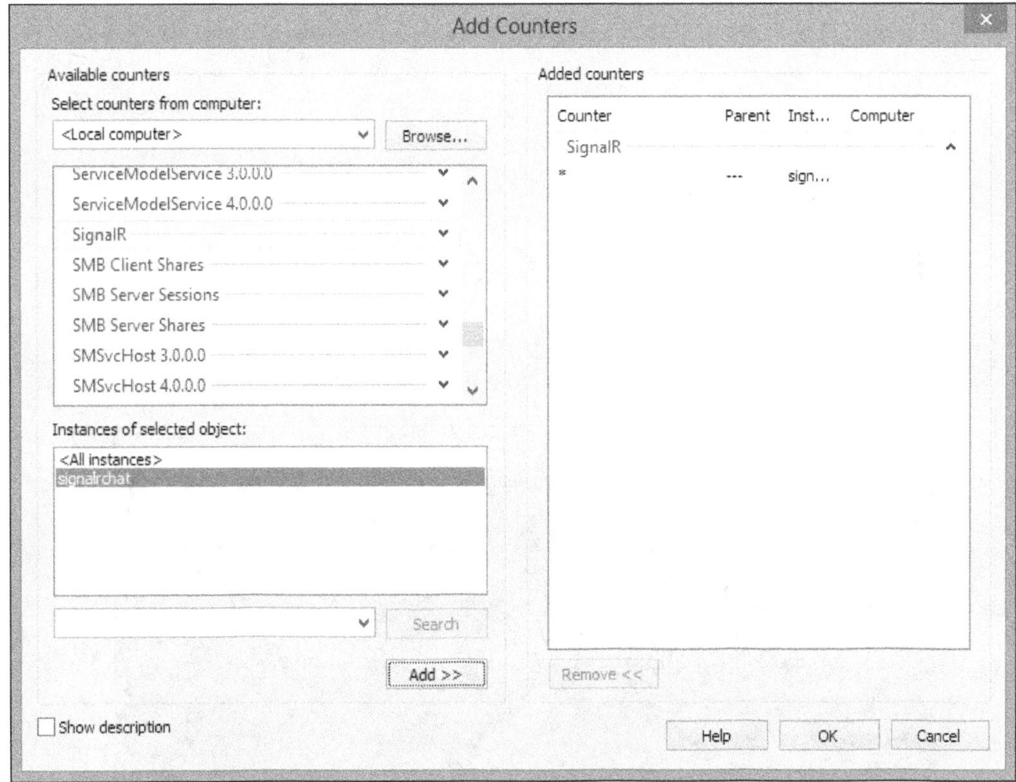

Once added, you can try out the app by sending messages and viewing the result in this graph:

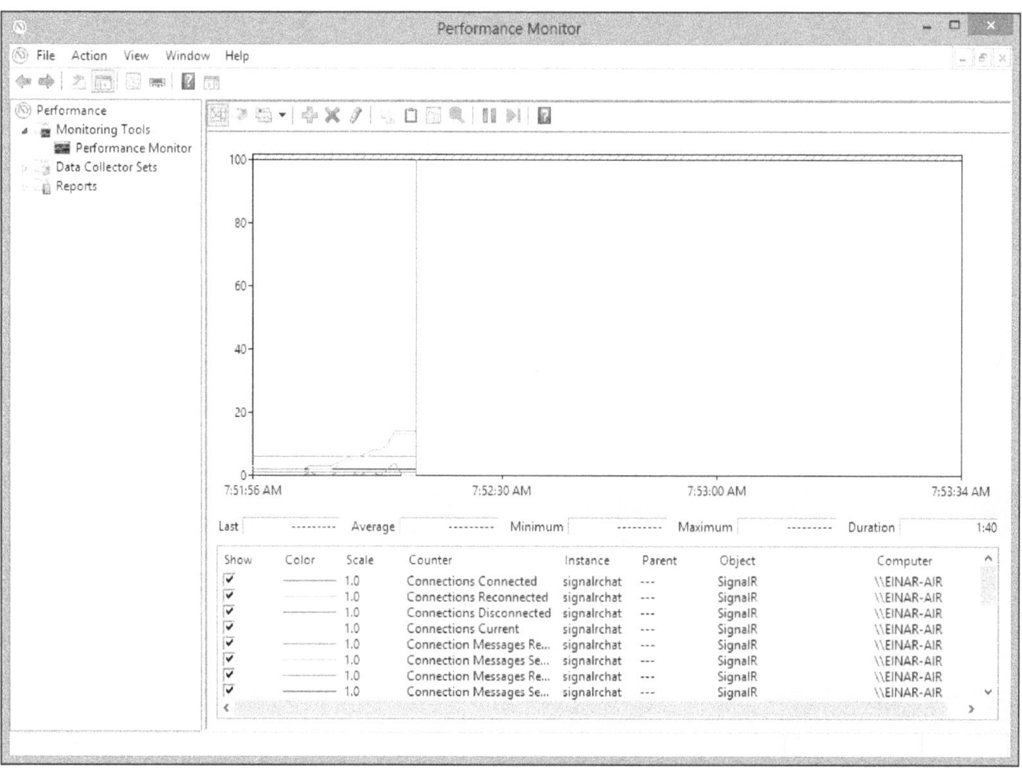

It's really important to disable any encounters that you might have enabled for debugging purposes on your production system because these will cause overhead for all messages. To disable it, you simply enter `signalr.exe upc` in the console from the same folder of the tools in which you enabled it, as shown here:

```
Administrator: VS2012 x64 Cross Tools Command Prompt

C:\Projects\SignalR_Blueprints\Source\packages\Microsoft.AspNet.SignalR.Utils.2.
1.2\tools>signalr.exe upc
SignalR Utility Version: 2.1.2.0

Performance counters uninstalled!


C:\Projects\SignalR_Blueprints\Source\packages\Microsoft.AspNet.SignalR.Utils.2.
1.2\tools>_
```

The browser

Inside all modern web browsers, you will be able to see the network traffic that goes on between the client and the server. The browser should be able to show you the details for each transport type. The following screenshot shows how this looks in Chrome for web sockets transport:

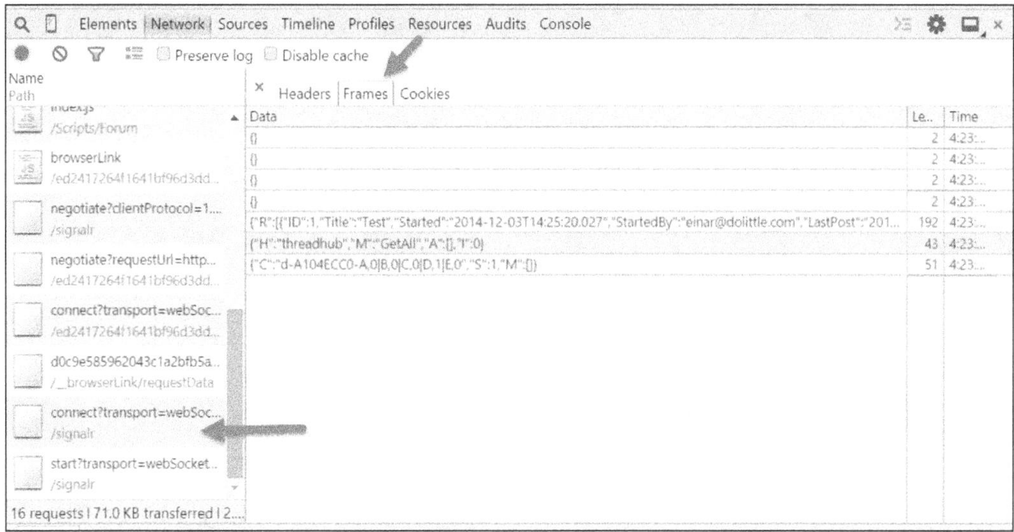

It shows the frames going back and forth for each message being sent either from the client or the server.

Summary

Debugging is not always a matter of attaching the debugger to the server code or the client code and stepping through. Sometimes, the secret is hidden in the data going back and forth and it's not that obvious to understand this with the debugger.

With logging enabled, Fiddler, the browser, and the performance counters, you should now be able to both debug and find potential bottlenecks in your system. Although, it might feel a bit primitive and different tools from what might be used to from just developing vanilla web apps, they are very detailed and should be of great assistance. Moving on, we will look at how to self-host SignalR in your own application and also how we can scale things out when there is more than one server involved, a scenario you will find yourself with typically in the cloud.

10
Hosting and Deployment

This chapter will cover how to host SignalR in different environments. Some solutions out here need to be self-contained and not rely on any server setup. We will see how to do this, ranging all the way to larger solutions where you need to scale out into a multiserver environment and even all the way into the cloud. When one has multiple servers and not necessarily controlling which server will be hit, we need to deal with this. In this chapter, we'll cover the following topics:

- Getting started with self-hosted OWIN
- Connect a .NET client to the self-hosted server
- Basics of messaging and how SignalR deals with them
- Using SQL Server to scale out
- Using Azure Service Bus to scale out
- Using Redis to scale out

At this stage, the developer should be familiar with how the server works and how to set it up in their own app. They should have a working sample of the chat working with the **Open Web Interface for .NET (OWIN)** server. The developer should also be familiar with how and why to scale out the messaging aspect of SignalR.

Self-hosting

Sometimes, you really don't want to have a big footprint on your application when you're deploying. You don't want to have the IIS dependency or other web server software, just your own executable and that's it. In combination with OWIN, SignalR supports this out of the box. OWIN is something to keep an eye on and get your hands dirty with, as this is what will make up the Microsoft web stack moving forward, not only for self-hosting but also for all kinds of hosts. It represents an abstraction that is not linked to any particular environment and makes it easier to move between different environments.

Let's get started by creating a new solution. This time around, the focus will be on how to achieve the technical solution of self-hosting and not what the solution does:

1. Open Visual Studio and create a new project by clicking on **New** from the **FILE** menu.
2. From the left-hand side tree, select **Visual C#** and then **Console Application**.
3. Name the project `Chapter10`, as shown in the following screenshot:

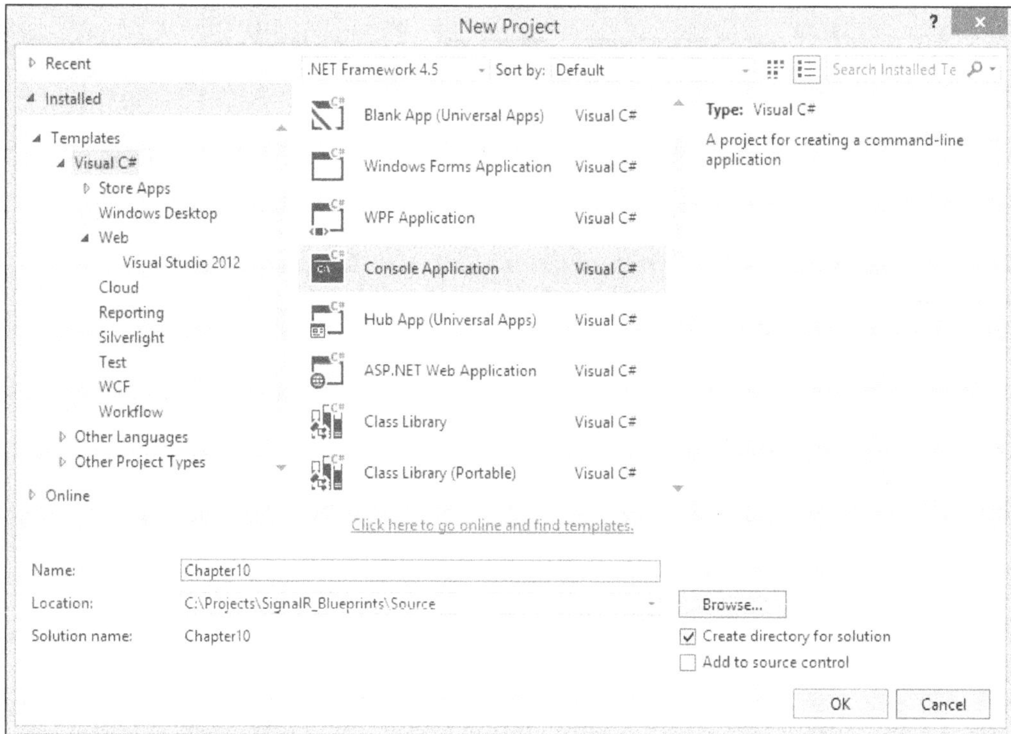

The packages

As shown in the previous chapters, we are going to download a few dependencies from NuGet. To do this, follow these steps:

1. Add a NuGet package reference, as described in *Chapter 1, The Primer*.
2. Right-click on **References** in **Solution Explorer**, select **Manage NuGet Packages**, and then type `Microsoft.AspNet.SignalR.SelfHost` in the search dialog box.
3. Select it and click on **Install**.

In addition to this, if you want to enable the self-hosted server to be available for clients coming from other domains, you will have to download a package called `Microsoft.Owin.Cors`, so add this package as well.

The code

As mentioned, this chapter will not focus on anything from a user's perspective. So we're just going to create the simplest chat, no authentication, no chat rooms or anything; just sending messages.

Let's start off with the server and how we initialize it. We will need a `Startup` class, as we've seen in previous solutions, but this time around, it's not being created by any package that we downloaded. In the root of the project, add a C# class file called `Startup.cs`.

Add the following `using` statements at the top:

```
using Microsoft.AspNet.SignalR;
using Microsoft.Owin.Cors;
using Owin;
```

Then make the class implementation look like the following code:

```
public class Startup
{
    public void Configuration(IAppBuilder app)
    {
        app.Map("/signalr", map =>
        {
            app.UseCors(CorsOptions.AllowAll);

            var hubConfiguration = new HubConfiguration
            {
                EnableJSONP = true
            };

            map.RunSignalR(hubConfiguration);
        });
    }
}
```

The first thing we need to do is to host SignalR at the `/signalr` route, which is default, and we could in fact have been using the `map.MapSignalR()` method if that's all we wanted to achieve. However, we want to enable cross-domain access for our server. Although this is not going to be used here, it's important to know if you want to enable any clients from any domain connected to your solution. The first thing we do is enable it through the `.UseCors()` method. Then, we tell the hub configuration that allows JavaScript clients to connect using a technique called JSONP. This allows web browsers to do cross-domain communication by telling the server to return JavaScript code that gets executed when the call is done. One reason for this approach is that browsers protect against cross-site scripting to avoid code from other domains or servers to be added. Another approach is that browsers include malicious scripts that could potentially take over your solution or simply just start recording keystrokes or capture changes in input fields on the page and send these back to the attacker. With this technique, we are circumventing the mechanism that is protecting us by asking it to return data in the form of executable JavaScript.

Now, we need to start a host that will then start the SignalR pipeline. Open the `Program.cs` file. Inside the `main()` method, place the following code:

```
using( WebApp.Start<Startup>("http://localhost:8181"))
{
    Console.WriteLine("Server running at http://localhost:8181/");
    Console.ReadLine();
}
```

This is all that's needed to get a SignalR server hosted; all we now need is a hub that will expose the logic that we want exposed.

Add a new class called `ChatHub.cs` to the root of the project. Make sure that you have the following `using` statements at the top:

```
using System;
using Microsoft.AspNet.SignalR;
```

Make the class look like the following code:

```
public class ChatHub : Hub
{
    public void SendMessage(string message)
    {
        Console.WriteLine("Connection {0} :
{1}",Context.ConnectionId, message);
        Clients.AllExcept(Context.ConnectionId).
messageReceived(message);
    }
}
```

All we do is expose a `SendMessage()` method that can be called by any client and it then just sends out this message to the console and to other connected clients.

Note the `.AllExcept()` method call. If you want to send a message to all the connected clients except for one or more clients, this is really handy. The method takes a param list of connection identifiers. In this particular case, we don't want to send the message back to the sender that we get from the `Context` property of the incoming connection identifier.

The client

We will need a client that can connect and send messages and also receive messages from other connected clients. Let's add a second project to the solution:

1. Right-click on the solution in **Solution Explorer** and select **New Project** in the **Add** menu, as shown in the following screenshot:

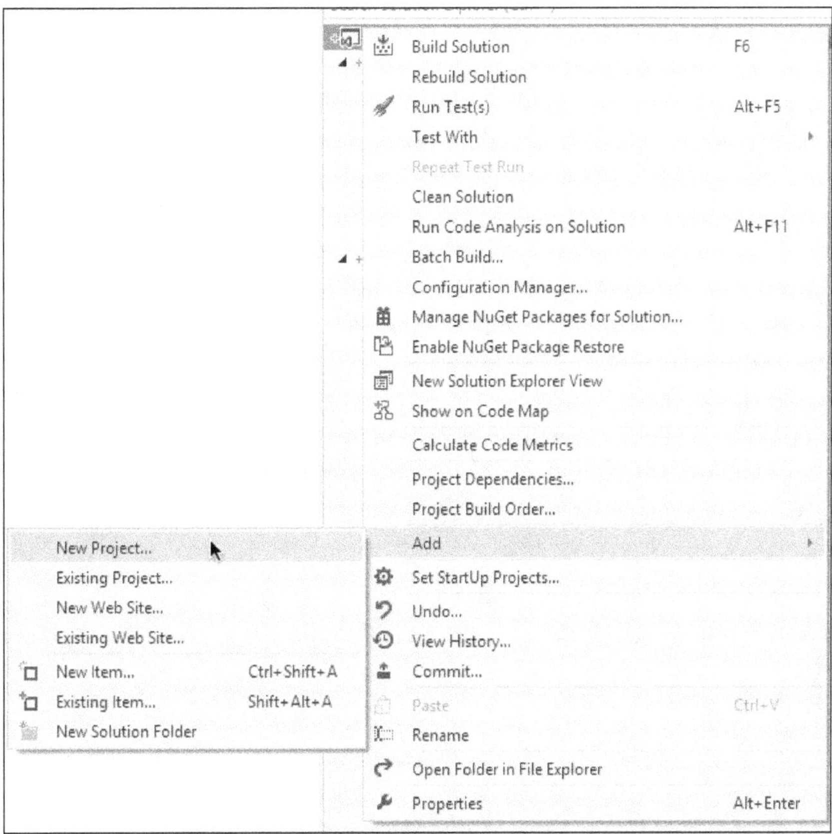

2. From the left-hand side menu, select **Visual C#** and then **Console Application**. Name the project `Chapter10.Client`, as shown here:

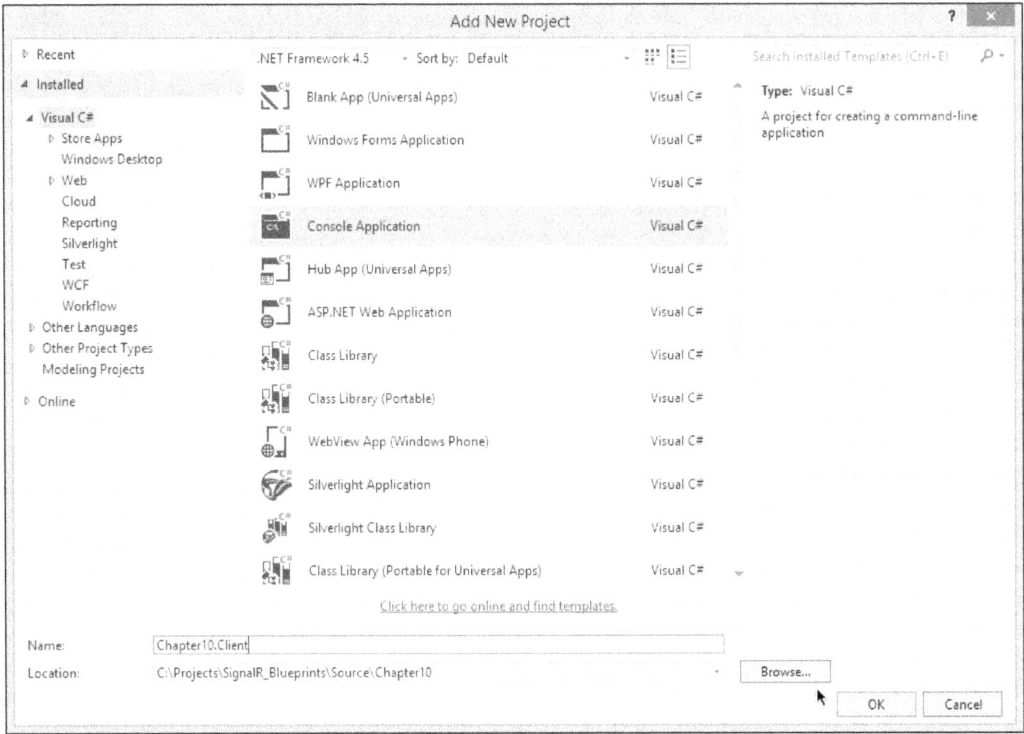

Again, we will need something from our good old NuGet. Add a reference to a package called **Microsoft.AspNet.SignalR.Client**. Open the `Program.cs` file in the client project. Insert the following code inside the `Main()` method:

```
var hubConnection = new HubConnection("http://localhost:8181");
var hubProxy = hubConnection.CreateHubProxy("ChatHub");
hubProxy.On("messageReceived", (string message) =>
{
    Console.WriteLine(message);
});

hubConnection.Start().ContinueWith(t=>Console.WriteLine("Connected
")).Wait();

for (; ; )
{
    var line = Console.ReadLine();
```

```
        if (line == "q")
        {
            break;
        }
        hubProxy.Invoke("SendMessage", line);
    }
```

As we've seen, with both the Windows Phone client libraries and the Xamarin, we create `HubConnection` and `HubProxy`. The API is exactly the same, making it very consistent to work with and easy to reuse knowledge.

Running both and typing `Hello` and hitting the *Enter* key should display a server looking like the following screenshot:

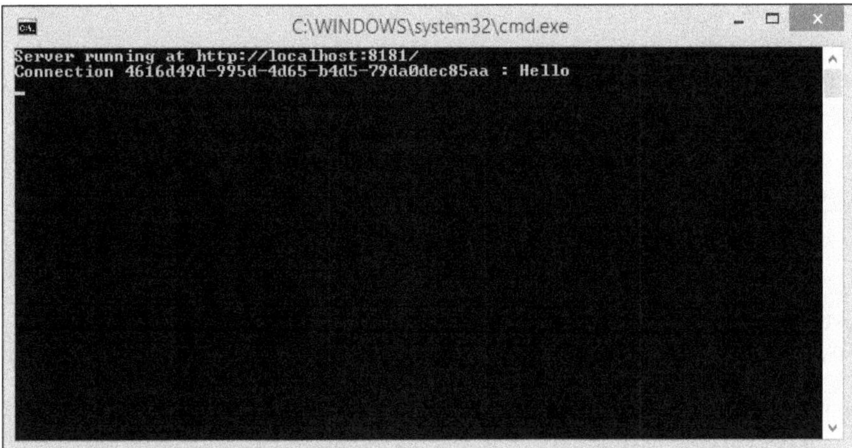

It will also display a client that looks like this:

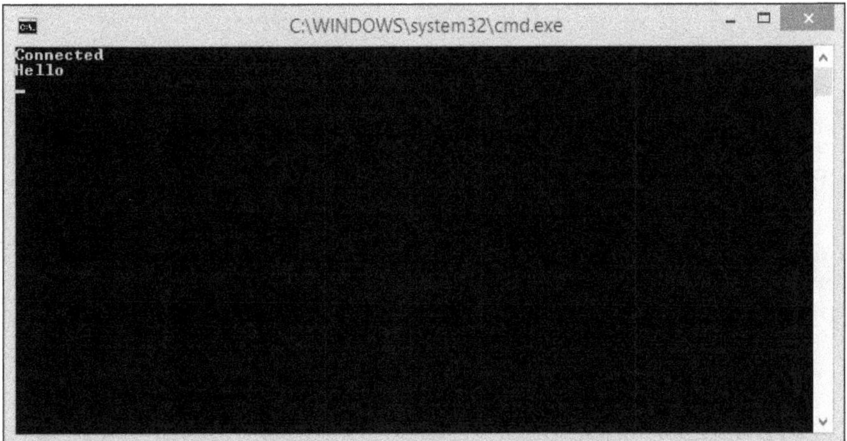

Scaling out

Underneath the covers, SignalR wraps all communication between server and clients into messages holding all the information with its origin, what the message is for, and the content of the message. By default, these messages are kept in memory in the process that hosts your SignalR-based solution. This means that having two servers will not have inter-process communication going on, so one client sitting on one server and another on a second one would not know about each other's messages. With the flexibility of SignalR at the core level of it dealing with this through well-defined interfaces, it is fairly simple to make it scale out for different technologies. This is something that the SignalR team has done as well; they do provide the ability to scale out in different ways. At the most, you can get support to use a Microsoft SQL Server for temporary storage of messages between servers, or use Windows Azure Service Bus to distribute the messages, or even the popular Redis to do this. There is a thriving community around SignalR and already a few more implementations for popular message buses and key-value stores to act as a backplane. Expect this to be a space that grows even more.

SQL Server

In your server project, you will need a package for the SQL scaleout option. Add a NuGet package reference to `Microsoft.AspNet.SignalR.SqlServer`. We are now ready to configure it. Open the `Startup.cs` file, before the call to `.RunSignalR()` or `.MapSignalR()`, we will add the configuration for SQL Server.

Add the following code before it:

```
GlobalHost.DependencyResolver.UseSqlServer(
        "Data Source=(local);"+
        "Initial Catalog=SignalRChat;"+
        "Integrated Security=True"
    );
```

The overload we're using is one that takes a SQL Server connection string. It could be any SQL Server you have either on-premise or in the cloud.

In order for SignalR to be able to use SQL Server as a messaging backend, we need to enable something called as Service Broker for our database. After creating your database, right-click on it in the **SQL Server Management Studio** and then select **Properties**. In the **Options** page, scroll down until you find the **Service Broker** section and enable the **Broker Enabled** flag, as shown here:

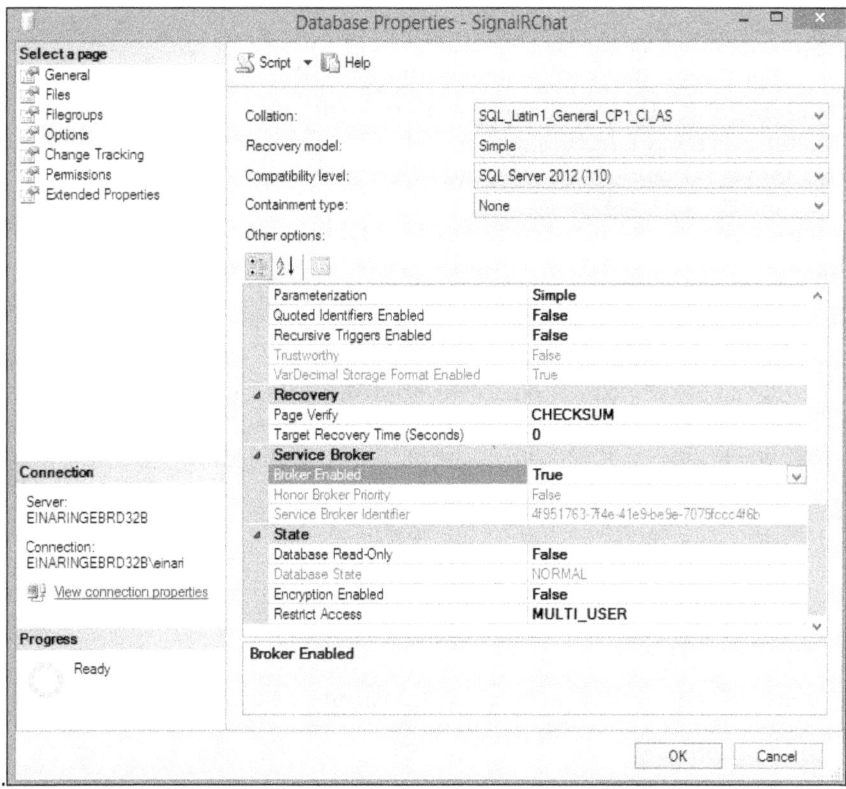

We should now be able to run our application and it will generate messages in the **SignalR_Messages** table, as shown here:

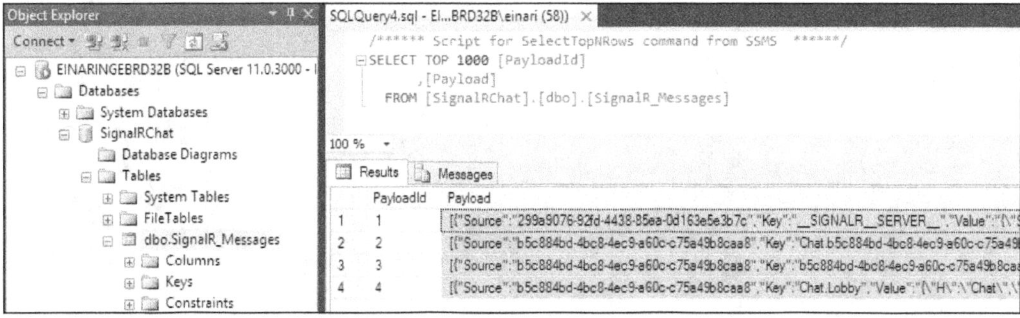

Redis

Redis is another option that can be used with SignalR to scale out. It's an open source distributed key-value store, very popular in the Unix space and is also adopted by Microsoft. Redis is fairly easy to get running on Azure or other cloud options. If you want to try things out with Redis locally, this is the procedure:

Download the source that Microsoft has published through their Open Tech initiative on GitHub at `https://github.com/MSOpenTech/redis`. Follow the guide here, build it, and run it. Once this is running, we can get going with configuring our chat application for Redis instead of the SQL solution.

Add a reference to the **Microsoft.AspNet.SignalR.Redis NuGet** package. Adding Redis is just as easy as adding with SQL Server. Go to the `Startup.cs` file and instead of using the `.UseSqlServer()` method, replace it with the following code snippet:

```
GlobalHost.DependencyResolver.UseRedis(
    "localhost",
    6379,
    "",
    "signalr.key");
```

This points us to the local Redis server running with a blank password, something you obviously would not have in production.

Run the server with clients connected; you should see the result in the Redis console output directly, as shown in the following screenshot:

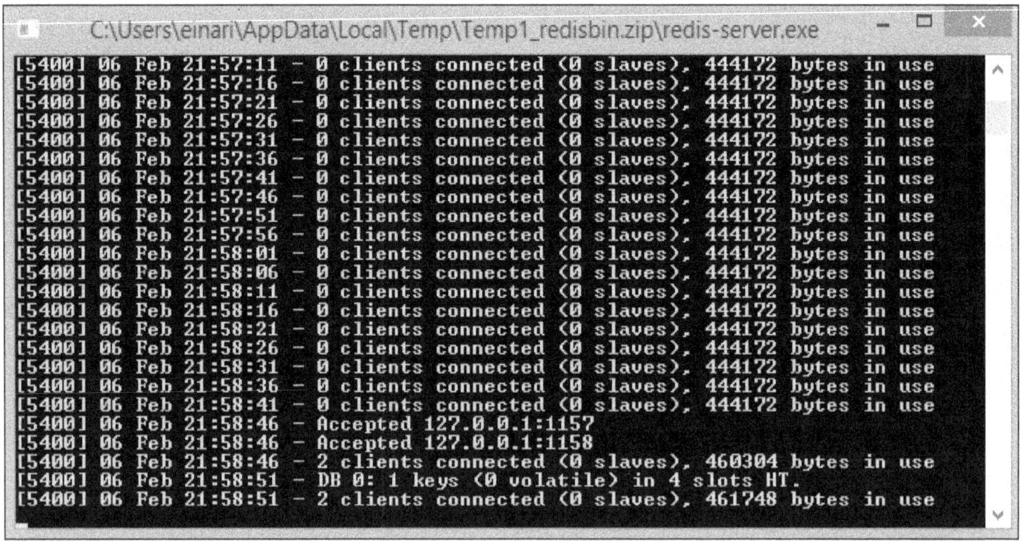

```
C:\Users\einari\AppData\Local\Temp\Temp1_redisbin.zip\redis-server.exe
[5400] 06 Feb 21:57:11 - 0 clients connected (0 slaves), 444172 bytes in use
[5400] 06 Feb 21:57:16 - 0 clients connected (0 slaves), 444172 bytes in use
[5400] 06 Feb 21:57:21 - 0 clients connected (0 slaves), 444172 bytes in use
[5400] 06 Feb 21:57:26 - 0 clients connected (0 slaves), 444172 bytes in use
[5400] 06 Feb 21:57:31 - 0 clients connected (0 slaves), 444172 bytes in use
[5400] 06 Feb 21:57:36 - 0 clients connected (0 slaves), 444172 bytes in use
[5400] 06 Feb 21:57:41 - 0 clients connected (0 slaves), 444172 bytes in use
[5400] 06 Feb 21:57:46 - 0 clients connected (0 slaves), 444172 bytes in use
[5400] 06 Feb 21:57:51 - 0 clients connected (0 slaves), 444172 bytes in use
[5400] 06 Feb 21:57:56 - 0 clients connected (0 slaves), 444172 bytes in use
[5400] 06 Feb 21:58:01 - 0 clients connected (0 slaves), 444172 bytes in use
[5400] 06 Feb 21:58:06 - 0 clients connected (0 slaves), 444172 bytes in use
[5400] 06 Feb 21:58:11 - 0 clients connected (0 slaves), 444172 bytes in use
[5400] 06 Feb 21:58:16 - 0 clients connected (0 slaves), 444172 bytes in use
[5400] 06 Feb 21:58:21 - 0 clients connected (0 slaves), 444172 bytes in use
[5400] 06 Feb 21:58:26 - 0 clients connected (0 slaves), 444172 bytes in use
[5400] 06 Feb 21:58:31 - 0 clients connected (0 slaves), 444172 bytes in use
[5400] 06 Feb 21:58:36 - 0 clients connected (0 slaves), 444172 bytes in use
[5400] 06 Feb 21:58:41 - 0 clients connected (0 slaves), 444172 bytes in use
[5400] 06 Feb 21:58:46 - Accepted 127.0.0.1:1157
[5400] 06 Feb 21:58:46 - Accepted 127.0.0.1:1158
[5400] 06 Feb 21:58:46 - 2 clients connected (0 slaves), 460304 bytes in use
[5400] 06 Feb 21:58:51 - DB 0: 1 keys (0 volatile) in 4 slots HT.
[5400] 06 Feb 21:58:51 - 2 clients connected (0 slaves), 461748 bytes in use
```

Azure

A third option that comes out of the box is the usage of Azures Service Bus, a distributed messaging system for Microsoft's cloud solution: Azure. We will cover it briefly in this book as it requires you to have the Azure SDK installed to properly do it. Once you have installed the Azure SDK, you will need to add a cloud project to your solution and add the web project as a website to the cloud project. When you have all this done, you need to set the cloud project as the startup project. The reason behind this is that it needs to be running inside the Azure emulator to be able to do this; it relies on infrastructure to do this.

Log on to your Windows Azure portal and go to Service Bus. Create a namespace if you already haven't at the top of the page, as shown here:

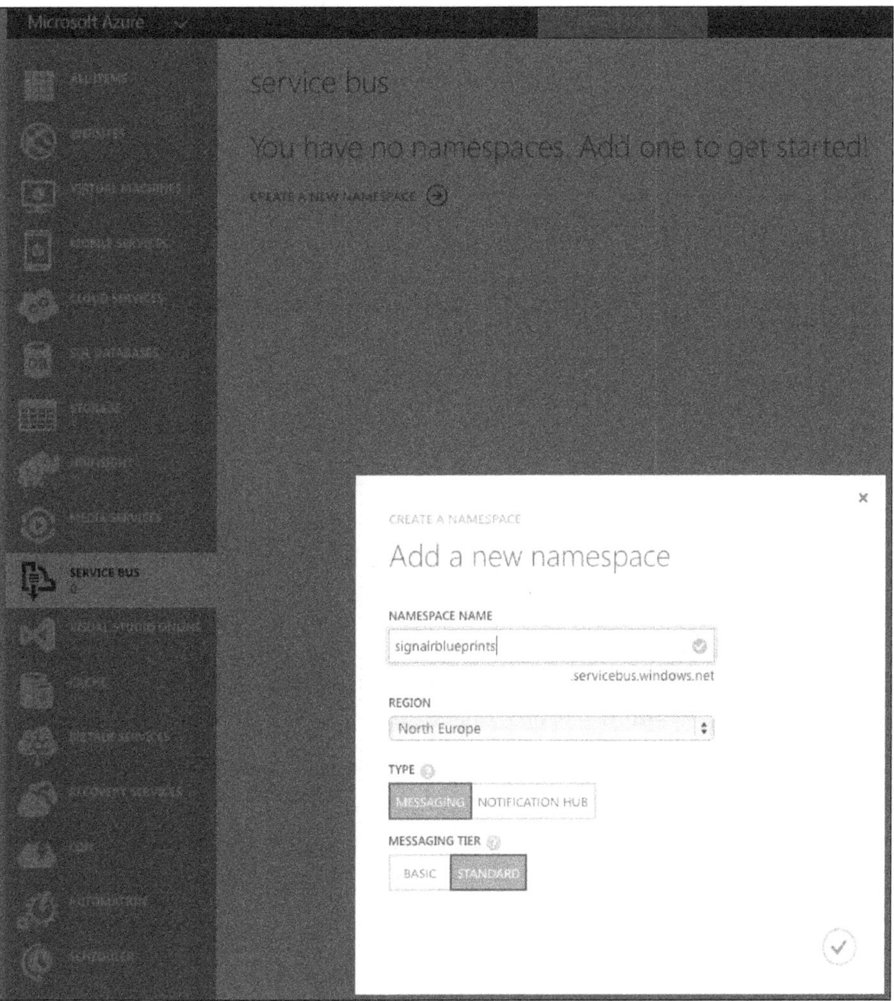

Navigate to the new namespace in the portal after creation. At the bottom of the page, you'll find a button called **CONNECTION INFORMATION**, click on it:

You will find the connection string that we need to use in our code. Copy it from the page so that you can put it in the code:

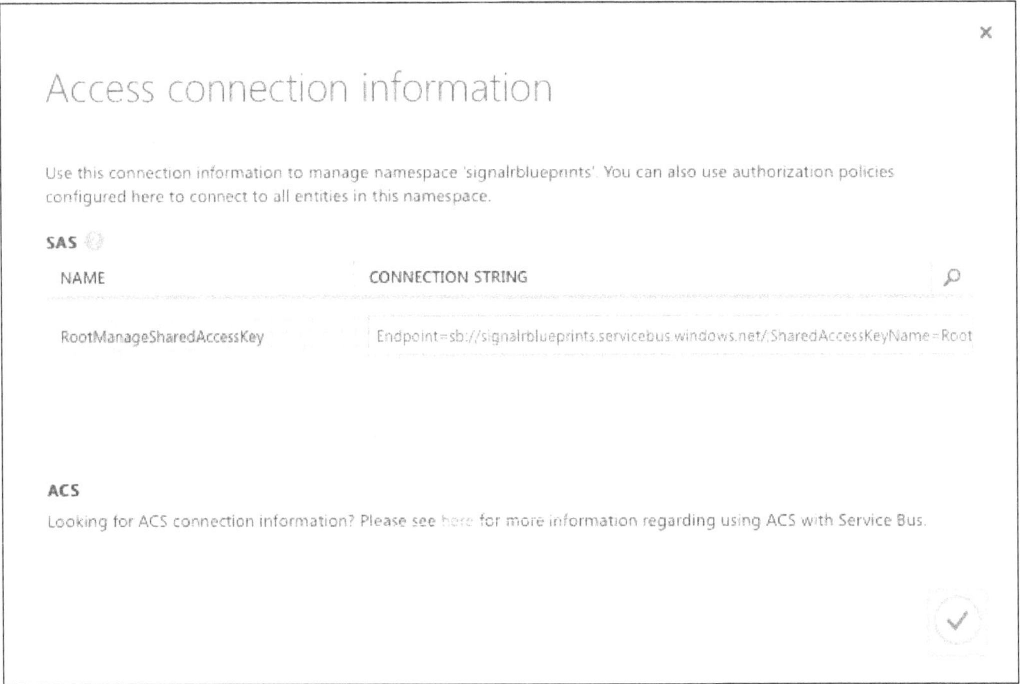

Back in Visual Studio, add a NuGet package reference called **Microsoft.AspNet.SignalR.ServiceBus** to the project. Open the `Startup.cs` file again and replace the `.UseRedis()` code with the following code:

```
GlobalHost.DependencyResolver.UseServiceBus(
    "your connection string from azure",
    "signalr");
```

You should now be able to run your solution on Azure and be ready to scale your solution any way you like.

There are other scale-out solutions available out here as well. For instance, the community has created RabbitMQ support. Also, the popular NServiceBus has a backplane implementation for SignalR. However, you might have an infrastructure in place that does not have any support yet or it might be proprietary to your system. Fear not, implementing support is fairly easy. At the heart of it all sits an interface called `IMessageBus` that you can build on top of. However, for the most part, you probably don't even need all this raw power. An abstraction for the scale-out scenario called `ScaleoutMessageBus`. It's a base-class that has methods to override and the most important one being the `.Send()` method. We won't get into details of building a bus here because the code for the existing ones is available and easy to read at the official GitHub site for SignalR at `http://github.com/SignalR/SignalR`.

Summary

Hosting any web solution in your own process can be very useful in many scenarios. With the details in this chapter, you should be well on your way to do just that and have SignalR be your transport for communication.

Another aspect that often proves to be a source of debugging nightmare is scale out. State being kept in memory on one server is not available on the second, leading to weird scenarios and result. This is also vital when applying SignalR in a multiserver environment. There is no guarantee to what server the SignalR is connecting to. If the client needs to reconnect, then the scale out option is very vital to the story. With the different options described in this chapter, you should now be able to scale in an on-premise solution as well as in the cloud.

You can find the entire sample code at `https://github.com/dolittle/SignalR_Blueprints/tree/master/Source/Chapter10`.

Although SignalR is very technical in nature and there are a lot of interesting things that it does technically, in my opinion, it's a tool to increase user experience. Users today are expecting more of our systems, they've grown accustomed to a certain experience they find in solutions such as Facebook and Twitter, and data is delivered almost instantly to them. Through advances in the mobile space, users have raised the bar of expectations in general. This is something even line of business apps should do their best to accommodate.

SignalR is not the only implementation. For platforms other than .NET, there are other options as well. For the .NET space, SignalR is the most familiar and most popular; in fact, I personally have yet to learn about any other solution (not that I have looked under every rock there is). I digress, the point is, what SignalR does: to take away all the "nitty gritty" details of how to keep a persistent connection between the client and the server, leaving you as a developer to think about the important things: delivering business value.

SignalR gives us the potential to avoid thinking about a few technical concepts we tend to spend time on: concurrency and staleness. Especially if we break things down to the smallest problem and are able to represent this in a message or a command, we can really start focusing on business value and our core domain. The concepts behind SignalR are the most important things to take away from SignalR; the messaging, the decoupling of your software, and how you can think differently about technical problems we tend impose on our system, such as concurrency and staleness. SignalR really proves that it's possible to take these things out of the equation, enabling us to write better, more responsive, and more user-friendly applications today. My default position today is to use SignalR no matter what; I see no point in not using it. In fact, I use it for all communication going back and forth with the server. Due to its nature, it feels more responsive. Also, I get new opportunities than I had before.

Real-time applications are a different ball game. It's about recognizing this rather than the technical aspect of it. I really hope that you've enjoyed this book and that it helped in opening the door to this ball game.

Index

D

E

F

G

H

I

Q

R

S

T

Thank you for buying
SignalR Blueprints

About Packt Publishing

Packt, pronounced 'packed', published its first book, *Mastering phpMyAdmin for Effective MySQL Management*, in April 2004, and subsequently continued to specialize in publishing highly focused books on specific technologies and solutions.

Our books and publications share the experiences of your fellow IT professionals in adapting and customizing today's systems, applications, and frameworks. Our solution-based books give you the knowledge and power to customize the software and technologies you're using to get the job done. Packt books are more specific and less general than the IT books you have seen in the past. Our unique business model allows us to bring you more focused information, giving you more of what you need to know, and less of what you don't.

Packt is a modern yet unique publishing company that focuses on producing quality, cutting-edge books for communities of developers, administrators, and newbies alike. For more information, please visit our website at `www.packtpub.com`.

About Packt Open Source

In 2010, Packt launched two new brands, Packt Open Source and Packt Enterprise, in order to continue its focus on specialization. This book is part of the Packt Open Source brand, home to books published on software built around open source licenses, and offering information to anybody from advanced developers to budding web designers. The Open Source brand also runs Packt's Open Source Royalty Scheme, by which Packt gives a royalty to each open source project about whose software a book is sold.

Writing for Packt

We welcome all inquiries from people who are interested in authoring. Book proposals should be sent to `author@packtpub.com`. If your book idea is still at an early stage and you would like to discuss it first before writing a formal book proposal, then please contact us; one of our commissioning editors will get in touch with you.

We're not just looking for published authors; if you have strong technical skills but no writing experience, our experienced editors can help you develop a writing career, or simply get some additional reward for your expertise.

SignalR Real-time Application Cookbook

ISBN: 978-1-78328-595-2 Paperback: 292 pages

Use SignalR to create real-time, bidirectional, and asynchronous applications based on standard web technologies

1. Build high performance real-time web applications.
2. Broadcast messages from the server to many clients simultaneously.
3. Implement complex and reactive architectures.

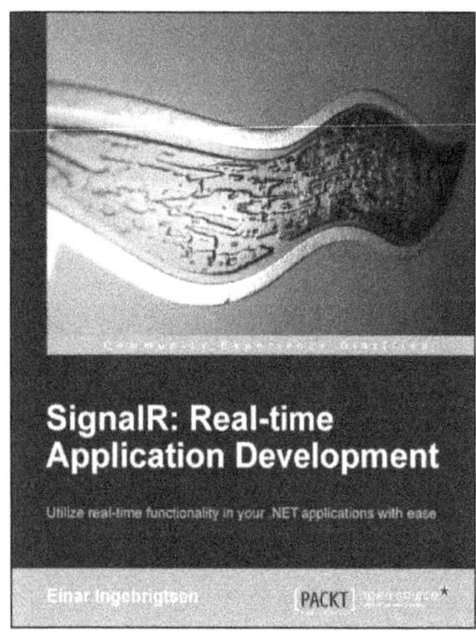

SignalR: Real-time Application Development

ISBN: 978-1-78216-424-1 Paperback: 124 pages

Utilize real-time functionality in your .NET applications with ease

1. Develop real-time applications across numerous platforms.
2. Create scalable applications that are ready for cloud deployment.
3. Utilize the full potential of SignalR.

Please check **www.PacktPub.com** for information on our titles

Storm Blueprints: Patterns for Distributed Real-time Computation

ISBN: 978-1-78216-829-4 Paperback: 336 pages

Use Storm design patterns to perform distributed, real-time big data processing, and analytics for real-world use cases

1. Process high-volume log files in real time while learning the fundamentals of Storm topologies and system deployment.
2. Deploy Storm on Hadoop (YARN) and understand how the systems complement each other for online advertising and trade processing.
3. Follow along as each chapter presents a new problem and the architectural pattern, design, and implementation of a solution.

AngularJS Web Application Development Blueprints

ISBN: 978-1-78328-561-7 Paperback: 300 pages

A practical guide to developing powerful web applications with AngularJS

1. Get to grips with AngularJS and the development of single-page web applications.
2. Develop rapid prototypes with ease using Bootstraps Grid system.
3. Complete and in-depth tutorials covering many applications.

Please check **www.PacktPub.com** for information on our titles

www.ingramcontent.com/pod-product-compliance
Lightning Source LLC
LaVergne TN
LVHW081339050326
832903LV00024B/1223